POINT BETSIE

POINT BETSIE

LIGHTKEEPING AND LIFESAVING ON NORTHEASTERN LAKE MICHIGAN

Jonathan P. Hawley

University of Michigan Press Ann Arbor, Michigan
&
Petoskey Publishing Co. Traverse City, Michigan

Published in the United States of America by
The University of Michigan Press and
The Petoskey Publishing Company
Manufactured in the United States of America

∞ Printed on acid-free paper

2011   2010   2009   2008   4   3   2   1

ISBN-13: 978-0-472-03318-8 (pbk. : alk. paper)
ISBN-10: 0-472-03318-2 (pbk. : alk. paper)

Library of Congress Cataloging in Publication Data on file

CONTENTS

PREFACE

"I'm not going to relax until we're past Betsie," mutters the chief engineer to a vessel's captain as their huge "laker" steams up Lake Michigan in late November's unsettled weather, lowered with ballast water to handle suddenly mounting seas.[1] Such caution has been common among generations of Great Lakes seamen who have learned by personal experience, or through tales of less fortunate mariners, to appreciate the power of the inland seas and the risks they can pose to vessels small and large.

The consequences of fierce storms on the lakes can be found in disaster bulletins such as the succinct notice in an August, 1855, issue of the *New York Times*: "The bark *L.M. Hubby*, of Cleveland, capsized off Point Betsey…. The crew, twelve in number, were all lost. COTTERELL, the mate, alone was saved."[2]

A year later that prominent newspaper carried a front-page story, originally appearing in the *Milwaukee American*, of the recent arrival in that western Lake Michigan port of the propeller *Globe*.[3] Those on board spoke of a "severe Northeast storm which prevailed at the foot of Lake Michigan and the head of Lake Huron…and of the loss of the propellers *Brunswick* and *Troy*, together with one of the crew of the *Brunswick*." The story continued, "Those sailors with whom we have conversed say that the storm in the region of Mackinac…was the most severe for several years, and anticipate that more disasters must have occurred to other fleets in that vicinity."

"When off the Manitou Islands," detailed the report of the northbound *Brunswick,* she "…was overtaken by the most severe Northeast wind that has been known on those waters for many months, and was unable to ride out the storm. She sunk in fifty fathoms water. The crew and passengers are saved, with the exception of one man, who was drowned, after reaching shoal water, from sickness and exhaustion. We have no further particulars." The other vessel, the upbound *Troy*, which had been hauling mixed merchandise to Grand River, Michigan, was reported to be a total wreck, having been driven onto rocks somewhere south of Mackinac where she quickly filled with water. The *American* advised readers that the "...passengers were taken to Point Betsie by the propeller *Plymouth*, all safe." The fact that workers were then constructing a lighthouse, at that otherwise isolated spot, may have prompted the decision to put the travelers ashore there.

One need not look so far back in time to find evidence of storms that proved devastating to vessels and crews. Even today, a crew cannot casually presume the structural integrity of their vessel should they encounter the extraordinarily powerful winds that sometimes arise on the Great Lakes, generating waves that are typically closer together than those with which ships sailing the oceans must contend. The continuing presence of U.S. Coast Guard rescue craft, along with helicopters capable of swiftly covering the entire region, confirms that even the massive vessels that now ply the Great Lakes, manned by highly skilled crews that have the benefit of the most sophisticated navigational tools, cannot ignore the risks of Mother Nature's fierce blasts.

The famed Armistice Day storm of November, 1940, whose southwest winds of up to seventy-five miles per hour swept across Lake Michigan, claimed three vessels, with the loss of fifty-seven people. Eighteen years later, the then-largest carrier on the lakes, the steel-hulled *Carl D. Bradley*, was caught in a vicious storm which broke her in half and sank her in northern Lake Michigan, taking to their deaths thirty-three of the thirty-five persons on board. And, as told in a famous ballad, the 729 foot, 13,632-ton *S.S. Edmund Fitzgerald*—the Great Lakes' most awesome vessel prior to the launching of today's generation of 1,000-footers—succumbed on November 10, 1975, to raging winds and smashing seas, taking her entire crew of twenty-nine to the bottom of Lake Superior. Yet, even with such history, it is sometimes said that crewmen of foreign-flag vessels sailing the lakes for the first time may dismiss their potential severity; before long, however, they are likely to accord these waters appropriate respect.

The year 1858, etched most notably in American history for two achievements—the famous Lincoln-Douglas debates in Illinois over slavery and the establishment of a stagecoach service from St. Louis to the West that pioneered coast-to-coast public transportation—also saw the completion of the lighthouse and keeper's dwelling at Point Betsie. Since then, its beam has served as an important landmark for captains and their crews on vessels large and small on northeastern Lake Michigan. The light is situated on a natural promontory slightly south of a vital passage between the Michigan mainland and the offshore North and South Manitou Islands. This welcomed, but nonetheless potentially perilous route, has also served as a refuge for vessels battling stormy seas. In 1865, as the close of the Civil War was followed by growing vessel traffic on the Lakes, a popular guide for vessels traveling up and down Lake Michigan, *Thompson's Coast Pilot*, described the important new navigational aid at Point Betsie as "a prominent light" and "a good leading mark for the Straits."

In similar vein, an early 20th century brochure promoting nearby Frankfort and Crystal Lake, sometimes called "the Lake Geneva of America," observed, "When the boat on which you leave Chicago or Milwaukee for Frankfort starts its trip, its course is set and Point Betsie is the objective. Twenty-four hours a day, winter and summer, this station is operated to protect Great Lakes shipping. Here you will find a picturesque lighthouse, only five miles distance from Frankfort...."

For centuries, vessels sailing or steaming toward the north end of 307 mile-long, 120 mile-wide Lake Michigan have passed through a "point of departure," between four and five miles off Point Betsie, where they have altered course. When fog or other inclement weather would obscure visibility, people on the shore would hear the distant whistle that signaled a ship's location and her change of course to the passage.

Likewise, southbound vessels have found Point Betsie a vital reference after passing the two Manitous. *Scott's New Coast Pilot,* published for the opening of seasonal navigation in 1895 when scores of schooners and steamers daily plied these waters, defined distinct courses starting from the light—to Chicago, Grand Haven, Milwaukee and Michigan City, as well as routes to nearby Manistee and, northwesterly across Lake Michigan, to the Sturgeon Bay Ship Canal and into Green Bay. Captains were told they could ascertain their location off Point Betsie in daytime by the landmark's then yellow brick, thirty-four foot tall tower, at night by its recurring beam and, amidst blanketing fog, by the uniquely timed blasts from the Point's whistle.

Federal "light lists" for Lake Michigan, published for nearly a century and a half, continue to inform mariners that they'll spot this treasured sentinel on a point at 44 degrees, 41.5 minutes north, and 86 degrees, 15.3 minutes west. And, as noteworthy as Point Betsie Light has always been to cargo vessels, its beacon has also been welcomed by coastal travelers on smaller boats. Generations of commercial fishermen and sportsmen, too, have an emotional attachment to this place, where anglers routinely catch salmon, trout, steelhead and whitefish within sight of the tower.

Land travelers, too, seek out Point Betsie, which is known as Benzie County's most historic and frequently photographed structure. They find the beautiful lighthouse in Lake Township, a short distance off M-22—the popular "Great Lakes Circle" route—about five miles north of the harbor town of Frankfort with which it has always been associated. Looking out over the "big lake," a traditional, local term that distinguishes Lake Michigan from the area's many inland lakes, visitors may spot a massive vessel passing along the horizon, her self-loading cranes outlined against the sky. She would most likely be one of the close to seventy self-propelled ships or large tug-barge units that now haul iron ore, limestone, coal, grain and other dry-bulk or liquid cargoes between Great Lakes ports. Thirteen of the newest vessels in the lake fleet are more than one hundred feet wide and about a thousand feet long, making them "super carriers" of a length nearly that of the famed Cunard liner *QE2*—ships almost as long, that is, as the Empire State Building is tall. The personnel aboard such a massive ship can off-load more than 60,000 tons of dry cargo in less than ten hours with their own equipment and be promptly underway again.[4] The modern fleet on the Great Lakes, whose ships can often be spotted on the horizon off historic Point Betsie, is truly a marvel of efficiency.[5]

From the black lantern room atop the circular tower, Point Betsie Light, still an official aid to navigation under the U.S. Coast Guard's authority, flashes nightly. But having decided that it no longer needs lighthouses to adequately protect mariners, the Coast Guard is turning most of them over to federal property managers for disposition to local governments and eligible non-profit organizations or, as a last resort, to be sold for commercial use as bed-and-breakfasts or other appropriate businesses. While a few structures at Point Betsie that once were important to the station's official functions have been torn down or owned privately for many years, the heart of the reservation—the lighthouse and associated support structures—now belong to Benzie County, with the non-profit "Friends of Point Betsie Lighthouse, Inc." managing the site and providing services to visitors.

The Coast Guard, now a key component of the U.S. Department of Homeland Security, has retained ownership of an adjacent vacation cottage. In addition to the charming historic tower and attached keepers' dwelling, today's visitors find buildings erected more than a century ago to house the fog signal apparatus and protect potentially explosive fuel, as well as an historically notable utility structure and a gift shop.

Long gone, or privately owned and maintained yet still important to Point Betsie's rich story, are buildings that for six decades housed lifesaving crews, their surfboats and shore-based rescue equipment on the lighthouse reservation. From this prominent coastal point, crews of the Coast Guard and its famed predecessor, the U.S. Life-Saving Service, conducted beach patrols and performed gutsy rescue operations, some of them of truly legendary scale. Those lifesavers share the legacy left by the many dedicated public servants who lived and worked diligently at Point Betsie, night and day, through nearly one hundred and forty years to protect human life and valuable cargo.

As was everywhere the life of America's tough and courageous coast-watchers, the people of Point Betsie's two stations knew joys and sorrows. They had to deal with seemingly unending tedium as well as with the occasionally desperate circumstances that could put their own lives at risk and result either in triumph or tragedy. Together with the wives and children who shared their experiences, these men not only have an honorable place in Benzie County's distinctive past, but are a noble part of the larger history of the U.S. Lighthouse Service, the U.S. Life-Saving Service and the U.S. Coast Guard.

On behalf of the generations of men, women and children who have rounded Point Betsie, this book recounts the protection that was so long provided them by its lightkeeping and lifesaving crews. Their memory is a treasure to be preserved and shared.

POINT BETSIE CHRONOLOGY

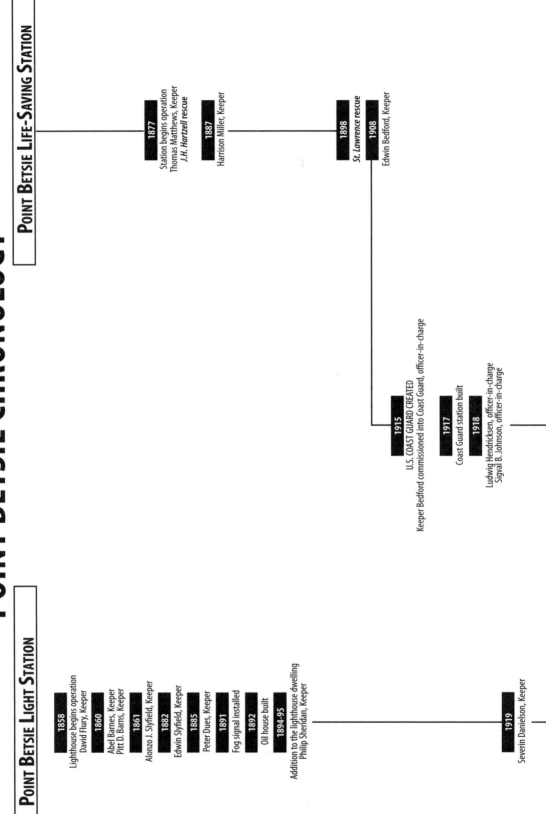

POINT BETSIE LIFE-SAVING STATION

1877
Station begins operation
Thomas Matthews, Keeper
J.H. Hartzell rescue

1887
Harrison Miller, Keeper

1898
St. Lawrence rescue

1908
Edwin Bedford, Keeper

1915
U.S. COAST GUARD CREATED
Keeper Bedford commissioned into Coast Guard, officer-in-charge

1917
Coast Guard station built

1918
Ludwig Hendricksen, officer-in-charge
Sigval B. Johnson, officer-in-charge

POINT BETSIE LIGHT STATION

1858
Lighthouse begins operation
David Flury, Keeper

1860
Abel Barnes, Keeper
Pitt D. Barns, Keeper

1861
Alonzo J. Slyfield, Keeper

1882
Edwin Slyfield, Keeper

1885
Peter Dues, Keeper

1891
Fog signal installed

1892
Oil house built

1894-95
Addition to the lighthouse dwelling
Philip Sheridan, Keeper

1919
Severin Danielson, Keeper

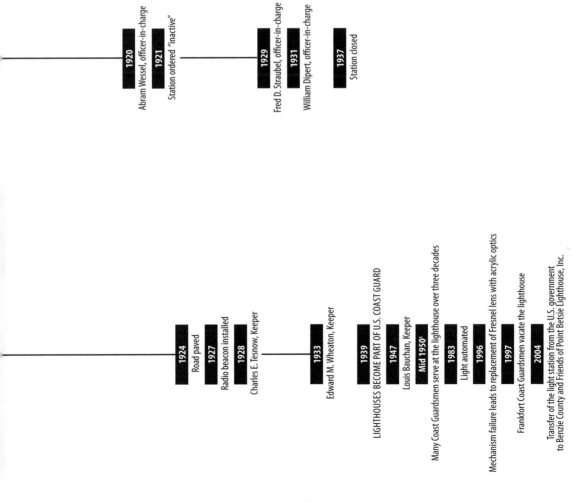

1920 Abram Wessel, officer-in-charge

1921 Station ordered "inactive"

1929 Fred D. Straubel, officer-in-charge

1931 William Dipert, officer-in-charge

1937 Station closed

1924 Road paved

1927 Radio beacon installed

1928 Charles E. Tesnow, Keeper

1933 Edward M. Wheaton, Keeper

1939 LIGHTHOUSES BECOME PART OF U.S. COAST GUARD

1947 Louis Bauchan, Keeper

Mid 1950s Many Coast Guardsmen serve at the lighthouse over three decades

1983 Light automated

1996 Mechanism failure leads to replacement of Fresnel lens with acrylic optics

1997 Frankfort Coast Guardsmen vacate the lighthouse

2004 Transfer of the light station from the U.S. government to Benzie County and Friends of Point Betsie Lighthouse, Inc.

CHAPTER ONE

EVERY NIGHT AT SUNSET

NOTICE TO MARINERS.
A NEW LIGHT-HOUSE

Has been erected at **POINT BETSIE,** *20 miles south of South Manitou Island, Lake Michigan. The tower and keeper's dwelling are of yellow brick and are connected. The illuminating apparatus is 4ᵗʰ order catadioptric, of the system of Fresnel, and will show a fixed white light, varied by flashes every 2 minutes. The focal plane is 45 feet above the level of the Lake, and the light should be seen in good weather a distance of 12 nautical miles.*

The light will be exhibited for the first time at sunset on the 20ᵗʰ of October, and every night after that during the season of navigation.

By order of the Light-House Board:
> *Wm. F. SMITH,*
> *Corps Topographical Engineers,*
> *Engineer 11ᵗʰ L.H. District*
> **DETROIT, MICH.**, *October 5ᵗʰ, 1858.*[1]

Each year, thousands of people visit Point Betsie Lighthouse and enjoy the sweep of Lake Michigan surf and sand that this historic sentinel commands. Over the past half-century alone, visitors would likely number more than two million. As at other beautiful spots of coastline, they come at all hours, from dawn, when the historic structure is highlighted against the still-dark lake and western sky, to the bright light of midday's sun, and most of all when sunset approaches.

Summer evenings are visitors' favorite time. Many, performing a ritual without which their vacation would be incomplete, wander the beach searching for a treasured

"Petoskey," Michigan's official state stone which the waves wash in not as abundantly as many visitors would like—from ancient offshore reefs. Children run and play in the sand or toss stones in the water; dogs ceaselessly retrieve sticks and balls from their masters. Other visitors gather around campfires or simply watch quietly as the sun, first round, then slightly egg-shaped and finally a fast-shrinking mound, slips down and away at the edge of the vast sea. Some in the gathering will be watching, hopefully and intently, to spot the elusive "green flash" that might immediately follow; some will simply enjoy the pastel afterglow that often spreads across the expansive western sky. And with dusk coming on, many of the crowd—keepers at heart—will glance at the old tower's top to be sure Point Betsie Light shines once again.

Mr. Smith's announcement on behalf of the Lighthouse Board alerted early Lake Michigan mariners to keep an eye out for a new beam of light from the east that would help them know their location and guide them along their way. The lighting, which came too late to be detailed that year in the annual, official U.S. *Light List* that typically has been released in mid-year, was the first of numerous steps to enhance ships' safety along this critical portion of the Lake Michigan shore. But operational details were soon known to mariners; to illustrate, the 1861 edition showed Point "Betsy's" light to be fixed, varied by a flash every ninety seconds (rather than the two-minute interval cited in the 1858 notice), and situated twenty miles south of South Manitou Island. Its beam, generated by oil burning lamps within a fourth-order Fresnel lens, was reported to be fifty-two feet above the lake and visible for ten nautical miles.

How did a lighthouse come to be located at Point Betsie? How does that light fit within the broader history of America's venerable coastal lights and their keepers? What about the lifesavers who, eventually working from this same beautiful site, rescued many whose lives were in grave danger?

To fully appreciate Point Betsie's place in history, one must look far back in time, for the point has been an important landmark for as long as man has coasted the Lake Michigan shore. Learning from the Native Americans who had fished, hunted, and farmed in the area, French explorers and traders marked the point on their maps as "Pointe aux Bec Scies" (or with slightly varied spelling or capitalization), their interpretation of the Indian "Un-Zig-A-Zee-Bee" which natives gave to a river flowing into Lake Michigan just a few miles to the south, where sawbill, or Merganser ducks thrived. The French name prevailed for both the river and prominent point to the north until shortly after the federal government and the first settlers became interested in the area, ultimately undertaking to improve access to the fine harbor which the river's broad mouth afforded.

In 1838-39, two years after Michigan entered the Union, brothers Alvin and Austin Burt surveyed the area for the U.S. to determine section and township lines. Their April 22 field notes appear to refer, in another slight corruption, to "Point Betsis" and to the nearby "River Aux Betsis"; the party recorded intersecting Lake Michigan and setting a "meander post" at a treeless spot which they further identified by observing that "Manitou Island" lay about 20 miles off shore.[2] Foretelling the marine traffic that would come to this coast starting only two decades later, the surveyors anticipated that the river mouth could be a good harbor for a settlement. The dredging several years after settlement of a deeper channel between Lake Michigan and the broad river made this a reality.

As American sailors became predominant on these waters and their countrymen founded coastal settlements, the name evolved into "Betsey," or sometimes "Betsy," for both the river that flows into the harbor at Frankfort and the distinctive land point to the north.[3] (Occasionally, 19th century writings end the word "point" with the letter "e"). "Betsey" or "Betsy" were the predominant spellings over the last quarter of that century, while today's prevailing form, "Betsie," achieved official recognition in the early 20th century.[4]

The first mariners to know this area well were the Ottawa and other Algonquian peoples who moved along the coast during the "Woodland" cultural epoch before the white man's arrival. They traveled along the Lake Michigan shore and its tributaries in large canoes, hunting, fishing, and gathering berries and other foodstuffs as well as moving between their summer and winter encampments. During the latter half of the 19th century, their canoes gave way to open "Mackinaw" sailboats designed to convey people and cargoes over these waters. Indians as well as early white residents were likely to travel Lake Michigan in these distinctive boats whose length ranged from about fourteen feet to nearly several times that size. Such craft were readily recognizable by their bowsprits and gaff rigs, the latter employing an upward-slanting spar coming off the mast near its top, from which the sail hung.

A French explorer, Jean Nicolet, is generally thought to have been the first white person known to venture into northern Lake Michigan when, in the early 1630's as an emissary for Governor Samuel de Champlain of New France, he may have been seeking a route to China. He is often described as dressing in elegant Chinese attire, which he might have been wearing, as some accounts suggest, when he landed at what is now Green Bay and met representatives of the local Winnebago.

Four decades later came the first recorded trip by white men along Lake Michigan's more dangerous eastern shoreline, a route that would take them past Point Betsie. This was the end of a long journey for the Frenchmen Jacques Largilier and Pierre Porteret, two associates of Father Marquette, the famous Jesuit missionary.[5] Seriously ill but struggling to get back to his St. Ignace mission, thus completing his second arduous visit within two years to Illinois tribes, Marquette died in 1675 somewhere along the Lake Michigan shore. (Frankfort residents presumably prefer historical analysis which identifies the mouth of the Betsie River, a few miles before the famed priest would have reached Point Betsie, as the probable location of his death. Other studies cite Ludington, about sixty miles south, as the likely site). Whatever the truth may be, Marquette didn't make it to Point Betsie, but his two compatriots subsequently resumed their shore-hugging, northward journey to the mission. This course would have taken them past the point and on up the coast. Hence, with the possible exception of unknown wandering fur traders, these Frenchmen would have been the first whites to paddle around the promontory and through the waters lying between North and South Manitou islands and the soaring, dune-lined mainland.

It seems reasonable to believe that even though Marquette didn't get to the Manitous, he must have heard about them. On his initial trip in 1673, Marquette had joined with Louis Joliet, a fur trader whom the Governor of New France had ordered to explore lands west of the Straits of Mackinac. Although Joliet's journal and other papers were lost when his canoe tipped over while he was returning to Montreal, memory enabled him to draw a map which first depicted Lake Michigan's islands. Although Joliet hadn't been to the Manitou Passage and didn't use that name, this early cartographer somehow managed to position the islands reasonably accurately.

Next among white explorers to see the Manitous and round Point Betsie was the famous Robert Cavalier Sieur de la Salle, the French explorer who headed south along the lake's eastern shore en route to the Gulf of Mexico in the fall of 1680. La Salle made a brief note of the islands, somewhat prophetically warning that they "...are a hazard on account of the sand bars which lie off them."[6]

One can presume that Native Americans camped on the beach in the vicinity of the point, as they did elsewhere along the coast. They surely knew the area well. An endearing and enduring tribal legend tells us that the giant Sleeping Bear Dune represents a mourning mother bear who, having crossed Lake Michigan to escape a raging forest fire, climbed atop the mainland shore where she waited, sadly in vain, for her two cubs. The two islands, named for the Great Spirit, are said to have been raised in their memory.

The first white campers at nearby Point Betsie may have been Henry Rowe Schoolcraft and Captain David Bates Douglas, who were members of the 1820 expedition led by Michigan Territorial Governor, Lewis Cass. The Governor's own homeward route took him inland and across Michigan Territory. Those who completed the trip by canoe pulled their craft onto the shore at what they called "Gravelly Point" and spent the night after the long day's forty-five-mile northerly paddle.

Contemporary campers can sympathize with them, for Schoolcraft's journal tells us their morning departure was delayed for a couple of hours by intermittent showers. Their journal also records a "...great uniformity in the appearance of the coast, which is characterized by sand banks, and pines. In some instances, a stratum of loam is seen beneath the sand, and the beech and maple are occasionally intermixed with the predominating pines of the forest; but our impressions in passing along the coast, are only those produced by barren scenery or uncultivated woods."[7]

The opening of the Erie Canal in 1825, which proved to have a profound impact on settlement of the Lake Michigan coast, connected the Hudson River with the Great Lakes. This enormous engineering achievement provided new opportunities both for travelers and the prospect of cheap shipments of agricultural goods from the new farms of the Midwest to populous eastern markets. Anticipating growing public interest, the U.S. Government began negotiating with the Indians in the mid-1830s, seeking to acquire lands for settlement. Through the Treaty of 1836, the United States gained control of the northern portion of the Lower Peninsula, as well as all of the Upper Peninsula. Thereafter, settlers began to swarm into the Michigan Territory, most of them coming by wagon over poor roads from communities in New England and northern New York, or by train followed by transfers to Great Lakes ships. Not long after Michigan achieved statehood in 1837, travelers could plan voyages over Lake Michigan on scheduled steamboats.

The state's population was soon growing at a truly extraordinary pace. From pre-statehood tallies of just under 8,900 in 1820 and a little over 32,000 ten years later, only five years after the Erie Canal's opening, the count shot upward to 212,000 in 1840—only three years after statehood—and sky-rocketed to more than a million people during the next thirty years. Viewed from another perspective, an 1836 record indicates that receipts from Michigan land sales in that year amounted to more than one-fifth of all such sales throughout the United States.[8] Michigan truly was booming country, and ships offered most people the best means of relocating to the Great Lake State. The early settlers found land in central and southern Michigan; significant settlement of the northwestern portion of the Lower Peninsula did not occur until after the Civil War. But along with growth at Chicago, Milwaukee, and other port towns in southern Lake Michigan, the settlement boom during the post-war decades served to build vessel traffic along the shore and generate interest in the erection of lighthouses. It wasn't long before travelers making long-distance trips into the lake country from eastern states were joined by those moving between newly established lakeside communities.

Frankfort Harbor in 1895.
The Benzie County Record-Patriot June 29, 1983.

POINT BETSIE AND THE TWO NEARBY MANITOU ISLANDS HAVE BEEN CLOSELY LINKED, NOTABLE LANDMARKS THROUGHOUT THE AREA'S MARITIME HISTORY. An 1857 guide observed, "On leaving Two Rivers [Wisconsin], the steamers usually run for the Manitou Islands, Michigan, a distance of about 100 miles. Soon after the last vestige of land sinks below the horizon on the west shore, the vision catches the dim outline of coast on the east or Michigan shore at Point aux Betsie, which is about 30 miles south of the Great Manitou Island."[9]

Apart from the canoes of the Indian traders, the earliest commercial boats traveling up and down the Lake Michigan shore were sail-powered vessels rigged as brigs, barks, or schooners. Generally, brigs were two-masted vessels carrying only square-rigged sails; barks were three-masted, the two forward masts being square-rigged and the mizzen mast carrying fore-and-aft sails, while schooners were two- or three-masted vessels that carried only fore-and-aft sails.[10] Having to sail without the benefit of global positioning satellites, radar and other navigation equipment common to today's commercial fleet, these boats often followed the shoreline to reach their destinations. Such a course could be a mixed blessing, for it placed vessels at the peril of shoals and submerged rocks upon which they might be quickly pounded to pieces.

Through decades starting early in the 19th century, the schooner—possibly inspired by the popular "clippers" but modified to better serve Great Lakes conditions—gradually became the dominant design owing to such vessels' ability to sail close to the wind, and by the relative ease of their management. Two types of schooner design were common on the lakes: nearly flat-bottomed, pointed-bow hulls that housed a centerboard that could be hiked to facilitate the vessel's passage over shallows into harbors, and scow-shaped, still flatter-bottomed hulls carrying two masts that, while slower of sail, could haul larger cargoes.

As historian Theodore Karamanski observes, "A remarkable feature of the schooner era on Lake Michigan was that it took place in the face of growing numbers of steamships on the inland seas."[11] Steamships gradually proved their popularity for passengers' travel and the shipment of time-sensitive goods, he explains, while sailing ships were a more economical means of transporting bulk cargoes. This pattern continued until the early 20th century when, but for the last tall ships that were able to hang onto a minor share of shipments into the early '30s, the benefits of steam overwhelmed wind-powered competitors.

The earliest steam-powered vessels on the Great Lakes were side-wheeling paddle boats. "Propellers," as the newer, screw-driven steamships were first commonly called, began to appear in the 1840s. Steamers of this propulsion proved themselves more economical to operate than side-wheelers and had a greater cargo capacity—important even though passengers provided the primary impetus for steam power. By the mid-1850s, the fleets of side-wheelers and propellers were about equal, yet sail-powered ships still out-numbered all the steamers by a four- or five-to-one ratio.

Karamanski adds, "The apogee of the age of sail on the Great Lakes was reached in 1868. [That was a decade into the operation of the lighthouse at Point Betsie.] In that year, 1,855 sailing ships were registered on the inland seas. While the number of sailing ships steadily declined thereafter, the actual total tonnage of sailing ships increased on the lakes, rising from 294,000 tons in 1868 to 298,000 tons in 1873. The building of larger clipper schooners accounted for this increase in tonnage."[12]

Shedding further light on the Lakes' schooner era, Karamanski reports, "Beginning in the 1860s, new three-masted vessels boasting 300 to 500 tons burden dominated the Lake Michigan grain trade. While some of these were rigged with a square sail from the foremast, more common was the use of another distinctive Great Lakes design: the raffe. This was a triangular sail set from the foremast that had nearly the pulling power of a square sail, but was not as difficult for a small crew to set."[13] Obviously, crew requirements had a major bearing on a cargo vessel's financial viability.

As the years passed and steamers were gaining dominance, designers and builders were yet showing their interest in sail power as they launched ever larger vessels. The trend culminated in the 1881 construction of the world's largest schooner—five-masted, both square- and fore-and-aft rigged, but nonetheless identified as a schooner —the celebrated *David Dows*. Doubtless an awesome sight, the ship proved to be rather short-lived. Within months of its launching, it collided with, and sank, a three-master, eliciting much ridicule. And after just eight years' total service, already having been converted into a towed barge like many other tall ships of the time, it went to the bottom near Chicago. Such re-makes were not confined to the grand sailboats; slow and shop-worn steam-powered ferries and cargo ships that once were the pride of their fleet often completed service gutted of machinery and wheelhouse, being hauled ignominiously around the Lakes as barges.

Surely, the tall ships were thrilling to watch and impressive, as well as challenging, to command. They were built to survive the lakes' tumultuous seas, yet capable of maneuvering in shallow waters. In the later years of sail, steam tugs typically towed them into and out of narrow harbor channels that could be tricky, if not impossible, to navigate under certain wind conditions; such assistance also enabled the ships to better maintain schedules and make more runs. "The mainmast of a Lake Michigan schooner frequently topped one hundred feet, and with all sails set these ships offered half an acre of canvas to the wind," writes Karamanski.[14] Together with the growing number of steamers beating their way up and down the coast, such rigs must have presented a magnificent sight to Point Betsie's keepers as they looked out for passing vessels.

◌

PASSENGER TRAVEL THROUGH THE "MANITOU PASSAGE," AS THE ROUTE BETWEEN THE TWO ISLANDS AND THE MAINLAND SOON CAME TO BE GENERALLY KNOWN, AND AROUND POINT BETSIE GREW RAPIDLY as the settlement boom reached the Lake Michigan country, the Erie Canal having opened the way to faster and more comfortable migration to the West from northeastern states and European countries. Hence, much of the early traffic was westbound—settlers bringing their goods to Lake Michigan ports. By the early 1840s, several steamer lines were competing for business on the route between Buffalo and Detroit, Chicago, St. Joseph, and other port communities. But as more towns along the shore developed, a two-way flow of commercial traffic emerged, with agricultural products and local goods moving about Lake Michigan and other Great Lakes ports. By the end of the Civil War, however, the nature of the trade was changing. Bulk goods—especially locally produced lumber and grains, iron ore from the Upper Peninsula, and coal from eastern deposits—became the predominant cargoes.[15]

As Midwestern cities grew and their economies expanded during the latter half of the 19th century, a packaged freight trade also flourished on the lake. Notes one study, "In 1905, annual receipts of 'unclassified freight' for the port of Chicago were 1,098,054 tons; out-shipments to other communities were 640,042 tons, or nearly half the amount of package freight received."[16] The writer added, "During the early 1900s, Duluth and Buffalo received significant amounts of package freight from Chicago. Each of these cities served as an important center for the transfer of goods inland by rail and/or canal. The return trade from Duluth was principally in iron ore, while Buffalo shipped back various merchandise and bulk quantities of coal for domestic and industrial use."[17]

Throughout the long history of Lake Michigan commerce, the Manitou Passage has been recognized as one of its most significant features. The passage afforded not only the most direct north-south route—significant since "time is money" in the shipping business—but provided refuge from western storms for a vessel managing to get behind the islands. Assuming a ship navigated the passage correctly, avoiding its shallows, it was a safe course. Writes a local marine historian, "Lake Michigan is long and narrow with its entire length exposed to the prevailing westerly winds. In a storm, boats must run directly into the wind to reach the protection of the Wisconsin shore or they can run for the protection of an Island. For vessels sailing out of the populous ports of Chicago or Milwaukee, the nearest islands are the Manitous. Thus, we have the combination of a narrow and dangerous passage and the best protection in 200 miles of Lake."[18]

Author Frank Barcus tells the moving story of the steamship *Illinois*, which battled a massive Lake Michigan storm for seventy-two hours before finally arriving three days late at its Chicago destination.[19] Captain John Stufflebeam, he observed, "...put not his faith in anchors nor yet in other works of man, but trusted his life and that of his vessel to a nobler creation." The vessel had been on a trip to Mackinac Island, fortunately carrying only freight on that trip. On the return, the ship stopped at Northport, then departed there at 3 a.m. "The lake was rough, but things didn't begin to look serious until a couple of hours later," Stufflebeam recounted:

> *We stood the rising gale and sea quite well for an hour. Then it began to snow and the storm broke all about us. We headed for the beach of South Manitou Island, but when we reached there found to our consternation that there were no docks, and it was impossible to anchor safely.*
>
> *I saw only one safe solution. We drove right into the land and forced the nose of the vessel up the beach. I kept the engines going slowly for fifty hours in this position. Their action helped us ride the seas continually smashing against us.*
>
> *At the end of fifty hours we were at last able to improve our situation. We succeeded after several attempts in throwing a line ashore, which we fastened to a large old tree. Then I could stop the engines and we remained securely fastened to that life-saving tree for the next twenty-four hours. Later we backed off and went on our way.*

The *Illinois'* tactic, running onto the beach, was not unique. Numerous skippers have followed this strategy, including captains of the Ann Arbor Railroad car ferries who, while steaming back and forth across Lake Michigan, sometimes set a course for the Manitou Passage to take advantage of its shelter from vicious seas on the open lake.

While the captain's seamanship enabled the *Illinois* to escape, the sheer number of vessels whose fates weren't so fortunate is convincing evidence of the risks these inland seas have posed for mariners. A 1972 study identified more than 3,700 documented Great Lakes wrecks;[20] undocumented wrecks would substantially hike that count. This author's findings indicate that although Lake Huron has posed the highest risk to vessels, second place—far surpassing Superior, the largest of the Great Lakes—goes decisively to Lake Michigan. The tally totaled 772 wrecks on Lake Michigan; Huron was the site of 1,212 wrecks, and mighty Superior—with a lower wreck count than the relatively shallow Lake Erie—was at 503.

Grounding has posed the chief peril to vessels traveling Lake Michigan waters, including the shoals in and about the passage. Countless ships have literally "gone to pieces" on sand bars within sight of the beach when their anchors have failed to hold in the face of high winds and heaving waves. Proximity to a beach often has been of little help or solace to victims of the powerful storms of late fall, when a person tossed into smashing, frigid surf is very unlikely to survive longer than a few moments.

While most such accounts relate to events in the latter 19th or early 20th centuries, haunting evidence of a more recent grounding yet lies just off the southwest coast of South Manitou Island. The rusting hulk is the *Francisco Morazan*, a "salty" which, while seeking to return to the Atlantic through the St. Lawrence Seaway, was driven

A barge works to free a grounded schooner near Frankfort before a storm would batter it.
Courtesy of Benzie Area Historical Museum

hard aground in a blinding snowstorm during the first night of December, 1960. Its Greek captain and crew had missed the proper course into the passage. In a rescue effort that illustrated the Coast Guard's modern capabilities, the captain's pregnant wife was air-lifted to safety by helicopter the following morning, while the captain and twelve man crew abandoned ship two days later, taking refuge aboard the Coast Guard's famed icebreaker, the *Mackinaw*.

For his classic 1899 account of the Great Lakes, J.B. Mansfield relied upon U.S. Government data covering the twenty-year period between 1878 and 1897 tallying a wreck total of 5,999 vessels, with 1,166 lives lost.[21] The schooner *Hercules* became the first known wreck in Lake Michigan, lost with all hands off Chicago in 1818. A recent estimate puts the total shipwreck count on the Great Lakes, over 300-some years of travel, at around 25,000.[22] The tally starts with the famed *Griffon*, the French explorer Sieur de la Salle's sixty foot, Niagara River-built ship that went to the bottom in 1679, most likely in northern Lake Michigan, returning from its maiden voyage with a load of fur pelts. That pioneer vessel had been sent home from Green Bay at the order of the famed explorer, who chose to continue searching overland for the route to China.

Passengers and crews aboard both sailing ships and the early steamers faced substantial risks, which also posed threats to valuable cargoes. Writers Harlan Hatcher and Erich A.Walter cite one authority's estimate that "…[O]f the 199 steamships on the lakes between 1818 and 1853, 14 burned, 4 exploded, and 36 were wrecked, a total loss of over 27 per cent" and added that sailing ships' records "…probably showed even greater casualties."[23]

Mark L. Thompson cites an 1872 publication by Captain J.W. Hall, reporting that a Detroit ship reporter had kept a record of Great Lakes shipwrecks through the 1871 season. In that single year, he recorded 591 founderings, collisions, groundings, and explosions.[24] With 2,475 vessels of all types operating on the Great Lakes that year—662 sailing ships, 682 steam-powered and the rest barges—there was about a twenty-five percent chance that a ship would meet with an accident. A prospective traveler might find such odds a trifle unsettling!

Thompson's analysis identifies the Great Lakes' waters that have posed the greatest peril. Not surprisingly, among them is "the disarmingly picturesque Manitou Passage" between the islands and the dune-lined bluff. While acknowledging that wreck figures are "sketchy," he says "…we know that the broken hulls of thirty-five ships still rest on the sandy bottom of the passage. More than fifty vessels are known to have wrecked around the Manitous, and that probably represents only a small percentage of the actual total."[25] Other counts of known shipwrecks within, or close to, the Manitou Passage and islands place the total at nearly sixty, with that number being swelled by a large number of undocumented wrecks—vessels thought to have gone down in the vicinity, of which no trace has been found. The prominence of these waters as a site for studying shipwrecks has led to the recent establishment of the Manitou Passage State Underwater Preserve, embracing 282 square miles.

❧

THE REPORTS OF EARLY TRAVELERS TO THE MANITOU PASSAGE OFFER INSIGHTS INTO THE CHARACTER OF THE AREA IN THEIR TIME, and confirm that the suddenness with which violent weather could arise was a common source of concern to them. Count de Castlenau, a European nobleman sailing through the passage, described the severity of its turbulence in this way: "We were a plaything of the giant waves....I have seen the squalls of the banks of Newfoundland....And the hurricanes of the Gulf of Mexico. Nowhere have I witnessed the fury of the elements comparable to that found on this fresh water sea."[26]

It was in the mid-1830s that passengers on the earliest steamships first became familiar with these islands as their vessels took the safe route through the passage or stopped there for fuel—the last such opportunity for a vessel taking a mid-lake southward course toward Chicago or another port. One of the first such references comes from a noted Englishwoman, Harriet Martineau, who, in describing her 1836 journey, observed that her fellow passengers were familiar with the native legends associated with the islands and Sleeping Bear Dunes. The islands had appeared deserted to her; however, the following year an American en route to Chicago reported that his ship had stopped at South Manitou Island for wood.[27]

In 1837, Lieutenant G.J. Pendergast of the U.S. Navy visited the passage, seeking to identify suitable locations for lights that might be helpful to ships transiting the area. He reported that the south end of South Manitou Island held promise for a lighthouse. With vessel traffic continuing to increase, his choice was seconded a year later by another Navy man, Lieutenant James Housman. Their recommendation reflected not only the potential hazards in the area, but the fact that South Manitou offered the only deep-water harbor between Chicago and the growing port towns at Lake Michigan's south end, and the Mackinac Straits far to the north. Their reasoning apparently found support in the Executive Branch and Congress, for construction began in 1839 on the first South Manitou Light, an investment of just under $5000 that would greatly aid mariners by marking the Passage's western side.

The Manitous became routine ports with the growth of steamer traffic. Given the fuel requirements of a 19th century steamer, accessible lands close to harbors represented attractive business opportunities to ambitious woodsmen and the owners of suitable forest tracts. When her steamship stopped at the Manitous for wood during an 1843 trip, the noted writer Margaret Fuller observed that the island's only residents were the cutters. Somewhat later, New Yorker Juliette Starr Dana wrote in her journal of an 1852 voyage that her side-wheel steamer, the *Baltimore*, had stopped at North Manitou Island for wood. While the fuel was hauled aboard, she said she took a walk in woods that "...cover the whole Island & are very thick & high."[28]

✦

THE AREA'S INITIAL WHITE SETTLEMENTS WERE ON THE TWO MANITOU ISLANDS. The first recorded settlers on South Manitou, William W. Burton and family, were active in the business of "wooding" for steamships in the latter 1830s and early 1840s; government timber apparently was his source, as his actual ownership of about fifty acres has been traced back only to 1849. Notably, Burton was also the first lighthouse keeper in northwest Michigan, being appointed in 1839 to the new South Manitou Light at an annual salary of $350. He was removed from the light-tending job after three years; one account suggests that wooding may have been judged to interfere with the performance of his government duties.[29]

While wood-cutters were also interested in harvesting North Manitou Island's forests, lack of a natural harbor deterred them for a time. But Nicholas Pickard began cutting there in the mid-1840s, and it is reported that by 1847 there were forty woodcutters and one family living on North Manitou.[30] A dock was first built on the island's southeastern coast; somewhat later, another was erected on the western side at a place where the high bluff briefly dropped close to the lake's level. That site held promise of good business as an alternative to South Manitou Island's western side, which is lined with soaring dunes and presented no naturally protected site where vessels could readily be loaded. The western side of North Manitou offered another benefit, as ships could find protection from the occasionally fierce storms out of the northeast. And Pickard's wharf facilitated the fueling of ships whose captains chose, under certain adverse weather conditions, to avoid the narrow Passage's perilous shoals.

An account by Albany (NY) *Evening Journal* editor Thurlow Weed of his summer voyage from Buffalo to Chicago for the 1847 Rivers and Harbors Convention offers an interesting perspective on travel in this region.[31] Weed traveled aboard the side-wheel steamer *Empire*, a luxurious, 260-foot vessel of over 1,200 tons—"extremely well arranged," he judged, for cabin and steerage passengers as well as freight. The vessel's fuel requirements shocked him; he reported that her boilers consumed six hundred cords of wood in a single such voyage, an amount he judged would require the clearing of more than ten woodland acres! Wrote Weed of his west-bound trip, "From Mackinaw our course is south....At 7 o'clock this evening we touched at one of the Manitou islands for wood. At this point all the steamers 'wood.' This island, some three miles by ten in extent, is only inhabited by the few persons employed in cutting and hauling wood. It is not even inhabited by animals. I saw none of the feathered race. Reptiles are seldom seen. And in the absence of all these, mosquitoes, finding no one to torment, come not to the Manitou island."

Weed also chronicled his return home, a route that first took him northward along the Wisconsin shore. He took note of the treacherous "Death's Door" strait, roughly across the lake and slightly to the north of Point Betsie, that was then the only link between Green Bay with Lake Michigan. With its associated islands, this area, also known by the French term "Port des Morts," is said to be the site of more shipwrecks than any other freshwater body in the world. Weed wrote, "These waters are seldom traversed, and human footsteps are rarely set upon these islands. A single lighthouse, with an occasional land-mark, is all that we have seen, indicating that our government has recognized the existence of this most interesting portion of our common country." In such isolated country, a lighthouse was, in fact, early evidence of the government's expanding interest in, and responsibility to, mariners on the Great Lakes. From Death's Door, Weed's vessel ventured across Lake Michigan to North Manitou Island. He wrote that its "...sand soil produces nothing but wood, though I do not understand why a soil that sustains a maple and a beech forest should not bear wheat, corn, and vegetables. There are some forty men employed here in cutting and hauling boat wood, for which $1.75 per cord is paid." He took note that the only resident family on the island came there from a town in his state of New York. Impressed by the island's isolation, he added, "From the last of October until May, they know nothing of what is passing in the world."

These accounts clarify how isolated northwest Michigan generally, and the Lake Michigan mainland coast and Manitou Passage, in particular, were in the mid-19th century. First at South Manitou Island, and then at Point Betsie nearly two decades later, the construction of a lighthouse was a truly remarkable step—something of a region's coming of age, signifying the presence of lake-borne commerce and settlement opportunities.

One other aspect of the region's early story that would have pricked the curiosity of an 1850s visitor relates to the islands. For forty years beginning in 1855, the two Manitou Islands along with South and North Fox Islands and the Beaver Island group farther to the north comprised a separate Michigan county. This came about because of the self-appointed rule of the Mormon King, James J. Strang on the more substantially populated Beaver Island. His followers elected him to the Michigan Legislature where, during his second term, he proposed creation of an island county. The legislative committee considering his proposal reported it favorably on grounds that "...a feeling of deep distrust and repugnance approaching warlike hostility exists between the different classes of people inhabiting the islands and the mainland." These tensions for the most part stemmed from religious and political differences between the "kingdom's" faithful and the island's previous settlers, some of whom remained on the island while others had relocated to the nearby mainland.

The initial proposal included only Beaver Island and the Foxes, but the Manitous were added to the measure during its consideration and became the source of the new county's name. Strang was assassinated in 1855 and his followers then fled or were driven from the island as prior occupants returned and newcomers arrived. Separate county structure for the islands no longer being justified, the two Manitou and two Fox islands were placed in Leelanau County, immediately north of Benzie, while the still more northerly Beaver group was awarded to Charlevoix County.[32]

As Lake Michigan traffic grew, interest rose in improving guidance for vessels using the popular Manitou Passage. The area's sole light, on South Manitou Island, had served to mark the passage's west side for more than a decade, but no aid served mariners' needs on the eastern, mainland side. The situation began to improve in 1852 with the construction of a light at Cathead Point, near Northport, marking the northern end of the passage. (Both the island and Cathead lights would be rebuilt on their sites in 1858.) The shore near Point Betsie, which northbound vessels following the shoreline had to round to the east as they set their course to the passage, was the logical southern location.[33]

❧

THE KEY STEPS THAT BROUGHT THE LIGHTHOUSE SERVICE TO POINT BETSIE BEGAN MORE THAN 150 YEARS AGO, literally in the final hours of U.S. President Millard Fillmore's term. Vital, formative steps continued throughout the administration of President Franklin Pierce, who succeeded Fillmore on March 4, 1853, and the project was completed early in President James Buchanan's term. A few background observations on the government's commitment to lighthouses will put the federal investment at Point Betsie in an appropriate context.

Americans' earliest experience with lighthouses began on Little Brewster Island at the entrance to Boston harbor, sixty years before Independence; the coast's first light was built there, financed by tonnage duties on ships entering and departing the colonial city. Shining first on September 14, 1716, that light was destroyed during the Revolutionary War, but was quickly rebuilt in 1783. A truly historic landmark, the Boston Light is the only U.S. beacon that is still tended by a keeper; this symbolic bow to history recently took on greater significance with the appointment of a civilian female, representing women's important place in lighthouse history, as keeper. The longest standing American light tower is at Sandy Hook, New Jersey; erected in 1764, that structure now lies within the Gateway National Recreation Area.

Illustrating lighthouses' importance to the commerce and well-being of the new nation, the federal government found itself dealing with them virtually from its start. The United States gained title to the existing lighthouses through the ninth law enacted by the Congress, which President George Washington signed into law on August 7, 1789. That statute placed administrative responsibility for lighthouses in the Treasury Department under its first secretary, Alexander Hamilton; a few years later, the task was delegated to the department's commissioner of revenue.

In 1820, the leadership of the facilities and personnel comprising the Lighthouse Establishment was assigned to the less visible fifth auditor of the treasury, Stephen Pleasanton, who would bear those responsibilities, in addition to his other duties, for over thirty-two years. Many lighthouses were built during his tenure, among them the original Great Lakes lights. Lights were first constructed at Presque Isle, near Erie on Lake Erie, and near Buffalo, on Lake Ontario; amidst some uncertainty, the Lake Erie light, completed in 1818, appears to have the stronger claim of being first. A year later, Congress provided for the construction of the first light in Michigan Territory, at the mouth of the Detroit River, and the initial Lake Michigan light was built at Chicago in 1832.

The need for additional lights on the Great Lakes was becoming apparent, and when Congress in 1838 gave authority for the division of the Lighthouse Service into eight districts, two of them were drawn to cover those inland seas. U.S. Navy Lieutenant James T. Homans was assigned to the western lakes and is said to have traveled more than 1,800 miles on an inspection tour that took him through Lakes Huron and Michigan to Chicago.[34]

Although Pleasanton's interests, commitment to frugality and administrative ability may have been appropriate for his other duties, they unfortunately did not lend themselves to a progressive approach to his expanding lighthouse responsibilities. During his long tenure, frustration gradually turned into outright condemnation of his policies. Sensing that America's Lighthouse Establishment was falling behind public needs and failing to benefit from technological improvements developed and deployed in Europe, Congress finally intervened in 1851; an appropriations measure required the secretary of the treasury to appoint a competent and prominent board who would evaluate the existing U.S. light network and chart its improvement.

❧

THE BOARD FULFILLED CONGRESS' EXPECTATIONS AND GUIDED THE NATION TO AN EXEMPLARY LIGHTHOUSE PROGRAM. Led by Navy Admiral William B. Shubrick, the panel promptly reported the following January that America's navigational aids were not only inadequate, but significantly inferior to those in place and being installed across the Atlantic. The investigative board recommended a complete reorganization of America's lighthouse functions. The panel also resolved a long-running controversy by calling for the use of an illumination system well known and widely deployed throughout several previous decades in Europe, developed by a French physicist, Augustin Fresnel.

These were bold recommendations, as they would fundamentally alter the country's lighthouse administrative structure and terminate use of a light apparatus advanced by Pleasanton's long-time technical advisor, Winslow Lewis. An American sea captain, Lewis had modified and patented a "catoptric" light system of earlier French design, which combined lamps and reflectors. Despite periodic improvements, the catoptric concept was inherently inefficient; severe light losses were unavoidable, and its reflective capabilities tended to deteriorate. Hence, only a fraction of the light generated by these lamps was visible from the sea. Despite these limitations Lewis had managed, through his personal association with Pleasanton, to block adoption of an alternative system.

The revolutionary Fresnel concept replaced the reflectors with stacked rings of glass prisms that were capable of intensifying light such that its visibility was essentially enhanced several-fold. The greater efficiency justified the Fresnel design's significantly greater cost (in end-of-19th century dollars, a Fresnel lens ran from more than $4000 to more than $8000, depending on its size). Flashes of light could be created by rotating panels containing "bulls eyes" around the stationary lamp, either inside or outside the lens. When differentiated from other nearby lights, the timing of such flashes would permit certain identification of a light from sea, thereby greatly boosting its navigational benefit. Lights were also "fixed," or non-flashing. When finally brought to America at the board's insistence, the Fresnel system quickly won universal adoption and acclaim.

Fourth-order Fresnel lens No. 468
Sleeping Bear Dunes National Lakeshore, Empire, Michigan.
Photo by author

Original 1856 fourth-order Fresnel lens, fixed beam, in use at Owl's Head Light, Maine.
Photo by author

The study panel also called for the direction of all federal lighthouse functions by an appointed board within the Treasury Department. This permanent board was promptly created, led initially by Admiral Shubrick, the study panel's chairman. The new Lighthouse Board proved to be a highly successful reform, directing lighthouse functions for more than 50 years.[35] Its leadership was ambitious, as new construction proceeded rapidly. By 1865, there were twenty-six lights on Lake Michigan; fifteen on Lake Superior; twelve on Lake Erie; ten on Lake Huron and seven on Lake Ontario, and on the ocean coasts the pace was similarly impressive.[36] Taking its responsibility very seriously, in 1868 the Board summarized its mission: "Nothing indicates the liberality, prosperity or intelligence of a nation more clearly than the facilities which it affords for the safe approach of the mariner to its shores."[37]

❧

POINT BETSIE LIGHT'S OWN ORIGIN STEMS FROM AN 1852 RECOMMENDATION BY THE NEW LIGHTHOUSE BOARD'S SUPERINTENDENT FOR THE UPPER GREAT LAKES. He called for erecting small lights, each said to be a $5000 project, at three sites: "Point Betsey, and two on Lake Superior—Grand Island harbor and Rock harbor, at Isle Royal."[38]

The Board responded, "Although…not possessed of the requisite detailed information to recommend these lights as being absolutely necessary, yet there can be no risk of a misappropriation of funds, inasmuch as the law provides that their necessity shall be reported on by the Topographical bureau before constructing them; and as the commerce of this rich mineral region is rapidly increasing, and is subjected to many natural obstacles, it is deemed just to recommend them to the favorable consideration of Congress."[39]

Acting with a clear sense of dispatch which reflected its historic interest in navigational safety, Congress promptly passed an appropriations measure for "Light-houses, Light-boats, Buoys, etc., and providing for the Erection and Establishment of the same…" that contained this pertinent language: "For a light-house on Point Betsey, Lake Michigan, five thousand dollars."[40] President Millard Fillmore gave this measure his signature on his final day in office, March 3, 1853.

It was early in President Franklin Pierce's term that attention was directed to finding a specific site for a lighthouse at Township 26 North, Range 16 West. Records suggest that a number of "reservations" for lighthouse purposes were designated within a stretch of government-owned shoreline from close to the mouth of the Betsie River to Point Betsie.[41] The earliest of these orders, covering an area just south of the Betsie River, was issued just a month after Pierce took office. Eleven months later came another reservation covering a 64.7-acre area a little north of the river, but slightly south of the site ultimately selected.[42] Both of these orders were subsequently rescinded on grounds they would not be needed for lighthouse purposes, thereby restoring these tracts to the public domain.

The Lighthouse Board's index of in-coming general correspondence cites a Point Betsie letter from the district office at Detroit, relating "to site selected for light house at Point marked on sketch enclosed," but this January 21, 1856, document unfortunately was lost in a 1921 fire that consumed or damaged many historically significant files held in storage at the Commerce Department.[43] There are, however, two other important clues to the identification of the Point Betsie reservation. One is a February 3, 1856, letter from President Pierce (its current location and recipient are unknown) that refers to a 9.52-acre tract; this land is cited as "Parcel #2" in a 1930 Federal Real Estate questionnaire that also refers to the Pierce letter. The other citation of interest is an entry in the Bureau of Land Management tract book that refers to a February 3, 1858, letter from the Lighthouse Board, relinquishing "...all of said reservation...by order of the President July 27, 1855, except the NW corner containing 9.50 acres."

It is worthy of mention that the tasks of siting and constructing Point Betsie Lighthouse, as well as other navigational aids, fell primarily to the administration of President Pierce, who is generally perceived as a "strict constructionist," i.e., one whose conception of the scope of Congress' legislative powers is profoundly narrow. But, perhaps because he resided in a coastal state, he was also a firm believer in lighthouses and federal navigation assistance—assuming that the scope of federal involvement was, in his view, properly defined. In his first annual message to Congress, Pierce directed the lawmakers' attention to "the eminently successful progress of the Coast Survey and of the Lighthouse Board."[44]

In a message accompanying his veto of an 1854 rivers and harbors measure, President Pierce further clarified his position. Having cited legal precedents reaching back to President Washington's administration, he acknowledged that, "In accordance with long-established legislative usage, Congress may construct light-houses and beacons and provide, as it does, other means to prevent shipwrecks on the coasts of the United States. But the General Government can not go beyond this and make improvements of rivers and harbors...." he opined.[45]

∾

WITH THE CONGRESS AND PIERCE ADMINISTRATION'S SUPPORT AND REQUISITE LAND FROM THE PUBLIC DOMAIN IN HAND, the way was clear for the Lighthouse Board to provide for Point Betsie lighthouse's construction. The Board drafted a contract and set of specifications detailing the project; on July 17, 1854, an agreement was signed between the U.S. Government and three contracting partners from Milwaukee, Wisconsin—Alanson Sweet, Luzern Ransom, and Morgan E. Shinn—the low bidders.[46]

The specifications for Point Betsie's lighthouse and keeper's dwelling also covered, with certain differences, such facilities at North Point on Milwaukee Bay and at the mouth of Michigan's Grand River. However, the government's actual contract with Sweet's firm was even more encompassing. In addition to Point Betsie ($3,200), it embraced the following construction projects and costs: North Point, Milwaukee Bay

($2990); Michigan's Grand River ($3500); La Pointe Harbor, Wisconsin ($4500); Rock Harbor on Lake Superior's Isle Royale ($4650); mouth of Michigan's Portage River ($4200); Grand Island Harbor ($4200); Point Iroquois, Lake Superior ($4500); mouth of Michigan's Eagle River ($3750); Round Island ($2940), and at the northern outlet of Lake Winnebago ($3000). Clearly, lighthouse building constituted a major opportunity in the middle 1850s for contractors on the Great Lakes, and Sweet and his associates vigorously pursued a share of the work.

⋙

THE CONTRACT EMPHASIZED that Mssrs. Sweet, Ransome and Shinn, along with their heirs, executors and administrators, were to meet all its stipulations and agreements. In a "workmanlike manner," they were to erect the buildings "...in every respect according to the drawings, plans and specifications provided by the Inspecting Engineer or agent for the Lighthouse Board." The contractors were obligated to "... construct, supply and furnish any and every omitted or defective part or appliance or accessory which may not be included" in the specifications, and to be guided strictly by the officer in charge of all the work without any additional charge or claim against the government. They were to furnish all the labor and materials and artificer's work necessary for the completion of the buildings.

An inexplicably optimistic contract provision, it would seem, set a completion date of September 30 of that same year—1854—for the buildings at the Point Betsie, Grand River, North Point and Winnebago; the other buildings were to be completed by August of the following year. Finally, the agreement stated that "...all the materials and workmanship herein contracted for shall be of the best quality and shall be subject to the inspection and approval of the Inspecting Engineer or Superintendent of Construction and accepted by him; and no payment shall be made under this contract for any material or work unless so accepted and received." That last sentence would prove significant in subsequent months.

⋙

THE SWEET FIRM'S INTEREST IN THIS WORK can be traced to an 1848 storm experience, during which a Captain Justice Bailey, sailing along the Wisconsin shore of Lake Michigan, sought shelter. He spotted an uncharted bay, mostly surrounded by forests, and having safely entered it and begun to explore the immediate area, came upon a limestone deposit. Captain Bailey reported his discoveries to his employer, Mr. Alanson Sweet, who was in the shipping business; his fleet of a dozen schooners generally hauled grain to Buffalo. Bailey's finding, Sweet recognized, could be turned into lucrative new west bound cargo. A New York native who had moved to Illinois in the early 1830s, Sweet had become involved in the lumber and building business there, then moved to Milwaukee in 1835 where he had built major buildings and was active in local political life.

A man of strong entrepreneurial instincts, he had found another opportunity in that city's newly emerging grain trade with eastern cities via the port of Buffalo. Acting upon Bailey's report, he had his crew build a pier at the natural harbor, and began lumbering and quarrying operations. The commercial promise of the area soon led to the state legislature's establishment of Door County, in which the settlement of Bailey's Harbor was centrally located. Sweet soon recognized that the town's commercial success depended upon construction of a lighthouse that would assist marine traffic; he then won the contract with the U.S. Government to complete that construction project, using limestone from his quarry to build a stone tower and keeper's dwelling that were used from 1852 to 1869.

Ultimately, Mr. Sweet's business results proved not as financially sweet as his name, but in the meantime his vessels and work on the Door County project facilitated his participation in the major round of lighthouse construction projects elsewhere on Lakes Michigan and Superior. The jobs at Point Betsie and other sites, several of which were embraced by the 1854 contract, attracted his attention, and he and his colleagues won the bidding.

∽

THE HAND-WRITTEN, DETAILED SPECIFICATIONS FOR POINT BETSIE'S CONSTRUCTION provided for a twenty-eight foot square keeper's dwelling, one and one-half stories tall, with a ten by twelve-foot shed adjoining the kitchen. The light tower was to be twenty-one feet, nine inches tall, from ground level to the lantern deck (the base of the illumination room atop the tower).

The brick walls of the house were to be one-foot thick; the brick walls of the ten-foot two-inch in diameter tower were to be sixteen inches thick. A six-foot deep cellar was to run under the entire house. The first floor of the dwelling, which was to be thirty-two inches above ground level and finished nine feet high, was partitioned into three rooms, two closets and an entry. The space above was to be three feet high at the eves; its ceiling, at its peak, was to be six and one-half feet high. The center of the lantern tower was to be eight feet, seven inches from the middle of the dwelling's end wall, and the tower was to be connected with the dwelling by a three-foot wide passageway at the second floor level.

All lumber was to be of fine pine or spruce, well seasoned and framed to the drawings' dimensions. The window caps and sills were to be of "dressed stone of approved quality"; the roof was to be covered with the best quality of slate, "well applied and secured with copper or composition nails and made secure from leaks around the chimneys with lead or zinc." The floors were to be of "white pine free of sap, shakes and knots, the boards not to exceed 8 inches wide, planed to an even thickness and well fitted and secured." The tower floor plates were to be of cast iron; so, too, was cast iron plate to cover the passageway and walls joining the house and tower, its ends "laid into the walls of both house and tower as they are laid up."

Cast iron was also specified for the cupola or ventilator in the lantern, and for capping the cistern, which was to be six feet deep and eight feet in exterior diameter, its interior being plastered with the best hydraulic cement so as to be water-tight. It would be furnished with a "good pump" or windlass, chain and bucket.

The glass for the lantern was to be of "French plate one quarter inch thick" and all the windows in the building were to be of "first quality crystal glass, all to be glazed and secured in the proper manner."

A superintendent or agent appointed by the Board was responsible for the location, position, and execution of the project. All construction tasks were to be done in a "faithful and workmanlike manner," and from these provisions there would be "No deviation whatever allowed or accepted without [the] previous consent of the Light House Board."

❧

THE FOLLOWING SET OF DRAWINGS DEPICTS POINT BETSIE LIGHTHOUSE AS ORIGINALLY CONSTRUCTED UNDER THESE SPECIFICATIONS. The plans include a side view from the south; a front view from the lake; the first floor's interior configuration, and the second floor's arrangements. Note that oil for the light originally was to be stored at the base of the tower (the only space allocated to this purpose initially), on the same level as the keeper's living and dining rooms and kitchen. As shown here, the tower and light were accessed from the second floor only, through a passage at the top of the stairway to the sleeping level's three bedrooms.

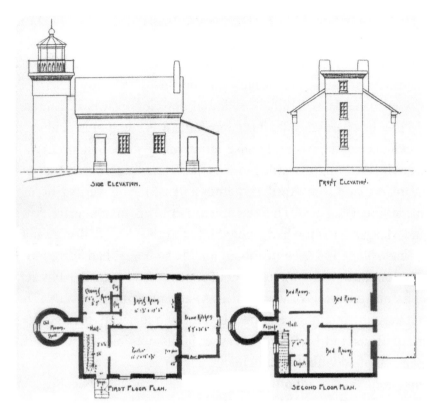

*Original Drawings, National Archives, reproduced in QUINN/EVANS ARCHITECTS'
Historic Structures Report: Point Betsie Light Station, 2005.*

❧

THERE ARE SEVERAL INDICATIONS THAT THE CONSTRUCTION
OF POINT BETSIE WAS NEARLY COMPLETE BY THE END OF 1857. The
Board's correspondence index references a January 4, 1857, report (consumed in the
aforementioned fire) by a district engineer regarding the completion of a contract for
Point Betsie signed by Alanson Sweet and the other parties. Also indexed but lost in the
blaze is a report by an Inspector Smith, from the steamer *Michigan*, on an examination
of the site. And there is an otherwise undated 1857 indexed letter from L. Sautter of
Paris, France (presumably of the firm of Sautter, Lemonier & Cie), relating to the
"illuminating apparatus" being shipped in cases to Point Betsie.

There is regional evidence, too. One source, in citing the establishment of the
colony of Benzonia about seven miles inland from the Betsie's mouth as "the first
event of interest in the settlement of Benzie County," added, "In the spring of 1858,
when the projectors of the colony arrived, there were a few white persons already in the
county." Among them, he noted, "There was a man at the light-house...."[47] Supporting

this description is a report from the Lighthouse Board itself, dated February 1, 1858, which describes Point Betsie in this way: "On the point of that name east side of Lake Michigan. A fixed light in a yellow brick tower. Building built 1857, has 4th order lens apparatus."[48] (In a report later that year, the Board officially described the light as flashing, rather than "fixed." Either the initial description was inaccurate or, perhaps more likely, the installation of the flash apparatus was completed slightly later.)

Solid evidence of the status of construction activity is found in a Lighthouse Board report of March 16, 1858, forwarded to the U.S. House of Representatives by Treasury Secretary Howell Cobb on April 9, addressing certain expenses of the lighthouse service on the Great Lakes.[49] This document reaffirms that Alanson Sweet, Luzerne Ransom and Morgan E. Shinn had entered into the July 17, 1854, contract on the basis of its "drawings, plans and specifications" and, in so doing, had agreed to be subject to the inspecting engineer or superintendent of construction, with no payment being made to them "...for any materials or work unless so accepted and received." The House was advised that the superintending engineer had refused to accept the lighthouses at Eagle River, Portage River and La Pointe because, in his opinion, the terms of the contract had not been complied with by the builders.

Details in that Board report listed five new lighthouses as being complete, each with a cost figure. Nothing had been paid to contractors for their work at Eagle River, with a cost of $4016.50, the report stated, saying that it should have been finished by the first of August, 1855, but was not completed until the end of June, 1857. When the engineer finally inspected the work that summer, he found "...numerous deviations from the contract, which, in his opinion, should prevent the payment of the contractors until they were made good and the contract was complied with." The contractors, however, had refused to accept his findings, and had requested that the Treasury Department intercede on their behalf.

With respect to Point Betsie the report added, it "...has not yet been accepted on account of its being finished too late in the [1857] season to admit of examination." The secretary advised the federal legislators that a special agent would be dispatched "as soon as the navigation of the lake will admit of his visiting the several points" where lights had been constructed. Presumably eager for payment, the contractors were also seeking the Treasury's approval of their Point Betsie work. There was also some question of possible cost over-runs at certain projects, including Point Betsie; it was reported only that "...the contractors have other claims, it is believed, of which this office has received no notice."

Finally, the National Archives' correspondence index makes reference to an October 3, 1858, letter to the Lighthouse Board (also unfortunately consumed in the Commerce Department fire) regarding a repair request for the tower. And a report from

Chairman W.B. Shubrick for the Secretary of the Treasury for the fiscal year ending June 30, 1859 reported that "The site of Point Betsey light-house has been protected."[50] These were the first of many repair needs, to both the terrain and its actual structures, that would be directed to the attention of district and national officials throughout Point Betsie Light's nearly 150 years of service.

❧

THAT 1859 REPORT OF THE BOARD ALSO SERVED TO ALERT CONGRESS to the challenge its key leaders were facing in striving to monitor the service's proliferating, but remote, facilities. In Shubrick's words:

The eleventh district, embracing the waters of Lakes St. Clair, Huron, Michigan, and Superior, and Green Bay, and their tributaries, is too extensive to be visited as often as is desirable without the aid of a steam tender. The sail vessel now employed in that district is constantly engaged, during the short season of navigation, in delivering supplies to the light-houses, and is therefore unavailable, if she were suitable, for inspection purposes. The consequence is, that the inspector is obliged to depend upon passenger steamers and railways as his chief means of transportation. But these, in but very few instances, carry him directly to a light-house, and he is consequently obliged to reach his destination from the point of deviation at a much increased expense and a great loss of time. A small propeller would answer the purposes both of visit and supply, and the increased expense of her maintenance, over that of the sail tender, would be amply compensated by the increased facilities of visit, and the prompt relief that might be carried to any given quarter in case of disaster. Personal visit and inspection being by far the most efficient means the board has at command to enforce due subordination and attention to their duties on the part of light-keepers, the change would seem to be a very beneficial one.

TO CONCLUDE DISCUSSION OF THE LIGHT'S ESTABLISHMENT, Dr. M.L. Leach, an early historian of the Grand Traverse region, described a notable event at the lighthouse. He said that two of the founders of Benzonia's Christian settlement, John and Charles E. Bailey, made several visits there during the summer of 1858 as they launched their colony. They would use a small boat to reach that inland destination, coasting the Lake Michigan shoreline from Glen Arbor, then sometimes portage across the divide between Lake Michigan and Crystal Lake, and complete their trip by paddling the nine miles down Crystal Lake to its eastern end, where the Benzonia settlement was taking root on a nearby hilltop. "Returning from one of these visits," wrote Leach, "they were once compelled by stress of weather to remain over Sunday near Point Betsey lighthouse, when Mr. C.E. Bailey improved the opportunity to preach to a small audience in a fisherman's shanty….The sermon was the first ever preached in Benzie county."[51]

Yet today, some visitors seem to find a spiritual quality in the beauty of this coastal spot that holds a prominent place in their memories. That worship experience nearly one hundred and fifty years ago was the first of innumerable vespers, weddings, and memorials conducted at the sentinel. And those advertisers whose strategies feature a lighthouse as a symbol of security and hope would find affirmation for their theme at Point Betsie.

The original Point Betsie Lighthouse as viewed from the northwest, with added protective works visible below the tower and the curtains drawn to protect the lens.
Photo, collection of author.

CHAPTER TWO

LIGHTKEEPING THROUGH THE YEARS

Technological advances in lighting, communications, weather forecasting, ship design, and navigation systems have consigned the human dimension of American lighthouses to the country's illustrious maritime history. This is not a recent development, but a trend which was easily spotted as much as a half-century ago by retired, or nearly retired, lighthouse personnel.

As one lighthouse admirer then lamented, "The keeper and his light has been shunted off the main track by the bulldozer of progress. With the old-time mariner and his three-stick windjammer he has been pushed high and dry on the lonesome shores of yesteryear. But even if he has no place among today's aids to navigation, the *old-time* keeper and his *old-time* light do have a place in our history. In his day, he not only did his best with what he had to safeguard the lives of seafarers, but often risked his own life to rescue the victims of the cruel ocean."[1]

Lightkeepers' extraordinary sense of responsibility for the safety of the rapidly increasing number of vessels and the crews they served is legendary. Maintaining the best quality of light possible was their critical task, whatever the fuel and illumination system at a particular tower might be, and however challenging the weather. Often, skill, ingenuity and stamina were demanded if a keeper was to fulfill that mission; a remarkable degree of dedication to one's tasks was an unending expectation.

The story of lighthouses and their keepers extends deep into history. Fires were set atop peaks as landmarks, it is believed, in pre-Christian times. Such fires would have been set to warn ships off dangerous shoals, or to help them steer toward harbor entrances and safe moorings. But the purpose was not always so salutary; fires were also the tactic of pirates intending to pillage a vessel by luring her aground. Even after the fires were commonly elevated onto towers in order to increase their visibility, the earliest lights were generally fueled with wood that was locally accessible. However, likely weary of the incessant hauling of heavy wood, the keepers of those primitive lights must have been relieved when lighter, longer-burning coal was found to be an acceptable fuel. Candles also came to be regarded as another convenient and popular alternative to wood. Their flame could be protected from bad weather within a lantern, but the intensity of candlelight was limited.

Lighthouse histories typically acknowledge the Roman days, then give more emphasis to the expansion of sea trading activity that followed the close of the Dark Ages. As shipping expanded through the years, Italian, French, and English firms became the leading innovators of coastal lights.

∽

AMERICANS' EXPERIENCE WITH LIGHTHOUSES dates back to 1716, when the first light was erected at the entrance to the busy port of Boston. Nearly three quarters of a century later, in 1789, President Washington approved legislation federalizing the existing coastal lights and their operations, about a dozen such sentinels were in place at key points along the Atlantic shore.

The first light on the Great Lakes was built by the British at Lake Ontario's Fort Niagara during the Revolutionary War, and lighthouse construction on the lakes remained an exclusively British and Canadian pursuit until the early nineteenth century. As already noted, the U.S. built lights at Buffalo and Erie, in 1818-1819, and the first two lighthouses on Lake Michigan were built in 1832 at Chicago and St. Joseph, Michigan. Construction projects continued thereafter, and in 1858 the Lighthouse Board reported the completion of four lights in the 11th District, including the Point Betsie structure.[2] There was something of a "chicken-and-egg" quality to the lighthouse construction movement, summed up in the popular adage, "If you build it, they will come." As historian J. B. Mansfield wrote long ago, "Lighthouses are not only aids to commerce, but they are the inducers or breeders of commerce, for where they are come ships." [3]

∽

THE EARLIEST LIGHTHOUSE LAMPS, first available for installation in Europe during the mid-18th century, used solid wicks. Improvements came through the years, leading eventually to the so-called "spider lamp" that consisted of a pan of oil with four wicks rising from it. This type was used extensively in American lighthouses beginning around the turn of the 19th century. They were the best available for their time, but the fumes they gave off would make it very difficult for a keeper to properly tend his light. The invention of a lamp that had a hollow circular wick, through and around which oxygen flowed, was a major step forward. This "Argand lamp," named for its inventor, Ami Argand, yielded a bright, smokeless flame whose power has been described as equivalent to seven candles.[4]

The next step in the Argand development sequence was the addition of reflectors, the most effective of such systems placing the lamp's flame at the center of a parabolic reflective surface. As mentioned previously, having been widely implemented in England and France, this concept was brought to the United States by Captain Winslow Lewis. The light from this lamp was brighter than the commonly used spider lamp, and significantly more fuel-efficient. A determined entrepreneur, Lewis patented the concept, then sold the rights to the government in 1810 under terms which mandated the installation of his system in all U.S. lighthouses, along with seven-year maintenance arrangements. His persistence blocked, for several decades, prompt American adoption of the far superior illumination system that Augustin Fresnel had developed in the early 1820s. Not until the early 1850s was use of the more effective and efficient "Fresnel lens" mandated for all newly constructed U.S. lights and those needing replacement.

The first commonly used fuel in these lights was whale sperm oil, but the forces of supply and demand resulted in sharply escalating prices. About the time the lighthouse was built at Point Betsie, the Lighthouse Board was actively pursuing alternatives. Long predating today's surging interest in biomass fuels, colza, a liquid made from cabbage and other plants, was an early choice. Then lard oil, which worked better than colza but was much cheaper than sperm oil, was found to produce an acceptable flame, especially if preheated. While sperm oil may have been used briefly at Point Betsie, lard oil seems likely to have been the standard fuel during the light's earliest years.

In the latter 1870s, the Lighthouse Service began to use mineral oil, better known as kerosene, which was produced either by heating coal (thereby obtaining "coal oil") or, through the later-developed process of refining, "petroleum." First refined in Canada, kerosene fueled the incandescent oil vapor lamps that were developed and widely installed in the latter 19th century as a major improvement, in terms of both brightness and efficiency, over the traditional wick-burning lamps. It was kerosene that Point Betsie keepers handled for many decades; the use of this highly flammable oil required the construction of a separate small building for storing a station's fuel supply, minimizing both the chances of, and the damage from, accidental ignition.

Finally, in the 20th century, electricity—the cleanest and safest source—reached most lights, including Point Betsie, and eventually facilitated their automation. As with the predecessor technologies, advancements continued to be achieved over the years. Point Betsie's illumination and Fresnel lens would at one time have a candle-power rating of 350,000, producing a beam visible for close to twenty miles. Today, a "VRB-25" optical system manufactured by New Zealand's Vega Industries, less beautiful in its form but sophisticated in design, revolves atop Point Betsie's tower. Also installed at many other Great Lakes light stations, this contemporary unit—said to embody "fresnel" features—has a range of about fifteen miles. It features six equal-size panels which rotate continuously around a small bulb turned on and off by a sensor. A microprocessor and changer automatically deliver replacement bulbs as needed.

᪣

IN UTILIZING ALL THE COMMON LIGHT TECHNOLOGIES OF THE PAST CENTURY AND A HALF, Point Betsie's history not only informs us of the routine operations of shore lights, but reminds us of the dedication demanded of their keepers. By the time of Point Betsie's establishment, senior lighthouse authorities had narrowed the use of political patronage for keeper appointments, insisting that persons selected be between eighteen and fifty years of age, preferably married, able to read, write and keep simple financial records, and possess skills requisite to performance of station duties.

In order to ensure consistent, high quality performance throughout the agency, the senior lighthouse command periodically issued explicit sets of instructions to all employees, detailing what might be termed keepers' "daily grind." Two such sets of instructions laid down in the fall of 1852 by the chairman of the Lighthouse Board, and approved by the secretary of the treasury, illustrate the requirements in place at the time of Point Betsie's construction and initial operation.[5] Copies of these provisions were to be posted both in the lighthouse and in the keeper's dwelling. One set, applying to stations manned by two or more keepers, consisted of thirty-eight provisions, while somewhat fewer requirements applied to lights tended, as Point Betsie soon would be, by a single keeper.

Both sets led off with the two most fundamental commands: "1. The lamps shall be lighted punctually every day at sunset, and extinguished at sunrise. 2. The lamps shall be kept burning, bright and clear, every night, from sunset to sunrise; and in order that the greatest degree of light may be uniformly maintained, the wicks must be trimmed every four hours, or oftener if necessary, and clean glass chimneys fitted on; and special care must be taken to cut the tops of the wicks exactly even, to produce a flame of uniform shape, free from smoky points."

The solo keeper, the instructions made clear, "...is held responsible for the careful watching and trimming of the light throughout the night, and is expected to be in attendance during the day, never absenting himself from duty without permission from the District Inspector....in which cases he must furnish an efficient substitute; any negligence will subject him to the severest displeasure of the Department."

The following summary of additional requirements applicable to single-keeper stations illustrates the detailed regulations with which a keeper was required "...to make himself perfectly acquainted":

- "The plate glass must be cleaned within and without, by night as well as by day, particularly of the drift snow, sleet, and the moisture which is liable to accumulate in the interior of the lantern, and must polish and clean the reflectors or refractors, and lamps; time the lamps, and put the light-room in perfect order by 10 o'clock, a.m. daily...."

- "Strict attention must be given to the ventilation of the lantern, taking care to keep the leeward ventilators sufficiently open to admit the requisite quantity of air to produce steady, clear, and bright lights."

- "The keepers of revolving lights [like Point Betsie] are required to give their particular attention to the MOVEABLE MACHINERY; to see that it is well cleaned in every part, and kept free from dust; well oiled with clock-maker's oil; uniform in its motions, without unnecessary friction of its parts; performs its revolutions regularly within the prescribed period of time; wound up at the expiration of regular intervals of time; the motive weight rests during the day upon a support to relieve the machinery and cord, and that the CORD is not in danger of parting from long use."

- "The keeper is held responsible for the safety and good order of the stores, utensils, and apparatus of every description, and for every thing being put to its proper use and kept in its proper place. He shall take care that none of the stores or materials are wasted, and shall observe the strictest economy, and the most careful management, yet so as to maintain, in every respect, the best possible light."

- "He shall keep a daily journal of the quantity of oil expended, and state of the weather, embodying any events of interest or importance that may occur. These shall be written in the journal books to be kept at each station for the purpose, at the periods of the day when they occur, as they must, on no account, be trusted to memory. At the end of each quarter he shall make up and transmit to the district inspectors...an accurate copy of the journal for the preceding quarter."

- "He is also required to take notice of any shipwrecks which shall happen within the vicinity of the lighthouse, and to enter an account thereof, according to the prescribed form, in a book furnished to each station for this purpose; and in such account he shall state, if practicable, whether the light was seen by any one on board the ship-wrecked vessel, and recognized by him, and how long it was seen before the vessel struck."

- "The light-keeper shall, under no circumstances, use Tripoli powder for cleaning the refractors, or silvered parts of the reflectors, nor any other cleaning materials than the rouge, whiting, buffskins, and cleaning cloths, etc., furnished by direction of the Light-house Board, and for the purposes designated in the directions to the light-keepers. Each package or parcel of rouge and whiting must be examined by the keeper before using it, by rubbing between his fingers, to ascertain that it is free from grit and other impurities…. The Tripoli powder shall be used exclusively for cleaning the backs of the reflectors, and other brass work of the apparatus."

Personnel policies under these regulations were notably stringent; the keeper had permission "…to go from home to draw his salary, and also to attend public worship on Sunday, but on no other occasion without the permission of the district inspector." If he became ill, he had to provide a temporary keeper, and promptly inform the district of his illness and substitute. A keeper was to present himself in a way that would reflect well upon the agency: "The light-keeper is required to be sober and industrious, and orderly in his family. He is expected to be polite to strangers, in showing the premises at such hours as do not interfere with the proper duties of his office; it being expressly understood that strangers shall not be admitted to the light-room after sunset."

All this for $350 a year, at the time of Point Betsie's establishment—and with a firm proviso that the keeper "…is prohibited from carrying on any trade or business whatever, which will take him from the premises, or in any other manner cause the neglect of his public duties." Concluding the comprehensive regulations was a solemn warning: "The breach of any of the foregoing Instructions will subject the offending light-keeper to the severest displeasure of the Department, and, in the absence of extenuating circumstances, to dismissal."

∽

THE LIGHTHOUSE SERVICE WAS NOT INSENSITIVE TO THE ISOLATION WITH WHICH MANY OF ITS KEEPERS AND THEIR FAMILIES HAD TO DEAL. One of the steps taken to address this reality was the establishment, in the mid-1870s, of traveling libraries—shelved boxes containing as many as fifty books, fiction and non-fiction, along with a Bible, that would circulate among a district's light stations as their supplies were delivered, most commonly by vessel.

∽

ORDERS ISSUED IN 1927 BY ESTEEMED LIGHTHOUSE COMMISSIONER GEORGE R. PUTNAM[6] illustrate changes that accompanied the then-typical presence of assistant keepers, as well as the increasingly widespread electrification of lights. These regulations also served to maintain—even to enhance—the standardization of procedures, the professional atmosphere and *esprit de corps* that not only marked Putnam's long personal tenure but characterized America's lighthouse administration over many decades. Adding to Putnam's outstanding reputation is the fact that he won from Congress an important benefit—a retirement system applying to the Bureau's staff and to its lighthouse employees.

The instructions to lighthouse keepers had not only become even more rigorous, but laden with a more bureaucratic tone that continued to reflect the agency's determination to standardize operations throughout the network of remote stations: "A strict observance of these instructions is required of all persons in the service, and each person shall promptly report to the proper authority any disobedience or infraction of the instructions coming to his knowledge." Similarly, read the second section, "Constant and faithful attention to their duties shall be required of all persons in the service, and no employee shall be absent from his station or duty without authority, except in case of serious illness, which must be reported at once to the proper officer. Unless absences without authority be satisfactorily explained, charges will be filed against the employee looking toward his dismissal or other disciplinary action."

Obedience and effectiveness were viewed as tightly linked. "All persons in the service are required to obey readily and strictly, and to execute with promptitude and zeal the lawful orders of their superior. They shall show to their superiors the proper deference and respect. No persons in the service shall join in, or abet any combination to weaken the lawful authority of, or lessen the respect due to his superior officer, or shall treat his superior officer with contempt or be disrespectful to him in manner or department." Critically important, and doubtless never far from a keeper's mind throughout a long, stormy night, was this provision: "No officer, keeper, or other employee shall sleep during his watch, or at his post, or leave his station or post before being regularly relieved. Violation of this instruction may be considered cause for dismissal."

Except where there was little or no necessity for the use of boats, the qualifications for lightkeepers read as follows: "Besides the requirements as to physical ability, the civil-service requirements as to experience and fitness include ability as a waterman or boatman accustomed to handling and pulling sail and motor boats in all kinds of weather, and in certain cases ability to properly handle and care for fog-signal apparatus and machinery. Ability to read and write is required in all cases."

Light stations were never to be left unattended; either the keeper or an assistant was to be present and on duty. Where there was no assistant, the keeper was required to arrange "...for some competent person to take charge"; a keeper's absence was not to extend beyond sunset, except in an emergency or unless authorized by the district's superintendent. While keepers were instructed to always be courteous to visitors, as the officer in charge of their station they were responsible for any damage visitors inflicted upon the property. No station equipment—the light, fog signals or other power machinery—was to be operated merely for visitors' benefit.

Watches were a regimen that essentially defined the twenty-four-hour day. At stations having one or more assistant keepers, watches were to be kept and "... so divided that an equal share of work and desirable hours of watch shall fall to the keeper and to each assistant." They were to be stood "...in such place and manner as to give continuous and the best possible attention to the light and the fog signal when in operation." At stations served by a sole keeper, he was instructed not to "...leave the light for at least half an hour after lighting, in order to see that it is burning properly...." He was also required to "...visit the light at least twice between 8 p.m. and sunrise, and on stormy nights the light must be constantly looked after."

Keepers were instructed to exhibit their lights "punctually at sunset" and to keep them "...lighted at full intensity until sunrise, when the lights will be extinguished and the apparatus put in order without delay for relighting. When not in use, the illuminating apparatus must be covered and the lantern curtains hung." As was usually the case on the Great Lakes, where navigation was generally terminated by ice, lights could be extinguished "...but must always be shown when it is at all possible for vessels to benefit by them."

Being responsible for their premises' cleanliness, keepers were to whitewash buildings and wash painted areas within lanterns. Station boats were to be painted "... lead color inside and out, with their official number, three inches tall, painted black on each bow under the letters 'U.S.L.H.S.' [United States Light House Service]."

A keeper having an assistant was required to issue supplies daily, if practicable in the aide's presence. "The exact quantities thus expended must be entered immediately in the record for entering expenditures."

Presumably for reasons of both economy and safety, the regulations pertaining to kerosene were particularly specific. The fuel was typically delivered to a station by a supply boat and stored on shelves in the oil house; from there it would be carried daily to the light in five-gallon brass cans, which were to be "completely emptied and cleaned before refilling." The proper fueling procedure was laid forth in detail. The oil was to be transferred to the brass can from the "transporting can" by which it was typically delivered. In the interest of fuel purity, the instructions informed crews that they were to "...pour off gently all except about 1 inch of the oil from the transporting can into the brass can. The remaining inch of oil in the transporting can is to be then drawn off in a can kept for the purpose and set aside for use in the hand and table lamps." That wasn't the only such precaution, however. When drawing oil from the brass can for the light, again the can's last inch of oil was to be set aside for routine lamps, and the oil was to be strained before use. In the case of oil vapor lamps, one more precaution was required: the oil was to be filtered the day before, and yet again the last inch was to be used for other purposes about the premises.

Crews were admonished to take all precautions against fire, maintaining liquid chemical fire extinguishers, and keeping ashes or sand available for use on burning kerosene, gasoline, or other flammable materials. Smoking was not permitted in any Lighthouse Service buildings other than the living quarters, and only safety matches could be used on the premises. Other strict requirements governed the use of alcohol that in some instances fueled incandescent oil vapor lamps. Such alcohol was to be kept in the original and five-gallon cans in which it was delivered to stations; the cans were to be stored separately from other fuels, placed "so that leaks will show up readily," and inspected weekly.

The commissioner was to authorize fuel allowances made to a light station. Where a government powerboat was assigned to a station, it was to have an authorized allowance of gasoline or other fuel. Such allowances "...are not to be considered as either a perquisite or an emolument, but solely to facilitate the work of the service," the regulations emphasized. There was a rule of thumb involved: "In computing necessary requirements it has been found that 1 pint of gasoline per running hour for each horsepower has proved sufficient, and allowances should be made on this basis, but consideration should be given to an adjustment to meet special conditions due to age, condition, or inefficiency of the engine, the total extra allowance for all causes not to exceed 25 per cent for any one station." There were even restrictions on carry-overs of such fuel from one year to another; such were to be used up and taken into account when requisitions were filled.

୶

DURING THE 1920s, WHEN ELECTRICITY REACHED POINT BETSIE AND MANY COASTAL LIGHTS, this safe and clean power source often was also run into the keepers' quarters. This convenience was not to be treated casually. Based on the lighting requirements of a dwelling containing six rooms of average size, the instructions specified that the amount of current to be paid for by the Lighthouse Service was not to exceed thirty kilowatt-hours per month; the number of lamps furnished by the service was not to exceed ten. A formula governed adjustments in living quarters of more or less than six rooms, and all current as well as lamps in excess of authorized levels were to be personally paid for by the keepers.

୶

WHEN A SUPERINTENDENT OR OTHER OFFICIAL OF THE SERVICE CAME CALLING, the keeper was required to give him one of the dwelling's rooms as an office and bedroom and to furnish him board and furniture, with reasonable compensation due the keeper. And when working parties of the Lighthouse Service came to a station, it again was the keeper's responsibility to find lodging for the party, either in outbuildings or in the dwelling. Meals were also to be furnished the workers, with compensation provided.

❧

KEEPERS WERE GIVEN SPECIFIC INSTRUCTIONS AS TO HOW TO MAINTAIN STATION STRUCTURES, including their washing and painting. Except when major structural repairs were involved, work of this nature was generally their responsibility. Painting was done only when necessary; parts "...shall be scrubbed, which will be done as often as necessary, and no paint shall be applied until the existing paint is worn thin. This applies to the exterior of buildings and towers as well as to the interior. In cases where the paint is excessively thick, cracked, peeling, or blistered, the same shall be scraped off and surfaces sandpapered before any more paint is applied."

Roofs were a special concern; all tin or galvanized-iron roofs, gutters, and leaders were to be painted once each year with two coats of red lead paint and then, when dry, with one coat of brown metallic paint. Ironwork was to be painted each year in similar manner. Window sashes were to be kept well puttied and primed with white-lead paint.

Specific colors were assigned for various lighthouse structures. Outside wooden structures were to be dark red, brown, or white, with red or lead-colored trimmings; towers were to be white; lanterns and gallery rails black; iron structures other than towers, brown; shutters red, green, or brown; iron walks, rails and steps, brown. As for interiors, iron floors, staircases and railings and interior ironwork in general, were to be brown. Interior walls, cellars, and outhouses were to be whitewashed, while the interior of lanterns and all interior woodwork was to be painted white.

The instructions included a recipe for whitewashing—since the days of Tom Sawyer, one might think, something of a lost art. The lighthouse administrators by experience had found this process to work "...on wood, brick and stone nearly as well as oil paint and is much cheaper: Slake half a bushel of unslaked lime with boiling water, keeping it covered during the process; strain it and add a peck of salt dissolved in warm water, 3 pounds of ground rice put in boiling water and boiled to a thin paste, half a pound of powdered Spanish whiting and a pound of clear glue dissolved in warm water; mix these well together, and let the mixture stand for several days. Keep the wash thus prepared in a kettle or portable furnace and when used put it on as hot as possible with painters' or whitewash brushes. The following formula for mixing whitewash when properly made and put on, gives a white that does not easily wash or rub off, viz: To 10 parts of best freshly slaked lime add 1 part of best Portland cement, mix well with salt water and apply quite thin. Whitewash must never be used on ironwork."

❧

RECORD-KEEPING AND COMPLETING DAILY LOGS AND OTHER MORE SPECIALIZED FORMS AND REPORTS—the infamous, seemingly unending paperwork that facilitates accountability in government—consumed much of a lightkeeper's time. In later years, records included the station's journal, watch book, fog-signal record book, record of absences, record of inspections, and an account of expenditures and receipts. There were separate monthly reports of a station and its fog signal; annual reports of property returns, requisitions and supply receipts, and still additional reports, when occurring or otherwise required, as follows: accidents to personnel; special or emergency requisition; receipt for supplies; surveys of public property; transfers of property. All information was to be submitted on specified forms.

Letters were to be sent to employees who had rendered commendable service to endangered persons or property, or otherwise performed their duty under hazardous or trying conditions, and the keeper was to advise superiors of such acts. To be determined by the importance and merit of the service provided, such letters would come from (1) the superintendent of lighthouses; (2) the commissioner of lighthouses, or, in the most extraordinary circumstances, (3) the secretary of commerce. Keepers and stations were also awarded commendations when inspections found them to have attained a "high efficiency." Keepers received the superintendent's "efficiency star" of gilt, or, when the favorable recognition spanned three successive years, the commissioner's star of silver, for display on their uniforms. Stations honored for performance, including Point Betsie, would receive an "efficiency flag" to be flown through the succeeding year.

Special letters, and in some cases telegrams, were required of keepers whenever any of the following circumstances arose: a failure or irregularity in the operation of the illuminating or fog-signal apparatus; storm damage to property; act of life-saving or aid to distressed persons; information as to defects in any other aids to navigation visible from the station or of which the keeper became aware; misconduct or inefficiency of subordinates, and other occurrences perceived to be worthy of prompt report.

∾

THE MOST STORIED AND IMPORTANT OF A KEEPER'S DAILY DUTIES were those bearing directly upon the quality of the light itself—cleaning the lens and lanterns, polishing brass, and trimming wicks to achieve a beam of maximum effectiveness. The task of keeping wicks in proper condition was so significant that keepers gained the moniker of "wickies"—a term which outlasted the use of wicks. And attention to brasswork presented keepers with similarly unrelenting duties, as poetically expressed by a keeper's published account:

POINT BETSIE

"Oh, what is the bane of a lightkeeper's life,
That causes him worry and struggles and strife?...
It's brasswork.
I dig, scrub and polish, and work with a might,
And just when I get it all shining and bright,
In comes the fog like a thief in the night.
Goodbye Brasswork."[7]

The complex glass lens was to be cleaned with a soft linen cloth and polished with a thoroughly dry buff skin. The general practice was to wash the lens every two months and to apply a rouge polish annually. To prevent the frosting of lantern glass, a small amount of glycerin was to be applied with a linen cloth. Reflectors were to be cleaned, then "...lightly dusted with authorized powder kept in a double muslin bag then rub[bed] lightly with a second buff skin, and finally with a third by passing over [a] reflector with a light quick circular stroke."

Tower windows were subject to breaking under heavy stress, and not infrequently from birds' impacts. Broken or cracked glass would have to be replaced promptly, in a specific manner: "After cutting, the edges of the glass should be ground level and smooth by rubbing on a cast-iron plate covered with sharp, wet sand, or rubbing with a block of coarse carborundum. To avoid breakage from oscillation about one-sixteenth of an inch must be left on all sides between the glass and its frame. The glass must be rested on thin sheets of lead or softwood."

As reflected in Point Betsie keepers' records, the revolving clockwork which created the light's distinctive flash would require periodic attention. The mechanism's carriage had to be cleaned and oiled, the old and gummy lubricant being replaced; the vertical driving shaft had to be monitored to prevent cutting or excessive wear of its foot, and the weight, whose gradual descent powered the rotating mechanism, was to be kept on a rest when not in use.

&

AT STATIONS EQUIPPED WITH FOG SIGNALS, AS POINT BETSIE CAME TO BE, KEEPERS WERE CONFRONTED WITH ADDITIONAL DUTIES. The manual held the keeper "...strictly accountable for the sounding of the signals during the whole time that weather conditions make the signal useful to navigation," adding, "It is especially to be borne in mind that it is better to sound the signal too much than too little." The fog signal was vital to a lighthouse's effectiveness in daytime, when a light would be ineffectual. The distinctively-timed blasts from the classic "diaphone" or another type of horn could be crucial to a mariner's ability to know his location and avoid any hazards in nearby waters. Generally, the fog signal would be required "...

—40—

when a given object can not be seen a distance of 5 miles" or when a passing vessel was heard to blow its whistle as a signal of its presence amidst fog. An account was to be submitted each year of the total number of hours a fog signal was sounded, and the amount of fuel it consumed.

Given the rapidity with which fog can envelop a coast, the signal required keen attentiveness on the part of the keeper and his assistants. The instructions stated: "Close watch must be kept for the approach of fog conditions, and every effort must be made by the keeper…to sound the fog signal at once on the actual approach of fog. The fog-signal machinery and apparatus must at all times be kept in a thorough condition of repair and preparation for use on the shortest notice; and when weather conditions warrant, all preliminary preparations must be promptly made for sounding the signal."

To insure the signal's readiness, the machinery was to be "…inspected and turned over daily by hand or other power." Customarily, duplicate sets were installed at each station in order that the signal's protection would not be interrupted by a mechanical breakdown. Hence, there were normally two systems to maintain. Steam-powered signals, such as Point Betsie's early ones, were to be operated at full pressure at least fifteen minutes each month. The two sets were to be treated equally, each receiving care as if it were the only signal on hand. Given the additional workload associated with fog signals, their installation at a station led to the assignment of one or two assistant keepers because a single keeper could not tend the light adequately at night and operate the fog equipment in daytime.

❧

IN SUMMARY, A KEEPER'S LIFE, especially a solo keeper's, was disciplined and rigorous; it was also often lonely, affording him and his family, if he had one, little opportunity for relief from the job's unending demands. The routine was clearly defined in official requirements that shaped his nights and days. But that was far from the full story; a keeper also had to be constantly prepared for the unknown—for any crisis that might arise on the neighboring seas or within a station's generally routine operations—especially at a site as remote as was Point Betsie in its initial decades of service.

In his insightful lighthouse history, Dennis L. Noble summarized keepers' services in appropriately eloquent and realistic terms: "Under the direction of the U.S. Lighthouse Board…America's keepers became a professional group that ranked among the best, if not the best in the world…. In recent years it has become popular to romanticize keepers and, indeed, it is easy enough to follow this path. It is important, however, to realize that lighthouse keepers were ordinary men and women who stayed by their lights and did the best job they could do under trying circumstances. Some performed their duties nobly, others had feet of clay, but anyone whose ancestors came to this country by sea, or who went down to the sea in ships, and reached port safely owes these ordinary men and women a great debt."[8]

CHAPTER THREE

POINT BETSIE LIGHT'S FIRST TWO DECADES

Point Betsie Light's early period features the legendary service of Dr. Alonzo J. Slyfield and his wife, Alice. A major figure in the history of northwest Michigan, "Doc" Slyfield was keeper of the new light for twenty-two of its most significant years. During much of his tenure his medical services were also sought by sick or injured residents of farms and scattered settlements throughout the county. And when Benzie County was formally organized, Slyfield also was elected to the office of coroner.

Slyfield's Point Betsie charge was the second-longest in its entire history and, given his early prominence, he is sometimes mistakenly identified as its first keeper. That recognition, however, belongs to David Flury, whose official service ran for a little over six months, from February 1, 1859, until his resignation in early August. On an annualized basis, Flury's salary, like that of other keepers at the time, was $350. Flury then served for about two years at Tail Point Light on Wisconsin's Green Bay, where a lighthouse replacing the original structure opened that year.

There is no clear explanation for the short gap between October 20, 1858, the officially announced start date for the Point Betsie Light, and Flury's first recorded day of service some three months later, as reflected in pay records. But given the lateness in the year, possibly Point Betsie was not regularly lit until February 1 or an even later date when the 1859 navigation season was underway. Alternatively, the compensation record could be incomplete, failing to include the light's brief operation in late 1858, prior to the seasonal shutdown.

Succeeding Flury on his departure date, at the same salary, was a Mr. Abel Barnes, but he died less than a year later, on July 30, 1860. Illness may have further limited his actual service, as the June, 1860, U.S. Census report contains an entry for thirty-six year-old Pitt D. Barnes, already listing him as the lighthouse keeper. Little is known about either of the Barnes, but the latter one apparently had been a resident of the nearby Benzonia area. Listed with him is Martha M. Barnes, age twenty-four; both are shown as having been born in New York state. (A much-treasured memoir written decades later by the Slyfields' son, Charles Burt Slyfield, gives Barnes' first name as Peter rather than Pitt, and indicates that as Barnes had no family of his own, his niece kept house for him.)[1]

The record confirms that P.D. Barnes officially assumed the keeper's duties on the date of Abel Barnes' death. But his service lasted only about a year; he was removed from the post on July 11, 1861. Politics could have led to his termination, as the inauguration that year of the first Republican U.S. president, Abraham Lincoln, prompted numerous new lightkeeper appointments, including that of a Dr. Slattery at the northern end of the

Alonzo J. Slyfield.
Courtesy of Jan Condon

Manitou Passage. Whatever the cause, the second Barnes was replaced that day by Dr. Slyfield, who thus became Point Betsie's fourth keeper.

❧

BORN IN CONCORD, VERMONT, ON JUNE 1, 1825, Alonzo Jeremiah Slyfield moved to Michigan's St. Clair County, on Lake Huron, with his family at age seven. Long before formal education became the route to a career in medicine, the young man studied the field and spent several years working with Indians, thereafter operating a drug store in St. Clair and practicing the "eclectic medicine" of his time. As best he could, he treated whatever health issue a patient brought him.

In 1848, Alonzo married a nearby resident, Alice J. Latham, who was a native of New York state. They would raise a family of seven children, three girls and four boys. Following a serious illness that interrupted his own medical work, Alonzo found an opportunity for steady employment as keeper of the lighthouse on Lake Michigan's South Manitou Island. The fifth man to serve at that historic station, he became its acting keeper on June 18, 1853, following his predecessor's resignation, and received the permanent appointment in September of that year. Thus, the young doctor and his wife found themselves doing something they likely had never anticipated—guiding ships from this sparsely populated offshore spot, where fueling steamboats bound for Chicago, Buffalo or points in between was the predominant way of life.

This light was South Manitou Island's first, having gone into operation in 1840. The wooden keeper's residence close to the beach was topped by a short tower mounted on the roof; the illumination came from Argand lamps and reflectors that comprised the common system at that time.

In 1858, the same year that the Point Betsie Light was officially established, South Manitou Lighthouse was replaced with a seven-room brick residence erected further back from the beach, and at a higher level. A white light tower was mounted on the roof. The new light system featured a state-of-the-art fourth-order Fresnel lens whose beam swept over the lake at close to seventy feet above sea level and was reported to be visible for a distance of fourteen miles. The station was also equipped with an innovative, mechanically operated fog bell and a lifeboat. Slyfield was in charge of the South Manitou beacon for six years, resigning the post in May, 1859.

❧

MUCH COULD BE WRITTEN OF THE SLYFIELDS' YEARS ON SOUTH MANITOU ISLAND, BUT ONE STORY PARTICULARLY STANDS OUT, for it illustrates the resourcefulness and dedication of a man who was destined for recognition as one of the Great Lakes' legendary lightkeepers. It is the account of Alonzo's rescue of the passengers and crew of the brigantine *J.Y. Scammon*, a vessel owned by the prominent Traverse City, Michigan, lumbering firm of Hannah, Lay & Company. A frightfully stormy night in June, 1854, found vessels in the Manitou Passage facing dangerous, gale-force winds out of the northeast, accompanied by six inches of snow that ultimately turned into a driving rain. As Slyfield recounted the experience, this was a "living gale" that threatened vessels caught in its path:

> The sea was running high, and seemed as though it could not grow larger, but still the storm increased....I saw the doomed vessel slowly nearing the beach, and, knowing she would soon be ashore if her anchors did not fetch her up, and among the breakers that were dashing and boiling and foaming while against the shore, and perhaps drown the crew, I came to the conclusion that something must be done to get communication to them. The thought came to me like a flash to write a note and send it to them in a bottle. I then took a small rope and bottle in my hands, held them aloft, and made signs to the crew to send me a small line, which they soon understood, and fastening a line to a buoy and throwing it overboard, was but a moment's work. It soon reached the shore. I attached the bottle containing the note and it was hauled on board, and the passengers, as well as crew, were not long in learning my design, and a shout of joy went up from every mouth. The note was, "Can I render you any assistance? If so, send word by bottle." The answer came back per the same trusty little messenger, saying, "Our big chain has parted, and the small one will not hold us long. Look out for us ashore." I patrolled the shore and in about an hour after that, the brig came on broadside. The men launched a spare spar over the rail, an end resting in shoal water. The mate mounted it and slid down, and wading through the water, was helped ashore. Next followed four ladies, who came ashore in about the same manner, the mate and I assisting them as they came in reach. And so all the crew were safely landed, much to their joy.[2]

Slyfield is said to have long treasured a spy-glass bearing the vessel's name, which he bought from its captain. As he would reminisce, "[W]hile in daily use it often reminds me of the wrecking of the brig nearly a quarter of a century ago, when the marine interest, now grown to gigantic proportions, was yet in its infancy."[3] Especially memorable, too, was what he learned had also happened that day:

> On our return with the shipwrecked crew to the light-house, we found that during my absence I had been blessed by the arrival of an eight-pound blue-eyed boy... and there was indeed a feeling of happiness in the station that night, and I felt satisfied that I had accomplished more that day than on any other day of my previous life. That child [Charles] has grown up to manhood, and from his early days has always been a careful watcher for the

safety of lives from wrecks; and has while quite young assisted me in saving the crew from another wreck, under similar circumstances. He has spent his whole life in handling boats in the surf, and on the old lake at his occupation of fishing. He, at such times, is careful, considerate and cool....[4]

Lucetta and Charles B. Slyfield, author family memoir.
Courtesy of Sue Whitcomb

Charles Slyfield's own recollections, written at age fifty-eight, offer fascinating insights into the family's life on South Manitou Island and later on a mainland farm and at the point. Charles could recall the building of the keeper's dwelling during the summer of 1858, when the workers boarded with them. And he remembered another schooner's grounding near the lighthouse that fall, its crew having lodged with his family while tugs sought to free the vessel from the beach. March, 1859, saw the birth of a brother, Edwin, who was destined to become a lightkeeper as well. That summer their father resigned as keeper at South Manitou in anticipation of moving his growing family to the mainland, on farmland he had acquired near Empire Bay.

Even this relocation proved adventuresome, and hence is a reminder of the Manitou country's harsh isolation. Charles recalled that the family stayed at the nearby Burdick residence for several weeks while his father was building a simple farm dwelling on the mainland. Mr. Burdick then brought the family, together with a few possessions, to their new home in his Mackinaw sailboat. Along the way, that beautiful July day turned windy; Burdick found he could not steer toward the farm and had to make landfall several miles to the north. Three-year old Mary, who had become ill during the crossing, died just a few weeks after their arrival while her father, believing she was recovering, was traveling back to St. Clair for business. Charles remembered her simple funeral and burial, without the presence of clergy, on a hill a half-mile from their new home.

∽

ANOTHER FRIGHTFUL EXPERIENCE FOR THE FAMILY came that fall when Alonzo, having readied the house for winter, returned alone to South Manitou Island in his open sailboat to harvest his potatoes. Three weeks passed, during which the family on the mainland had no word from him. Charles' mother grew anxious as the days passed, and they faced the prospect of wintering on their own should he have perished. But then came a quiet night, and she took the children to the shore where she built a bonfire. Possibly guided by that light, Alonzo arrived that night, accompanied by a sailor who also had been marooned on the island and leapt at the chance to get off before winter closed in. Alonzo's return, he explained, had been delayed by persistent winds that prohibited him from attempting to re-cross the Manitou Passage alone in his small vessel.

The Slyfields lived on the farm for almost two years, growing crops, fishing for whitefish, hunting, trapping, and tending cows, chickens, and turkeys. Hence, upon the taking of the 1860 U.S. Census, thirty-three-year old Alonzo described himself, as did most area residents, as a farmer.

∽

ANOTHER BIG CHANGE FOR THE FAMILY CAME ABOUT A YEAR LATER, at the end of the summer of 1861, when Alonzo obtained appointment as keeper of the still new Point Betsie Lighthouse, fifteen-some miles south of his farm. With modest but stable income again at hand, the family prepared to relocate once again, hauling their goods down the coast by boat. However, after the lighthouse was closed for the season as navigation ended, the family returned to the farmhouse for that winter.

Point Betsie was a rather isolated spot when Alonzo Slyfield and his family began tending its light. Charles Slyfield later recalled only two residences close enough to be thought of as "neighbors"—Joseph Oliver, who had a place a mile north of the Point on the shore, and Richard Weston, who lived about a mile east on the shore of Crystal Lake. About four miles south of the light, a few residents were clustered at the mouth of the Betsie River, constituting the beginning of what would become the community of Frankfort. They operated a small store, blacksmith shop, and lumber mill whose wood products were shipped to Chicago on the *Trenton*, a brig-rigged scow.

There was also the Greenwood family, who had settled on the south side of the Betsie River in the mid-1850s; from this start grew the village of South Frankfort, which later changed its name to Elberta. In the words of Allen Blacklock, the village's historian, "Here on the shelves of their large kitchen were kept the scanty supplies of the community which John Greenwood brought in from Portage and Manistee. Here, many a weary traveler traveling the 'Traverse City Trail' found food, warmth and lodging. Here, many a group of victims of the many shipwrecks along the Lake Michigan Shore, following the shoreline south to 'Civilization', found shelter and supplies. Here they often rested for days at a time...."[5] This trail was merely a meandering footpath through the forest, marked by blazes; it was the only land route to the "outside world," a term used rather facetiously now, but in those days invoked in all sincerity.

While companions for a family residing at the lighthouse weren't numerous, there was no lack of boats to watch; Lake Michigan was "full of sail vessels," Charles would remember. Thinking back to the family's first year at the point, Charles wrote, "I have seen over one hundred [sailing ships] in sight from the tower of the Lighthouse at one time."[6] He also remembered finding a new mainsail that ominously had washed ashore south of the light that fall, with boom, gaff, blocks, and lines attached, its origin unknown.

While people were scarce at Point Betsie, pigeons weren't. In the spring of 1862, he recalled, flocks were so thick at the lighthouse that "...it seemed as though there was no end to them. They flew along the big sandhill next to the woods...and Father would go there and shoot them out of the flocks as they passed and we then had a plenty of fresh meat." Trout were abundant, too, right in front of the light. The younger Slyfields would troll for them from a small rowboat their father built. And there was one other exciting family event at the lighthouse that summer, the birth of another Slyfield, Elmer.

As already noted, traveling from the area involved substantial effort. In early 1863, before passenger service from this vicinity was generally available, Alonzo again headed for St. Clair. To get started on the long overland trip, he had to walk the beach for some thirty-five miles to the community of Manistee, where he could catch a stage, as there was yet no rail service north of Muskegon. When he finally returned from downstate, he brought Charles a memorable gift, his first gun. The boy would use it for many years while hunting game with his dog, "Hero."

Also memorable later that year was the trip Charles' mother, his sister Ella and baby brother Elmer took to visit relatives in Illinois. Illustrating summer travel at that time, they boarded the *Trenton* at Betsie River [as Frankfort was sometimes identified], to sail to Chicago. As Charles recalled the journey:

> They were caught in a gale that carried away one of her square topsails but she went through alright and they landed safely in Chicago. They were gone about six weeks and returned on a steamboat to Glen Arbor and there got an old fisherman...to bring them up to Point Betsie in his boat. They gave him $10.00 to make the trip and Ella had to work her passage by steering and bailing as he had to tow the boat along the shore for the wind was against them and he had no one to help him but the passengers, his boat leaked pretty bad and kept her busy. He got within about a quarter of a mile of the Light and could not get any farther, account of the sea and wind, so he landed them with their trunks, etc., and set his sail and went back home, and they walked the rest of the way.[7]

To live at Point Betsie in the Slyfield era was to live off the land and water when possible, making use of what Mother Nature would provide. Fish, game, fruits and berries were essentials that could be found there. Now and then, goods came with adventures such as one in 1863 when, through the spyglass, the Slyfields observed the propeller *General Taylor* passing to the north several miles out on Lake Michigan, with the wind blowing in from the west. Visibly taking on water, the vessel labored on; her crew, seen through the scope, was desperately lightening it by rolling cargo barrels off the gangway. Their efforts proved insufficient; it eventually went to pieces in the Manitou Passage. But some six hours after the ship had passed Point Betsie, those wave-driven barrels were showing up on the beach. Alonzo and Charles walked as far as the Betsie River, rolling the barrels out of the surf. They retrieved about sixty of them, all filled with flour, enough to meet their family's and others' needs for several years. Afterward, Alonzo headed up the beach and alerted his neighbor, Joe Oliver, to this opportunity; he and his son scavenged the shore farther to the north, finding another forty barrels.

❧

IN LATE FALL AND EARLY WINTER, WINDS OFF LAKE MICHIGAN AT POINT BETSIE CAN BE BRUTALLY COLD, THE SPRAY FROM THE WATER VIRTUALLY ENCASING THE PLACE IN ICE. Charles wrote that during the winter of 1864, the thermometer's mercury dropped "clear to the bottom," his father then taking the instrument inside the house for fear that it could break. After closing for the season, the Slyfields moved to a farm near Elberta, but Charles and Ella stayed in a log house in nearby Benzonia with a housekeeper from January to mid-March so that they could attend their first "real school." In early spring, Alonzo borrowed a horse and sled, driving the children back to the lighthouse by traversing the nine-mile length of Crystal Lake on ice.

The next winter, when the family decided to stay together at the lighthouse, Alonzo hired a teacher to come from Benzonia for three months during the fall. By that time, in response to the needs of Benzie Countians, Alonzo had resumed his medical practice (providing all required services, including dentistry) in addition to fulfilling his duties as keeper of Point Betsie Light.

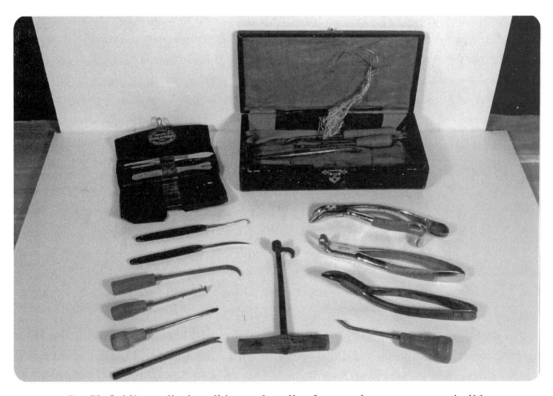

Dr. Slyfield's medical toolkit, tooth-puller front-and-center, sutures in lid.
Courtesy of Myra Elias
Photo by author

The doctor made numerous trips that winter to the inland settlement of Almira to treat poor, ill homesteaders who lived in houses that afforded inadequate protection from the bitter cold. The journey to his patients was arduous; he would follow the Lake

Michigan beach several miles north to Otter Creek, then snowshoe through the back country over four-foot depths. Paying tribute to his father, Charles recalled:

> *I have heard him tell of wading Platte River eighteen times that winter and standing on the ice to dress himself which could not have been a very pleasant job. He never got very much for his services as the people were too poor to pay much but I suppose he had the consolation that he had done some good. Surely these people would have suffered more had it not been for him.*[8]

That winter of 1865, a year which would bring the assassination of President Lincoln and the concluding actions of the Civil War, was a tough time for the country as a whole, and the effects of the struggling economy were felt as well at Point Betsie, Charles would recollect:

> *[I]t was "...rather pinchy times for us at the Light. We did not have any butter to speak of because there wasn't any to be had, nor any fresh meat only what I used to kill, partridges, squirrels, rabbits, etc., and they were not very plenty. Spring came at last and the pigeons never failed to come each year to gladden the hearts of the early settlers after a long winter on a diet of rusty salt pork and salt fish, if a person was lucky enough to have even them.*[9]

Two years later, when the government was recovering from the war's financial burdens, the Lighthouse Board reported that a new roof was needed on the Point Betsie dwelling and a repair party came to do this substantial job. (Maintenance of the roof would prove to be an unending challenge, as high winds out of the southwest or northwest have tested the durability of whatever material has been installed.) Charles remembered that the original slate roof was replaced that year with shingles, and that other repairs were made. Doubtless of even greater excitement to the family, the year 1867 brought a substantial salary boost for Alonzo Slyfield and other lightkeepers, from $350 to $560 per year.

Only a year later, with Point Betsie Lighthouse then ten years old, the Board pointed to some additional maintenance problems. Four thousand dollars were needed for repairs and renovations at both Point Betsie and South Manitou Island[10], the top authorities advised, while also saying separately of Point Betsie, "This station is greatly in need of repairs; the plaster has fallen in many places, and the floors are considerably decayed. Some of the foundation stones of the tower have become displaced; they should be replaced and the entire foundation repointed."[11] This recommendation resulted in the construction of a wooden bulwark to protect the sandy rise on which the lighthouse was situated, and strengthening of the tower with concrete.

THE CLOSE OF THE CIVIL WAR LED TO AN INCREASING POPULATION IN PREVIOUSLY SPARSELY SETTLED NORTHWEST MICHIGAN, as veterans came home and were joined by colleagues from the military who had heard of the area's attractiveness and emerging economic opportunities. The government responded to appeals for improvements at the mouth of the Betsie River, which held great promise as a largely natural harbor. In preparation, large hemlock trees were felled and cut into square timber. Charles remembered that on a beautiful June day, his father was scanning the horizon from the light tower with his spyglass and saw an inbound dredging outfit— a couple of tugs, a dredge, dump scows, pile driver, and other materials needed for the harbor work. Knowing the importance of this sighting, Alonzo penned a note which he then attached to Hero, and told the family dog to go to town, which he could do in about fifteen minutes. "Someone there took it off and read it so the town was aroused and ready to receive them when they arrived." Charles mused that Hero "…would go to town and carry a note but you could not send him back until he got ready to go. I think that was the first telegraph in this part of the country…."[12]

The following winter, Charles and Alonzo were scavenging lumber and scraps, piling them at the lighthouse for rafting to town where they intended to build a house, with fence and sidewalk. A man was hired for the basic construction and Alonzo lathed and plastered the interior; thus, the family acquired their own winter quarters in Frankfort, where a school had been started. At about this time, Alonzo again made the long trip to St. Clair, from which he returned with apples (Benzie County was not yet a big fruit producer), a cow, and a "Singer"—said to be the first sewing machine in town, which doubtless was soon kept busy making clothes for the large Slyfield family.

The Slyfields also decided to supplement the keeper's pay by fishing with nets off Point Betsie. Young Charles and his father made floats, packing boxes and other equipment, ordering gill nets from Chicago. They started with fifteen nets, each several hundred feet in length, setting them about a mile out on Lake Michigan. They would retrieve the nets and salt their catch, shipping the fish to market via schooner or steamer. Charles would remember:

> *Propellers would always stop in those days if the lake was calm, when we flagged them for they knew there was not any way for the Lighthouse Keepers to get away or ship anything. The Benzonia people would come to the Light in early days of the colony and have Father put them aboard some passing propeller so they could get away from the wild and wooly part of the country and when they came back they would get the boat to go close in at Frankfort and some one would come out with a sailboat and take them ashore.*[13]

The Lighthouse Board's annual report of November 6, 1869, advised that repairs had been executed at Point Betsie and "...measures have been taken to prevent the displacement again of the sand, which rendered necessary the replacing of some of the foundation of the tower." (To this day, the movement of sand off the beach has been a major problem at the Point, especially when fall's gales sweep across the beach and nearby dunes that are not yet sheltered by covering snow.)

The winters of 1870 and '71 saw Charles and Edwin staying in town for schooling, while the rest of the family lived at the lighthouse. The boys, who would go home for weekends, made some spending money by salvaging parts off old schooners and burning them to get the bolts and other iron for which the blacksmith would give a penny and a half per pound. This was about when a state roadway, now M-22, was rough-cut through the woods, but as Charles remembered, "...it was none too good." When his three aunts came to visit from St. Clair, they traveled by boat through Lakes Huron and Michigan and hired a lumber wagon to take them down to the lighthouse—the road trip itself being day-long and exhausting.

❧

TWO SCHOONERS WERE DRIVEN ASHORE BY A NORTHWESTERLY STORM IN THE FALL OF 1870, the *H.B. Steele*, about a mile south of Platte River, and the *Comet* about a mile north of the lighthouse. They had both been heavily loaded, the *Steele* with cordwood and the *Comet* with 23,500 bushels of oats, and storm-tossed Lake Michigan would take its toll. Charles later chronicled the rescue of the latter vessel's sailors by his father and himself—a task for which early lighthouse keepers had to be constantly prepared:

I got up early and saw a man coming from the north, about forty rods away and he appeared to be naked, but as he came nearer I saw that he had underclothes on and was bare headed. He came and knocked and I went to the door. He said that he was from the schooner, Comet, aground the point and that was all he could say, he was so near frozen. I had him come in and set by the fire while I called the rest of the family. Father got him some dry clothes and as he warmed up he told us of their sad experience in that terrible gale. It seemed that they were bound north and when near the Manitou Island the wind which had been east, shifted suddenly to the northwest and in her sails jibing, broke her fore peak halyard so their foresail was useless, and they could not keep her clear of the point as they were trying to run before the gale up the lake. After they came on the bar about thirty rods from shore he said he had swam ashore with a line tied around his body but was so cold and used up that he could not tie it, but wound it around a root. He then came up to the Light to get warm and see if he could get any help for the rest of the crew.

After breakfast Father and I took a number of long buoy lines and went back with him to the wreck. There were a number of men there when we arrived and we all went and got a large sized flat bottomed skiff that was a short way from there and dragged it abreast of the wreck and tied the line that the mate had brought ashore to her bow and our buoy lines to her stern and the men on the vessel pulled the skiff out and two men would get in and we would pull it ashore again and kept this up until all the crew were safely landed....[14]

As Charles succinctly appraised this effort, "There was a piece of lifesaving that would compare favorably with the more modern appliances as there was nothing to save but the men and we done that in short order."[15]

Charles recalled that the winter of 1871 was the last that the family lived at the lighthouse; thereafter, they occupied it throughout the period of navigation. He also remembered that pigeons were so plentiful that summer among the dunes behind the lighthouse that he could bring down six or eight with a single blast of his shotgun.

ONE CAN ONLY SPECULATE, BUT KEEPER SLYFIELD AND HIS FAMILY PROBABLY SENSED SOMETHING FORBODING IN THE SKIES ON OCTOBER 8, 1871, and days thereafter, when Chicago as well as large tracts in northeastern Wisconsin, just across Lake Michigan, were ablaze in tragic fires fed by strong winds and tinder-dry woods and structures. Two hundred and fifty people lost their lives in Chicago's famous blaze that destroyed much of that city. But more than 2000—the overwhelming majority of its residents—died in explosive fires in and around the small community of Peshtigo, Wisconsin, and surrounding areas in Oconto and Door counties, where vast areas of ground were literally burned bare. Simultaneous fires elsewhere in Michigan were also costly, but fortunately considerably less so in human terms. Though no deaths were reported in Manistee, about 1,000 people were made homeless, and a substantial part of the city, thirty-five miles to the south, was destroyed.

IN OCTOBER, 1872, THE SCHOONER *ISLAND* WAS WRECKED on the shore at Frankfort, having missed the piers leading into the harbor. As expected, Keeper Slyfield reported the nearby wreck, judging the vessel itself to be a total loss, although insured; fortunately, the crew of five and the large cargo were all saved.[16]

During most of the summer of 1873, the maturing Charles wrote that he and brother Edwin "...stayed at the Point and attended the Light most all the season and the family lived in town." Some years later, as we will see, "Doc" Slyfield would become the target of criticism, from outside his own agency, for leaving the light in charge of his boys. But perhaps because the importance of his medical service was recognized by his superiors, there is no evidence that the Lighthouse Service, which had not assigned him an official assistant, faulted his behavior. Nor is there indication that any serious consequences arose during his sons' tending of the light. As Charles elaborated, "Father was doctoring most of the time. He would come to the Light once in a while to see how we were getting along. Ed and I had lots of fun hunting that summer, pigeons, partridge and squirrels. We called the woods back of the Light our butcher shop and when we wanted fresh meat we would go out there and kill what we wanted and we wanted fresh meat most every day."[17]

Soon thereafter, the young Slyfield men took to fishing more seriously, building a thirty-foot, two-masted sailboat which they kept in Frankfort harbor, from which they set pound and gill nets off the town, off Point Betsie and in nearby Platte Bay. Charles, Edwin, and Joe Oliver, Jr. worked together; Alonzo would go from the Light on horseback and help clean the fish when he was needed. Catches were usually abundant and prices were low; Charles reports he could sell trout for $1.25 and whitefish for $2.50 a hundred, salted.

Keeper Slyfield recorded in his journal the wrecking of the schooner *Sinai* on November 4, 1873, saying the lightly loaded lumber vessel bound from Milwaukee to Ludington went ashore at Ball Hill, a mile north of Frankfort.[18] (The ship apparently had been driven far off her intended course.) One man was lost, Slyfield noted, his body being found about a mile and a half north of the Light; an inquest was held and the remains taken to Frankfort for burial. Just ten days later Slyfield described another area wreck, that of the propeller *City of Boston*, bound from Chicago to Buffalo. Loaded with corn, hogs and feed hay, it went ashore south of town in a southwesterly gale accompanied by snow. No lives were lost, he reported; the crew remained in Frankfort until they were taken aboard a steamer headed to Chicago. Their ship, however, was a total wreck. He wrote, "Broke in two; in this gale of wind the *City of Boston* will go to pieces. She was burst open soon after she struck the beach,"[19] as the fall season's heavy toll on shipping continued.

Annual reports of the Lighthouse Board contain brief entries during the 1870's for Point Betsie, generally indicating that repairs had been made but without disclosing many details. A notable entry by Slyfield in his journal on August 18, 1874, recorded the visit of a supply steamer to the lighthouse. The keeper reported that the goods were "all safe," and, noting a piece of good news, "...the Inspector thinks he will recommend that a boat be allowed at this station." A bit of history is associated with such a boat, for six years earlier, in the fall of 1868, the district inspector had written to the chairman of the Lighthouse Board, estimating a cost of $2,474 for the purchase of fourteen new boats and associated equipment required for light stations. He had added, however, "The Light Keeper at Point Betsie has a Boat suitable for the Station [possibly his

Mackinaw] which he will sell to the Lt. House Board with Boat House and Ways for $100.00 and I respectfully recommend that it be purchased."[20] Either Slyfield's boat was not acquired pursuant to that recommendation or, perhaps more likely, a replacement craft, according to records, was required six years later.

Significant repairs at Point Betsie Light were logged in October, 1875, when a cement deck was built across the front of the tower; this job, the Keeper predicted in his journal, "...will be the best work ever done at this station."

～⁄‹〉

A NEW AND EXCITING DEVELOPMENT WAS IN PROSPECT FOR POINT BETSIE THAT FALL, AN ADDITIONAL SERVICE THAT WOULD PROVE TO BE OF GREAT VALUE TO MARINERS. Keeper Slyfield made a note that on October 3, 1875, a steamer had brought men to identify an appropriate location on the lighthouse reserve for construction of a station of the U.S. Life-Saving Service. Their choice, he recorded, was a spot on the beach a little over six hundred feet south of the light. On the following day, Slyfield noted that lumber had been landed. Construction apparently was underway at least by early spring; on June 1, 1876, Slyfield reported that "Mr. Bushnell came to finish up the life-saving station." Tangential to this activity is a journal entry of June 29 by Slyfield in uncharacteristically scribbled hand-writing: "Thought I was partially sunstruck." Judging by his script, the Keeper seems to have come up with a good self-diagnosis; perhaps he'd spent more time than usual on the open beach under a bright sun, monitoring the project.

On July 3, the inspector came to examine the new building, finding that the roof and some interior work would have to be re-done before it could be accepted by the government. But the process of opening the new station went forward; in September, the steamer *Andy Johnson* brought necessary equipment to the facility—lines, oars, grapples, grindstone, and so forth. And on October 20, 1876, reported Slyfield—exactly eighteen years from the officially announced start of the Point Betsie Light's operations—Captain Thomas E. Matthews and his surfmen took charge of the new Point Betsie Lifesaving Station. Thereafter, at least during the navigation season, the Slyfields would have company at the point. Though there is some inconsistency in the records, Matthews' crewmen apparently were on-site rather briefly that fall; the station closed for the season on November 30 when poor weather led to a cessation of vessel traffic on Lake Michigan. Point Betsie Light was also discontinued for the winter at the same time.

～⁄‹〉

THIS ACCOUNT OF POINT BETSIE LIGHTHOUSE'S FORMATIVE YEARS CLOSES WITH AN ACCOUNT OF A NEARBY TRAGEDY WHICH

DOUBTLESS BROUGHT SADNESS TO THE SLYFIELDS, THE LIGHTKEEPING FRATERNITY, AND RESIDENTS OF THE REGION. Slyfield wrote of forty-three-year-old Aaron Sheridan and his thirty-three-year-old wife Julia; Aaron, who had served in an infantry regiment during the Civil War, had lost an arm to a Confederate ball relatively late in that brutal conflict. A farmer by prior experience, he had learned of an opening as lightkeeper at South Manitou Island—Slyfield's own first post as a keeper. Aaron Sheridan had no personal experience with lighthouses or boats, but his status as a wounded veteran had likely boosted his employment prospects at this island station. Surrounded by their six children and actively aided by Julia, Aaron had tended the isolated light for twelve years, from 1866 to 1878. As Alonzo Slyfield described the crisis that suddenly befell this family:

> Mr. Sheridan, Wife and Child was drowned while crossing the channel from Glen Arbor to the South Manitou Island. He was the principle Keeper, his wife one of the assistants of the South Manitou Light Station. They were highly respected by all. It appears the Boat was a Boat furnished by the government for Light House Keepers. They were crossing home to the Island when the Boat capsized and lay on her Beam end. They stood on the Center Box as long as they could. Mr. Sheridan let go first and caught his wife as he fell into the water. A young man who was with them still clung...and hollered so loud they came from the Island to his assistance. The accident happened about a mile from the Island. Just before Sunset, it was dark before the help arrived. The baby was lost when the Boat first capsized. The Sheet was found tied fast to the Boat. That was the Cause of the accident in all probability. Sheets should not be tied or fastened in squally weather.[21]

The five surviving Sheridan boys were taken back to Illinois, to be raised by their grandparents. The Sheridan's son, George, and eventually grandchildren and other descendants, would follow Aaron and Julia's example, serving as distinguished keepers at Lake Michigan lights.

Such were the realities of daily life and work, the routine aspects and the perils, at and about Point Betsie Lighthouse during its illustrious first two decades of service.

CHAPTER FOUR

LIFESAVERS JOIN LIGHTKEEPERS AT POINT BETSIE

Just as early lightkeeping activities at Point Betsie are best viewed in the broader context of American lighthouse history, the fascinating story of Point Betsie's lifesaving station should be interpreted within its own, distinctly separate, historical setting.

The U.S. Government's involvement in lifesaving began in 1848, about sixty years after the new federal authorities had so promptly assumed the responsibility for lighthouses. Congress heeded the appeals of Representative William A. Newell (NJ) to address the growing menace of coastal shipwrecks by providing surf boats and other equipment to aid stricken sailors on these vessels. The legislators responded with an appropriation of $10,000 "...for providing surf-boats, rockets, carronades, and other necessary apparatus for the better preservation of life and property from shipwrecks on the coast of New Jersey lying between Sandy Hook and Little Egg Harbor."[1]

As notable as Newell's initiative was, non-governmental efforts to assist victims of shipwrecks had begun much earlier. The Humane Society of Massachusetts was formally organized in 1791; this group, which had been operating for several years, built ocean-side huts that could provide protection to shipwreck survivors, stocking the shelters with food and blankets. Over time, these facilities were erected at additional spots along the state's coast; the effort was later expanded to include "lifeboat stations" equipped with boats and other essential equipment that could enable rescue workers to reach stricken mariners.

Each of these stations had a keeper, but the crews were voluntary—an arrangement which was also to appear, years later, on the Great Lakes. While efforts of this nature spread along the Atlantic coastline beyond Massachusetts, offering a welcomed if primitive level of assistance to wreck victims, it was soon recognized that more needed to be done. Critics pointed to an increasing number of horrifying wrecks, many of them resulting in the drowning of hundreds of immigrant men, women, and children within sight of their new homeland. The voluntary crews, whose members sometimes lived a considerable distance from the station and could not respond quickly to an emergency, was one problem; maintaining the facilities and equipment was another. While the boat stations were in some instances sited at a lighthouse where they could be somewhat protected, all too often the facilities and equipment deteriorated or went astray, leaving the assistance of less benefit than what had been promised, with dire consequences for the wreck victims.

As these deficiencies became increasingly evident, public pressure mounted for more effective measures. Congress responded in late 1854, authorizing the secretary of the treasury to establish new stations, make repairs where needed, appoint supervisory personnel, and hire a keeper for each station. The crews, however, remained voluntary; they were to be paid $10 for saving of life (later changed to $10 for each rescue attempt, irrespective of the outcome), and $3 for each drill they completed. While progress was made, the results were still inadequate to the rising demands upon the lifesaving mission. The major weakness remained the essentially voluntary status of the crews, which seriously compromised their opportunity for needed rescue training and drilling.

THE NEED FOR LIFESAVING INITIATIVES ON THE GREAT LAKES CAME TO BE RECOGNIZED AT ABOUT THE SAME TIME. In the mid-1850s, the Treasury Department sent fifty-one Francis metallic surfboats, costing $450 each, to various locations on the inland seas. The design of these twenty-six and one-half-foot metal boats, named for their manufacturer, was based on a cedar craft commonly used along the New Jersey shore. Some of these boats were sent to lighthouse keepers—among them, Alonzo Slyfield of the South Manitou Island Light or to other government officials on the lakes who were to care for them. Others were sent where an individual or group would post a bond, the terms of which required them to care for the property and use it whenever an opportunity came to save life and property from a shipwreck. Apparently, that was the situation at North Manitou Island where Nicholas Pickard was the bonded party.[2] While this was again a step in the right direction, its effectiveness was undercut by an absence of other essential support; no shelters for the boats were provided, nor was needed equipment for the boats sent, or wagons for rapidly transporting them to a possible rescue site.

Little is known about the actual use of the Francis boats on the lakes, as reports were not required and the government had virtually no capacity to make inspections at the widely scattered locations. Generally speaking, lifesaving operations between the mid-1850s and the early 1870s were not effectively coordinated or managed; training was still ineffectual, and it seems that boats and other essential items of equipment were not always used effectively by lighthouse keepers or properly maintained by the bonded parties who were expected to personally cover their expenses. But to look beyond that rather negative overall assessment, it should be recognized that the lifesaving capacities which did exist were highly valued by rescued sailors and their loved ones.

≈

THE SITUATION WOULD BEGIN TO PROFOUNDLY CHANGE AFTER ESPECIALLY DEVASTATING WEATHER HAD HIT THE ATLANTIC AND GREAT LAKES COASTS IN LATE 1870 AND EARLY 1871, when over two hundred people lost their lives in more than eleven hundred shipwrecks on the lakes alone. The fledgling lifesaving "system," having been shown to be inadequate, bore the brunt of the criticism for these great losses of life. Having seen enough to conclude that more drastic federal action was required, Congress appropriated $200,000 in April, 1871, to enable surfmen to be hired where, and for what period of service, the secretary of the treasury determined necessary.

Early 1871 also saw the appointment of Sumner I. Kimball to head the Revenue-Marine of the Treasury Department, the customs-enforcing agency under which the federal lifesaving functions were placed. Kimball, who was destined to become a legendary public administrator, launched a study of the lifesaving capabilities of his agency, finding it riddled with political favoritism and poorly operated. He immediately set out to restructure the service and upgrade the stations' personnel and practices. Full-time crews, generally numbering six men, were to be hired; the best of local manpower was to be recruited, and—like lighthouse personnel—keepers were to administer their stations in accordance with rigorous regulations and standards.

Expansion was rapidly underway. In 1873, Congress funded a study of possible locations for additional stations on the Atlantic shores and Great Lakes. The following year Kimball put a national classification of stations into place. So-called "complete life-saving stations" (sometimes also known as "first-class stations") were to be fully staffed and equipped with a surfboat, rockets, and other supplies; "lifeboat stations" were to be sited in populated areas—likely at a harbor entrance—where the keeper could quickly summon volunteers to man the boat in an emergency; and unmanned "houses of refuge" were to be provided on the remote Florida coastline as shelter for wreck victims.

Soon thereafter, three lifesaving districts were created to cover the five Great Lakes. Each district had a superintendent in overall charge of his stations and their operations, who maintained records and sent out supplies and crew pay. The annual salary of Great Lakes district superintendents was $1,000; in the early years, each keeper made $200 a year for his service, and full-time surfmen made $40 a month over the season. An assistant inspector was also assigned to each district; since by this time travel in the lakes region was not as arduous as it had been, he was to regularly visit each facility and report to the chief inspector. In approving this organizational enhancement, Congress also authorized the establishment of new stations on the lakes; ultimately, Lake Michigan, with its long stretches of unrelieved coast affording few natural harbors, would have the most stations, thirty-one.

A station's effectiveness was largely due to the ability and dedication of its keeper. Long ago, historian J.B. Mansfield ably described the program in his classic study of the Great Lakes:

> Each station has a keeper, the best that can be obtained from the athletic race of beachmen, a master of boat craft, and the art of surfing, and skilled in wreck operations. The keeper selects his own crew, who are, however, subject to the decision of the examining board. He is by law an inspector of customs, having authority for the care of stranded property and against smuggling. He preserves inventories of all property belonging to his station, and journalizes daily the life at the station, sending weekly transcripts of his journal to the general superintendent for his information. He keeps the station and equipment in order, commands the crew, steers the boat to wrecks, conducts all the operations, and governs his station precincts.[3]

Kimball's top assistant, James H. Merryman, described the specific requirements to which a keeper was to adhere in evaluating potential crewmen:

> The selection of his men, upon whose fidelity and skill depend not only his success, but oftentimes his life, as well as the fate of those whom he is expected to succor, is very properly confided solely to him. Both keeper and men are chosen from among the fishermen in the vicinity of the stations, who are most distinguished for their ability as surfmen. Drawing their first breath within sound of the surf, they pass through childhood viewing the sea in all its moods. In early youth, they make their first essay in the breakers, and from that on to manhood advance from the least important oar through regular gradations, until the most skillful reach the command of the boat. This life gives them familiarity with the portion of the beach upon which they dwell, and its bordering currents, eddies, and bars, and an intimate acquaintance

with the habits of the surf. It is an erroneous notion that the experience of the sailor qualifies him for a surfboatman. The sailor's home is at sea. He gives the land a wide berth, and is never at ease except with a good offing. He is rarely called upon to ply an oar in a small boat, particularly in a high surf, and his vocation gives him little knowledge of the surfman's realm, which is the beach and a portion off the sea extending but little beyond the breakers. The number of mariners who are annually lost in attempting to land from stranded vessels through the surf in their own boats, sorrowfully attests this fact. On the other hand, the most expert surfman may not be, and often is not, a sailor, though generally he has an excellent knowledge of every part of a ship and her apparel...[4]

Lifesaving station crews originally consisted of seven men, that number being the minimum oarsmen in the surfboat (three on each side) as well as the keeper, who handled the long steering oar. With all of the men in the boat, there was no one to assist from the shore, in either its launching or recovery, or maintain watch while the lifeboat was in use. Only after years of persistent efforts did the service obtain sufficient funding to provide for an additional crewman who would fill this void in station operations. Not only would there be someone at the station who knew where a rescue effort was underway, but he would also be available to receive reports of other emergencies that might arise while his colleagues were away on duty, and he could direct them to the second crisis upon their return.

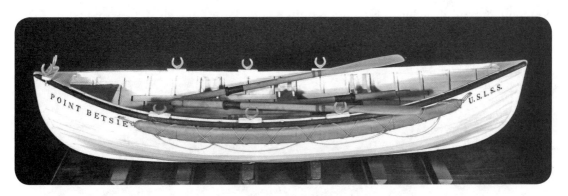

Scale model of the Point Betsie "Monomoy" surfboat. [5]
Photo by author

⌇

BACKED BY THE NEW INTEREST AT THE FEDERAL LEVEL, THE PROCESS OF SITING AND CONSTRUCTING NEW GREAT LAKES STATIONS WAS UNDERWAY PROMPTLY. In October, 1874, Kimball and Merryman selected

Lake Michigan's Point Betsie, known to them as Point Aux Bec Scies, as a lifesaving station site, and in April, 1875, the Lighthouse Board gave its approval for use of land within the lighthouse reservation for this facility. In mid-1875, a contract was approved with W.E. Bushnell for its construction, at a cost of $3,000. In late 1876 or early 1877, when the first full lifesaving crew was engaged and on-site, the station was ready for operation. Another complete station went into operation at about the same time on North Manitou Island, near Pickard's wharf. A lifeboat station, manned by volunteers and under the command of Captain Harrison Miller, of whom much more will be said later, apparently had gone into service on Beaver Island just months earlier.

Other stations would follow, as the service sought to provide a network of rescue capabilities up and down the Lake Michigan coast: on the north side of Manistee harbor in 1880; on the south side of Frankfort harbor in 1887 (relocated to the north side in the mid-1930's), and on South Manitou Island and at Sleeping Bear Point in 1902.[6] Hence, state-of-the-art navigational aids of that era—both lights and lifesaving components—were then in place within, and at the approaches to, the heavily traveled Manitou Passage.

A complete lifesaving station featured a ground-floor boat room, where the rescue boats, lifecar and apparatus-loaded beach cart were kept, and a kitchen or messroom; upstairs were sparsely-furnished sleeping space and storage. During the active season, which on Lake Michigan generally ran between the first days of April until the cessation of coastal navigation in early December, this was home to the keeper and his crew. Somewhat later, very basic housing would be available for married surfmen.

"Home, Sweet Home" for a Point Betsie family man.
Courtesy of Michigan Maritime Museum

∽

TO PARAPHRASE MERRYMAN, THE LIFE OF A SURFMAN WAS OFTEN MONOTONOUS, THOUGH FAR FROM LETHARGIC. For the most part, the routine centered on daytime drills and nightly beach patrols that could extend into the day when storms or fog closed in on the station. And just like their neighbors at the lighthouse, the keeper and crew had to clean and maintain the station and most of the equipment; this included keeping the boats and rescue apparatus in top working condition, which could be rather challenging when the items had been battered in rescue operations.

The station grounds included an area for practicing the technique of rescuing persons aboard vessels stranded on offshore bars. A "wreck pole" or "drill pole" was erected on the beach that represented the mast of a vessel from which a "victim" would be brought to safety, over a distance of about seventy-five yards, by breeches buoy, a device which resembled a pair of strong shorts beneath a life-ring that was suspended from a pulley. Once an adequate line had been positioned between a wreck and the shore, the breeches buoy could be pulled outward from shore to stranded seamen and hauled back, bringing the occupants, one-by-one, to safety over the stormy surf.

Drill Pole at Point Betsie Life Saving Station.
Courtesy of Michigan Maritime Museum

As speed was critically important if lives were to be saved from ships that the surf would soon pound to pieces, the drills sought to make this procedure as orderly as possible. No keeper could be satisfied with a lethargic performance by his crew, nor would a keeper's superior officers tolerate lackluster leadership on his part. An exacting procedure had to be followed, in each drill or actual rescue. Each surfman bore a number, usually reflecting his experience and capabilities, that ranking determining a man's role. The crew would first haul the beach cart to the drill site with lines like a harness, the odd-numbered personnel being on the cart's left and evens on the right. When the keeper called "action," the men set up the Lyle gun that was used to fire a line several hundred yards out to the "vessel"; the breeches buoy would be set up and sent out, and the "victim" pulled to safety. Both economy and efficiency being valued, the amount of powder consumed and the time it took to complete the procedure were carefully reported for each drill and actual use. After the initial weeks of the season when new crewmen were "learning the ropes," drill completion times of more than five minutes were deemed unacceptable; times of about four minutes showed the sought-after level of proficiency.

A "Rescued Sailor" arrives safely during a Point Betsie beach drill.
Courtesy of Michigan Maritime Museum

The training of the lifesaving crews was conducted under the overall direction, and periodic inspection, of officers of the Revenue-Marine. The breeches buoy exercise was but one element in a station's weekly routine; stations tended to follow a common schedule throughout the country. All season long, unless the crew was exhausted from rescue service or the weather was truly prohibitive (after all, stormy weather was when rescues would most likely be needed), Mondays were typically given over to boat maintenance and practice with the beach rescue apparatus, including the timed breeches buoy drills. Tuesday was boat practice day; on Wednesdays the crews practiced flag signaling; Thursdays brought more beach apparatus work, and Fridays found crews practicing artificial respiration—in the service's parlance, "resuscitation of the apparently drowned."

↭

BEACH PATROLS WERE THE OTHER DEFINING EVENT FOR THE CREW OF A LIFESAVING STATION. It was through these nightly patrols that a wrecked vessel, or one in imminent danger of grounding, might be discovered, be informed by flare that someone was aware of its plight, and the lifesaving station alerted to undertake a rescue of the crew. Except during the time of longest daylight, regulations required the fulfillment of four patrols each night, in both directions from the station, from sunset to 8 p.m.; 8 p.m. to midnight; midnight to 4 a.m., and 4 a.m. to sunrise. Nightly, each of the six surfmen at a station had to take his turn. In the view of the service's high command, this was another justification for adding a man at each station. As reiterated in the Life-Saving Service's 1880 Annual Report:

> It is no little matter, as everyone will concede, for these solitary men to be compelled to plod and grope for miles over rough levels of the seaside in the icy darkness, watching meanwhile the obscure offing for endangered ships, while all the world lies comfortably in bed. No man among these crews ever gets a whole night's sleep during the eight months of station duty. From sunset to dawn the beach must be patrolled, and for the space of at least four hours each member must perform this duty. It hardly needs to be said how wearing such a life is to the crews.

It was the keeper's solemn duty to ensure that the beach was patrolled. At many stations, a crewman was to meet his counterpart from the next station and exchange marked tokens with him to prove to the two keepers that the patrols had been completed. In circumstances such as at Point Betsie, where distance between stations precluded patrol connections, a more sophisticated proof system was employed. The surfman carried a clock on his patrol; when he reached a post at the end of his route, he used a key kept there to enter the time. It was the keeper's job to be sure the posts and keys were in place and that the clocks were not tampered with; the latter had paper dials that were regularly sent to the district superintendent for inspection. A surfman's repeated failure to mark the clock could trigger serious consequences for him, including dismissal.

These beach walks amidst the darkness and cold winds of fall and spring had to have been rigorous experiences, to say the least. Going one way or the other, from the station or back to it, the patrolman might face wind blasts that could force him to walk backwards over a log and boulder-strewn beach to gain some measure of relief from the biting winds and blowing sand. The surfman customarily carried a lantern, but in bad weather it could become encrusted with sand so that its flame would barely outline hazards lying in his way. Sometimes the walker had to find his way by whatever natural light remained. On August 31, 1880, Point Betsie Keeper Matthews would record in his journal the text of a letter from General Superintendent Kimball to District Superintendent William Louthit in Grand Haven that had been circulated to the area's stations:

> *As complaint has been made that vessels have mistaken the lights carried by patrolmen on the Life-Saving Service for light-houses and beacon lights: you will instruct Keepers in your district to prohibit the carrying by the men of the Service of lighted patrol lanterns except in dark or stormy weather, when a lighted lantern would be necessary to enable the patrolman to find his way safely. During clear and moonlight nights the lighted lantern does not seem necessary and its discontinuance is therefore ordered.*

❧

THROUGH THE COURAGE AND DILIGENCE OF LIFESAVERS AND THEIR LEADERS, major progress was being made in assisting shipwreck victims on the Great Lakes and Atlantic coast. And, as recognition grew of the importance of lifesaving activities and of Sumner Kimball's outstanding leadership at the national level, efforts were mounted in Congress to separate these functions from the Treasury's Revenue-Marine and give them their own identity within the federal bureaucracy. In 1878, Congress approved the creation of the United States Life-Saving Service as a separate entity within the Treasury Department; President Rutherford B. Hayes completed the process in the only appropriate way, naming Kimball its General Superintendent. Forty-four years later, at age 81, Kimball would retire from the post, having provided distinguished leadership from the agency's inception until the creation of the United States Coast Guard through a merger of the Revenue-Marine and the Life-Saving Service.

❧

THE SPRING OF 1877 MARKS THE OFFICIAL START OF LIFESAVING OPERATIONS AT POINT BETSIE, and also the beginning of a sixty-year span during which lifesaving and lighthouse operations were conducted there, side-by-side, under the direction of separate federal agencies. The lifesaving station's first keeper, Captain Matthews, was to serve there, with distinction, for a decade. The 1880 U.S. Census records the household as the forty-eight-year-old Matthews, his twenty-nine-year-old wife Mary, who was from Nova Scotia, an eleven-year old daughter Rose, and an aunt who assisted in housekeeping activities. Like many of the early lifesaving keepers, it appears that Matthews had sailed the Great Lakes, ultimately as a captain, before turning to land employment.

From an historical perspective, these initial years constitute the fascinating period when lake mariners' survival was heavily—sometimes critically—dependent on the respective services of the light and lifesaving stations. One might argue that the importance of the keepers and crews of both lighthouse and lifesaving services on the lakes peaked in the late 19th century and the following two decades; while their successors would become better equipped, so too would be the vessels they were charged to protect. But given the characteristics of the vessels and the limited ability of mariners of the historic period to forecast weather and outrun sudden storms, each crew knew then that their effectiveness might well mean the difference between life and death—for both their own personnel and those whose well-being the crews were sworn to protect.

Each station had its specialization of mission and was accountable to superior officers at both district and national levels. Employees of lighthouses and lifesaving facilities operated with different management regulations, pay schedules, inspections, etc. U.S. Life-Saving Service stations became Coast Guard facilities upon that agency's formation in 1915, whereas lighthouses were not added to the Coast Guard's responsibility until 1939. By then, the Point Betsie lifesaving station, and others, had been closed due to budgetary constraints or having been deemed outdated or redundant. In Point Betsie's case, its rescue capabilities had been turned over to the Coast Guard's station at the busier entrance to the nearby Frankfort harbor, from which speedy, motorized lifeboats covered the area's waters.

❦

THE TWO POINT BETSIE KEEPERS' ACCOUNTS PROVIDE INSIGHTS INTO EARLY LIFE AT THEIR STATIONS' REMOTE, SHARED LOCATION. Each keeper was responsible for his own station's mission, but in his records would sometimes comment on the activities of the other keeper and his crew. As was typical where the two types of stations shared a location, each knew the challenges the other faced as well as the strengths and weaknesses he brought to the task. While personnel of the two stations were comrades and friends, and routinely aided each other, there were circumstances when jealousies and resentment between them came to the surface. Frictions sometimes stemmed from the higher pay that lightkeepers and their assistants enjoyed under their agency's much longer history and, initially, a more powerful voice among Washington policy-makers, even though the routine duties of lifesavers called upon them to lay their own lives on the line while attempting to save others.

Lightkeeper Alonzo Slyfield's journal[7] offers a few insightful references to the Point Betsie lifesaving station's initial years of operation. Having noted on April 8, 1877, that his lighthouse was "fitted up ready for lighting" to open the season despite the cold north wind, the ice banks having virtually departed, he commented that the new "Life station commenced running" only on April 24. Throughout that summer, Slyfield would make nearly daily journal entries, mostly simply recording the weather. On September 1, however, he noted, "Life station not open yet", and eight days later followed up with the comment, "Life Station men came at 3 o'clock to open the station for the fall term...." His comment implies that initially the rescue station may not have operated throughout the mid-summer, but only in the spring and fall when storms were most likely to threaten lake shipping.

Slyfield had a horse at Point Betsie at this time, noting on July 11, 1878, "Went to Frankfort Horse Back" and recording one day that fall, "Station crew mounted boat on carriage first time. Towed boat from Frankfort to Platte River with horse." (Slyfield was certainly referring to the lifesaving crew, as apart from family, he had no assistants of his own.)

Some unexplained issue apparently arose for lifesaving Captain Matthews in the spring of 1879, as Slyfield wrote on April 21 that an examination was underway, by a visiting inspector of stations, into complaints against him. While Slyfield noted that the result was yet unknown (and no further evidence of this issue is available), the immediate consequences must not have been too serious for Matthews, for he led the Point Betsie lifesavers for eight more years. Whatever the episode amounted to, however, it proved to be a harbinger of difficulties that would arise later in his career.

Slyfield's journal recorded a fuel problem at the light on May 19, 1879: "Light burnt bad cause lamp oil leaked through side. I have soldered it tight—it flowed all the oil out & overrun the receiver." A lightkeeper had to be his own "fixit" man, and "Doc" Slyfield, fortunately, was both diagnostician and repairman. In the same vein, he wrote the following summer that "...my flash paines were not regulated from 8 o'clock until one. I worked at it, oiled all the wheels under the carriage and put on all the weights. I watched it for 2 hours. It flashed regularly. But...when I went to my light at 8 o'clock it was stopped. Today I have taken off all the wheels. I find a pin which holds a wheel was split in two at the point so it bound the wheel tight to the shoulder of the arm. It runs well since I put in a new pin."

A keeper also had to provide for himself and his family. On November 22, 1879, Slyfield wrote, "Killed Bear." Numerous deer kills were also recorded in the journal, which closes with a characteristic December 16 entry, "Discontinued light for 1879, all articles packed away for the winter."

∾

THE FOLLOWING YEAR OF 1880 WOULD PROVE ESPECIALLY EVENTFUL AT POINT BETSIE; as such, it offers many insights into activities at the stations, both routine and dramatic. The year began typically, lifesaving station Keeper Matthews reporting on April 1 that his crew was "...all assembled at the station and [had] commenced to clean house." He gave his daily weather report, recorded which crewman took each patrol assignment, and classified the passing vessels—just two schooners on that early season day. The vessel count shot upward, thereafter; on April 9, Matthews recorded three barks, one brig, nine steamers and fifty-three schooners passing and noted that "...all craft passing this station thus far this spring have been going to the northward. No vessels have passed from the Straights up to date." Farther to the north, the Straits of Mackinac, it seems, were still frozen, blocking long-distance southbound traffic.

In the spring of 1880, when Alonzo was fifty-five and Alice was fifty-two, the Slyfield family consisted of the parents and seven offspring. Daughters Ella and Mary Ellen were living outside the home; twenty-six-year-old Charles was generally engaged in commercial fishing. Living at home were brothers Edwin, age twenty-one, who also fished; seventeen-year-old Elmer, and fourteen-year-old George. The youngest child, daughter Jessie, was just nine. By that time their father had resumed his medical practice, serving the area's residents in addition to tending Point Betsie Light, and in Alonzo's judgment the boys were old enough, and had acquired sufficient understanding of the light's operations, that they could fill in for him at the light if an emergency called him away. Such was Alonzo's journal entry that April 5th: "Went to Frankfort to see sick boy. 2 sons at light to take charge."

As would happen in several later instances, this didn't sit well with Keeper Matthews at the lifesaving station, who treated Alonzo's absences differently in his own daily chronicle.[8] Thomas Matthews wrote on April 13: "Duty compels me to note on this Journal the very bad way Point Betsey Light has been kept this spring. I do not wish to do A.J. Slyfield any injury, but the light has been neglected so much and my crew so often passing remarks upon the light that I am obliged to make note of it. This morning the patrol see that the light did not revolve and was burning very dim—time 3:30 a.m. Watched it until near five OC, and weather being hazy and many vessels & steamers passing. Surfman LaCore went to the Light House, woked up some boys who were sleeping there who got up and fixed & put the light in running order. The Keeper is in the habit of leaving boys at the light in charge. I must say the light has been very much neglected all this spring."

By mid-summer, the passing vessels were frequent and of diverse types. On July 20, for example, five barks, two brigs, thirty-eight schooners, twenty-seven steamers and one sloop were recorded. And toward the end of that year, storms would place many Great Lakes sailors, aboard vessels of all types, in great jeopardy.

∽

THE MIDDLE OF OCTOBER, 1880, FOUND NUMEROUS VESSELS THROUGHOUT THE LAKES SUCCUMBING TO FEARFUL WINDS AND WAVES, WITH A STAGGERING LOSS OF HUMAN LIFE. Point Betsie's rescuers, ably led by Captain Matthews, were destined to answer duty's call with a performance that earned them national recognition and a measure of distinction within the annals of U.S. lifesaving that survives to this day.

As Lightkeeper Slyfield's journal of October 16 records, the day brought a southwest blow, with hail, rain, and snow, to Lake Michigan's coast. Keeper Matthews' own description is similarly revealing; he recorded high surf at midnight, heavy surf at sunrise and tremendous surf throughout the balance of the day. Westerly gale-force conditions over the next four days continued to make for hazardous sailing or other lake activity. Derived from his hand-written original version, and in terms common to the Life-Saving Service, here is Matthews' report documenting his crew's courageous response to the crisis they faced that day:

> Word came that there was a vessel ashore 1 mile South Frankfort. Left the station with beach apparatus at 8:45 a.m. to go to the relief of Sch. **J. H. Hartzell** of Detroit loded with Iron ore, ashore one mile south of Frankfort Pier and about 300 yards from the beach. [A]rrived with the apparatus at scene abreast of the wreck 10:30 a.m. first shot fired 10:40 a.m.; line fell onboard but fouled with the wreckage. [H]auled line and shot ashore again. [R]ecoiled line, fired second shot 11:30 a.m., line caught by the crew of the wreck. Crew all up in the fore crosstrees. 12:10 main mast fell over the side. [H]ull breaking up. Current is so strong that the crew are making very slow work hauling the whip off but they succeed getting the tail block at 2:30 p.m. I did not get a hawser but for fear of pulling mast out…if we get them at all it must be done with the single whip and that way soon as the hull is breaking up fast. Sent out breeches buoy first and brought the mate ashore first. [W]e

learned from him that the Capt. and 5 sailors & cook was still left onboard, the last named being a woman and she very exhausted. I took the desperate chance of sending out the life car by the single whip which we succeeded in doing. I run it up to the crosstrees and two sailors got into it - a signal was made to haul ashore. We landed them all right but the car was fearfully battered up. [W]hen asked why the woman did not come in the car they said they could not do anything with her. [T]he cover of car ...had been bent all out of shape. [W]e could not make it tight but it was the only thing we could do. I gave the order to haul it out again which was done by about 50 men: out she went and right up to the crosstrees. [N]ow they surely will send the woman this time, but no, the Capt. and 2nd mate came this time. [W]hen asked the reason the woman was not brought the answer was that she was past all help. [T]he car is badly stove and flange of the hatch or cover is all bent and warped so that in places...a person could slip in their hand. B]ut it getting dark and 2 men and the woman still on the wreck. I concluded to send the car again but with very little hopes of her reaching the masthead again. [A]s soon as she met the first breakers over she went, keel up and remained keel up until she reached the wreck and I supposed so full of water that we would not be able to raise her to the masthead by small whip but it must be tried. [I]t is our only chance. [T]he hull is going to pieces fast and the mast is swaying about fearfully. [T]here is nothing for us to do but to run the car up, which is done by fifty men, the last chance is at hand. [I]t is now so dark that we cannot see who or when the people will get in. [W]e wait about fifteen minutes. [T]hey surely must be in the car. I give the order to lower away and down she comes and is knocked keel up the moment she comes to the water. The people are terribly excited and strain and pull to bring the car ashore as soon as possible. [M]en run to get the woman out of the car but when the car is opened no woman is there. [T]he two men are asked why the woman was not brought and the answer was the woman was dead. I asked both men myself if they were sure the woman was dead. [T]hey both said the woman was dead and as stiff as a board and they could do nothing with her. It was now pitch dark and if I called for volunteers to go out for the dead woman and should lose them which was a hundred to one the mast would come down and they would be lost. I therefore concluded to suspend operations. [W]e let go of the whip and hauled it onshore. The mast fell during the night. The next morning the lifesaving crew picked up the apparatus and returned it to the station. I have forwarded wreck report to Dist. Supt. Up to this date the body of Lydia Dale (October 20th, 1880) has not been recovered.[9]

A Lyle gun and projectile for shooting a line to a wrecked vessel. [10]
Photo by author

Faking box on which a light line is wound, then removed, in preparation for being fired to a stricken vessel, minimizing the risk of its becoming tangled. [11]
Photo by author

The life car was a key piece of equipment that resembled a totally enclosed, cigar-shaped tube, blunt-ended, made of iron or copper. Its top was convex, with a hatchway through which several people could enter, then draw tightly closed (assuming it hadn't been damaged during rescue attempts). In the original cars people had to lie down; some later models were higher at the ends, allowing them sitting room outside a narrower center where the hatch was located. Riding in total darkness inside what must have seemed like the proverbial sardine can, breathing stuffy air while being pounded about by the surf could not have been a pleasant experience, but it was often the difference between life and death. Suspended on rings from a hawser that had been stretched between a stranded ship and the shore, the car would be pulled out by the ship's crew, loaded, then pulled to shore by the lifesavers. Practicing its deployment was a vital exercise at Point Betsie and other stations. And when it was put to actual use, the car was likely the only means of rescuing otherwise doomed mariners.

A life car for rescuing sailors from a stricken ship, its hatch opened.[12]
Photo by author

MATTHEWS' FIRSTHAND, GRAPHIC ACCOUNT OF THE HARZELL RESCUE POINTS TO THE LEVEL OF EFFORT THAT THE SERVICE EXPECTED OF HIM AND HIS ABLE CREW. When duty called, the lifesavers of Point Betsie immediately put into use the diverse skills they had sharpened through their unending drills, under conditions that required great strength and endurance.

There is, however, much more to be said of this great story, crucial elements of which enrich the more comprehensive and polished account that the U.S. Life-Saving Service published in its 1881 Annual Report. The *J.H. Hartzell* wreck was the first disaster with fatal consequences to occur that year within reach of the service's personnel. Irrespective of the loss of Dale's life, which certainly was not the rescuers' fault but much lamented by them, the effectiveness of Point Betsie's crew and Matthews' leadership did not escape recognition at the agency's highest level.

Sketch drawn by investigating officer showing circumstances of the wreck and rescue.
Courtesy of Claudia Lewis

A more thorough review of the *Hartzell* episode must begin with the sound decision of Captain William A. Jones to await daylight before taking his vessel into the harbor's channel, which at that time consisted of a narrow course between two piers running straight out from shore. Having arrived at about 3 a.m., the schooner lay off the narrow entrance in a southeast, or offshore, breeze. But then came a nightmare with which sailing vessel captains often had to cope, a sudden shift of the wind to the southwest, its strength rapidly intensifying to gale force. When the ship would no longer respond to her wheel and began to drift toward shore, the captain dropped both anchors and set a distress signal. Despite having two anchors on the bottom, she continued to drift toward land, soon striking a sand bar and turning her bow to shore. The waves immediately began to crash into and over the hull and the vessel soon foundered, her stern in about sixteen feet of water and her bow in even deeper water. The crew's only chance for survival was to get above the waves by climbing the foremast, hoping that someone would spot them and attempt their rescue. Four men are said to have carried the seriously ill and weak Lydia Dale up the foremast and lashed her onto planks they had nailed across it. Exposed to the elements despite attempts to shield her, she quickly grew delirious.

The young son of a local fisherman saw the wreck through the storm's gloom and alerted his father, who in turn notified nearby residents. A crowd of citizens gathered on the beach and built a fire, then used pieces of driftwood to spell "LIFE-BOAT COMING" against the soaring bluff, thereby offering a glimmer of hope to the mast-clinging crew. A young man named Woodward had immediately left by horseback for the closest lifesaving station, miles to the north at Point Betsie. He arrived at the station early in the morning, hastily explained the crisis to Keeper Matthews, who promptly ordered out the beach cart and rescue apparatus. Loaded with the Lyle gun, breeches buoy, lines heavy and light and other essential equipment, five crewmen—Leonard Rohr, J. Manuel, Marvin La Cour, J.W. Stokes, and Martin Barney—were soon hauling a wagon weighing close to a thousand pounds. The station's sixth surfman, Charles La Rue, was out on a southward beach patrol at the time, but was to later join the rescue party.

Just the story of the crew's arduous journey to a site on the shore opposite the wreck, the only possible location from which a rescue could be undertaken, is heroic. As the service later described it and other details for Congress and the public[13]:

> *The expedition had set out upon a terrible journey. The Point au Bec Scies station is upon the lake-shore, north of Frankfort, south of which town the wreck lay, and the intervening river and the harbor piers making out into the lake from the town made it impossible, in any case, to arrive at the wreck by following the line of the coast. The only way was to make a circuit through the woods and around the rear of the town, where the bisecting river could be crossed by a bridge in that locality, and the beach south of Frankfort gained. The shortest route, not less than seven or eight miles long, was by a road which led off the beach to an intersecting road leading to the town, but to gain this it was necessary to travel two miles from Point au Bec Scies along the beach, and the beach was now submerged by a swashing flood constantly bursting against and washing away the steep banks of the lake*

shore, battering the escarpment with inter-tangled masses of logs, stumps, and trees, and of course rendering the way impassable. The expedition was therefore compelled to lengthen the detour by taking an old trail or cart-track, which had been pioneered by the Point au Bec Scies light-house construction party several years before for the transportation of materials.

Point Betsie life savers ready for drill, roped to beach cart.
Courtesy of Claudia Lewis

This road wandered through the woods, along winding ravines and up steep, soggy sand-hills. Across these acclivities the way was so difficult that the men and the horse, tugging and straining at the cart together, could only make ten or fifteen yards at a pull without pausing.

When the men had finally pushed and dragged the cart to the intersecting road, they were fortunate to encounter a buggy bearing another party who was seeking to alert the station to the *Hartzell's* crisis. The keeper got into the buggy and they headed on, looking for additional help. They met others along the way, who hastened back to the station with horses to bring its lifecar, should that be needed. The surfmen eventually received assistance in the form of a team of horses, enabling them to pick up their pace. At about 10:30 a.m., they reached the base of the high dunes that separated them from the lake and wreck site. There they faced another big challenge:

So steep was the ascent that man and beast had fairly to climb, and almost to hoist the cart after them. Nothing could have been done but for the aid of a crowd of sturdy townsfolk, who had assembled there, and, anticipating the arrival of the life-saving party, had cleared away with axes and handspikes a great deal of the undergrowth and fallen trees. Even with these impediments removed, so precipitous was the acclivity, that it took the united efforts of twenty-seven brawny men, by actual count, and a span of stout horses, to gain the summit, only about twenty feet being made at a time.

Through the frantic efforts of crewmen and other citizens who had put their muscles to the task, the cart had reached the dune's top and a pathway to the lakeshore had been cleared, but their challenge was far from over. The rescue party then faced a frightful sight, "...a precipitous bluff nearly three hundred feet above the sea" with no place near enough to the wreck from which to fire a Lyle gun that would send its projectile and line to the wreck, except a ledge that was about two hundred and fifty feet below them. Using the lines on the beach cart that were wrapped around trees, they gradually lowered the cart; when the lines proved too short, the men provided the drag, keeping the cart from plummeting to destruction on the beach. In this way they finally completed the descent to the ledge, from which Matthews and his crew mounted the rescue that he so movingly recounted.

There are several additional elements to this extraordinary story, beginning with the facts surrounding the sole fatality, cook Lydia Dale. Irrespective of the crews' insistence that she initially was too traumatized to enter the lifecar, subsequently too weak or confused to cooperate with her colleagues to get her into it, and finally that she had died on the wreck, there was much public concern—even some outright hostility—toward the *Hartzell* survivors for having left her. The traditional mandate, "Women and children first," doubtless came to many minds, and the anger over the crews' lack of respect of this principle is sometimes voiced as an explanation for the crew's hasty departure from the community. And, when Dale's body was found on the beach more than two weeks later, a coroner's inquest attributed her death to drowning—the cause of death of this single woman, of unknown age and parentage, which appears in Benzie County's records. She is thought to have been buried in an unmarked pauper's grave in the local cemetery. Curiously that hand-written official record also shows an alias, "Harriett," and a virtually illegible last name. Nothing more is known about the alias' recording—in handwriting which is close to, if not the same as that in the rest of the document—but it apparently was an addition to the original entry.

Given the victim's undisputed illness and the effects of exposure and exhaustion that attended the vessel's destruction, it seems certain that the woman had become delirious, perhaps even unconscious, while lashed to a mast being battered by icy winds—but dead? That will remain forever unknown, but there seems little likelihood that her limp body could have been lowered into the small hatchway of the swinging car. It also seems certain that Keeper Matthews made the right call in deciding against risking volunteers' lives by sending them out to the wreck, with darkness setting upon the still heaving sea.

Another key aspect of the rescue, one which the chiefs of the Life-Saving Service emphasized, was the essential role played by some fifty to sixty local volunteers—farmers, fishermen, sailors, lumbermen, whatever—in working alongside Captain Matthews and his hardy fellow lifesavers. Without them, the heroic rescue could never have been mounted, much less succeed in saving the seamen's lives.

Never ones to miss an opportunity to bring great accomplishments to the attention of the public (and, perhaps more significantly, to the appropriations committees of the Congress), General Superintendent Kimball and his staff paid fitting tribute in their annual report to the captain, crew, and supportive citizens of the area:

The conduct of the life-saving crew in toiling to the wreck from such a distance, and despite the formidable obstacles interposed by the wild country and the October gale, is admirable; and also all they did and endured when once abreast of the sunken vessel. It might be said, however, that they acted under the obligations of official duty. But no abatement can be made in the tribute which belongs to the throng of great-hearted volunteers, who served with them so staunchly. Without any compulsion or requirement, other than their own manly hearts supplied, they were there with the men of the station from first to last. Hour after hour, patiently, sternly, they stood braced on the slanted front of a crumbling precipice, without food, without rest, beaten by wind and rain and hail, mired by the muck of the hills, choked and blinded by the sand-blasts, often half engulfed by the sliding soil, strained and aching in every muscle and sinew by the very act of standing on the steep and yielding acclivity, and by the racking pulling and hauling upon the ropes of the life-car, and never turned their faces from the wreck until the last being whom it was possible to save from the wreck was in safety among them.

The *J.H. Hartzell* rescue is rightfully viewed as one of the outstanding achievements in the history of the U.S. Life-Saving Service's operations on the Great Lakes. It is a story that everyone who has known and loved Point Betsie and the communities nearby should admire. It is said that the lifesavers were so exhausted after their ordeal that rather than return to the station, they slept in homes around town to recover their strength; one couldn't make it even that far, sleeping instead at a house by the beach. Then the drama was over, and the crew had to haul their equipment through the woods and over the sand to the station, and resume their preparations for their next call to duty.

✍

AS THE YEAR'S SERVICES AT THE ADJACENT LIGHT AND LIFESAVING STATIONS WERE DRAWING TO A CLOSE, on the 14th of December Slyfield recorded a snowstorm and wrote that he had come to the light that day to close up. His son Edie had killed a deer, he said—a much welcomed supply of food, no doubt, for the long winter. The Keeper concluded, "Discontinued light for 1880…packed things away in store room. Carefully covered lenze."

Such are the stories of service to sailors on the lakes, whether they featured the keepers of lights, keepers and crews of stations of the U.S. Life-Saving Service, or simply courageous private citizens facing up to the maritime perils of their time and place.

CHAPTER FIVE

DUTY, DRAMA AND DRUDGERY AT THE POINT

The closing decades of the 19th century and first twenty years of the 20th century comprised an especially active period at Point Betsie's lighthouse and lifesaving station, as each of the crews, working side-by-side, bore responsibilities that could determine whether mariners traveling along the coast of this sometimes tumultuous inland sea would live or die. The substantial fleets of aging schooners and steam-powered cargo vessels, passenger ships, tugs and fishing boats brought increasing significance to the network of lights and rescue facilities on the coasts of the Great Lakes.

Today's admirers of Point Betsie might be startled to hear that the Lighthouse Board once favored the tower's replacement. The importance of this light was never an issue; in fact, the value attributed to it was implicit in repairs regularly made to the charming structure, including continuing fortification of the tower's foundation to protect it from Lake Michigan's erosive power.

In 1879, the Board had first sought funds to expand Point Betsie's service to mariners by adding a steam-powered fog signal. (The first steam-driven horn on Lake Michigan had been installed years earlier at the South Manitou Island station, producing a four-second blast every minute. It improved upon a mechanical bell that had been installed four years earlier.)

But in its June 30, 1880, report to Congress, the Board's appeal for a new structure at Point Betsie was more strident, renewing concerns over the contractor's performance that had been raised at the time of the lighthouse's completion:

> *The great increase of commerce makes a corresponding increase in the power of certain lights necessary, especially in that at Point Betsey, Lake Michigan, near which four-fifths of all the lake commerce passes.*

This is one of the most important lights on Lake Michigan. The present light has never given satisfaction. The tower was built by contract in 1858 and the work was miserably done. A new tower with sufficient height to put the focal plane 100 feet above the lake should be built, and the fourth-order lens should be replaced by a third-order. An appropriation of $40,000 is recommended for this work.

But as is often the case, the wheels didn't turn rapidly in Washington; the combination of bureaucratic inertia and parsimonious appropriators in Congress combined to result in the preservation, to this day, of the tower and other original elements. A pattern took shape: whether new bricks and mortar, equipment installations, or additional personnel were at issue, change would come to Point Betsie quite gradually.

In April, 1880, Keeper Slyfield wrote to request an assistant, saying a second man at the lighthouse was a "necessity," but an inspector denied his appeal several weeks later. In annual reports over the next two years, the Board reiterated its recommendation, with no more success than previously, for the tower's replacement. Meanwhile, daily life went on as usual at the light; with the essential help of his family, Alonzo performed all the tasks associated with light-tending, making necessary repairs as best he could and keeping up the station as the explicit instructions required. Looking down from the lantern and its surrounding observation deck, he could also observe the Point Betsie lifesavers faithfully going about their daily drills and setting out on their nightly north- and southbound beach patrols.

South view from the tower, toward lifesaving station, boathouses, drill pole, etc.
Courtesy of Claudia Lewis

◆

A SURFMAN EMBARKING IN DARKNESS ON HIS FOUR-HOUR PATROL COULDN'T BE SURE OF WHAT HE WOULD ENCOUNTER, EVEN ON A CALM LAKE MICHIGAN NIGHT. On the 23rd of April, 1881, John M. Lee returned to the lifesaving station from his 4 a.m.-to-sunrise beach patrol and reported to Keeper Matthews that he had found a bottle containing a fly leaf, ripped from a book, bearing the following penciled note: "The boat is breaking, the Captain's washed over board." The communication was signed by James Eldridge, aboard the steamer *Alpena*. [1]

Nearly three months later, Surfman E. P. Karvand, making the 8 p.m.-to-midnight trek, returned with a liquor flask that he found on the beach near the station. Inside the flask was a slip of paper on which, in pencil, was this message dated October 16th at 3 o'clock: "On Board the Alpena. She has broke her port wheel, is at the mercy of seas, is half full of water, God Help us, Captain (Napier) washed overboard." The note was signed by Geo. Moore of 856 South Halsted St., Chicago, Illinois. On the back was the sentence, "The finder of this will please communicate with my wife and let her know of my death."

The *Alpena* was a well-known, wooden paddle-driven passenger steamer operated by the popular Goodrich Transit Company on its routes between Chicago, Grand Haven, and Muskegon. Built in 1866, the nearly two-hundred-foot-long vessel was in her fifteenth year of service when she departed Grand Haven for Chicago on the warm evening of October 15, 1880, Captain Nelson W. Napier apparently anticipating a smooth one hundred and eight-mile voyage. She carried a crew of about thirty and a passenger count of more than forty, but the latter figure has never been precisely determined and the total number aboard could have been close to one hundred.

She was sighted on-course by several other vessels until about midnight, when powerful winds and rapidly falling temperatures slammed their way across Lake Michigan, damaging or wrecking close to one hundred ships, among them, as already described, the schooner *J.H. Hartzell* lying farther northeast, just off the harbor at Frankfort. Driven off-course by powerful waves and winds, and perhaps also hit by a tornado, the *Alpena* completely broke up some twenty-five miles off Kenosha, Wisconsin, with the loss of everyone aboard. Over several days, identifiable wreckage and bodies came ashore; the *Alpena* was the year's single worst disaster on Lake Michigan.

◆

LIFESAVERS ALWAYS HAD TO BE READY FOR ACTION, whether the seas were calm and a crisis on the lake might not be expected, or when surf was smashing over the bars and obviously placing in jeopardy vessels, passengers, and cargoes up and down the shore. By this time, Point Betsie and most other lifesaving stations were manned by seven surfmen and their keeper when fully staffed, as Kimball had finally convinced economy-minded legislators of the merit of the larger crew complement. It meant that the usual six men would be available to row the rescue craft, with the keeper manning its steering oar, while the additional man could continue on duty as the station's lookout in the event another crisis were to occur within sight – a not uncommon reality given the large number of vessels that could be caught in suddenly stormy seas. The extra man also afforded the keeper some flexibility in case of a crewman's illness or leave, and in case the keeper was incapacitated, there would still be six men to row while the No. 1 surfman, subbing for his boss, would man the steering oar.

Point Betsie lifesavers' daily litany of drills, broken only by the occasional need to respond to an actual shipwreck or other emergency, would continue month after month, year after year. At 10 a.m. on May 12, 1881, thick morning fog lifted and, as Keeper Matthews recorded in his journal that day, "…the lookout discovered a vessel about five and half miles to the northward of this station with no sail set except the peak of the foresail." The crew also saw that a steamer was standing near the said vessel. Matthews reported that the steamer, apparently having ascertained the sailing ship's condition, began moving away to the south and west. Captain Matthews launched a boat, intercepted the "propeller," and asked what the schooner's problem was. He was told that the schooner was the *Advance*; its port bow was "stove in," it was full of water and there was no one aboard. It was apparently the victim of a collision with another vessel amidst the heavy fog that had earlier settled over the lake.

Returning to the station, the Keeper dispatched a man to Frankfort for a tug that would be needed to tow the ship if his crew succeeded in keeping it afloat. While the cook prepared their mid-day dinner, the crew readied the surfboat with equipment that would likely be needed to save the vessel. After the meal he took his surfmen to the wreck, leaving one at the station. After a "pull" of about seven miles, they boarded the *Advance* and found her loaded with shingles. About a third of her load apparently had been lost over the side. By the time the tug arrived, the crew had cleared the wreckage and hoisted a large anchor which had been knocked overboard by the impact of the collision. Matthews allowed that this "…was no pleasant job as the vessel's decks was two feet under water." The wind having shifted to the north, the men "...hoisted the fore stasail and the foresail as well as we could and headed her for Frankfort."

They soon met the tug, which took the schooner in tow, and at about 9 p.m. the *Advance* arrived off the town and went aground nearly two hundred feet off the south pier. When it became apparent that the entire deckload would have to be removed to get the ship into the harbor, the Keeper and his crew went into town to get some supper, then returned to the boat at 11 p.m. and spent the night unloading shingles onto a scow that the tug had brought. The next morning they were able to maneuver the schooner to safety between the north and south piers; meanwhile, Matthews had telegraphed the captain at Manistee, where he and his men presumably had been taken by the other colliding vessel, to advise him that his schooner was now in Frankfort. The Keeper sent four of his men back to the station to attend to their duties, while he and the two others maintained watch over the wreck until the *Advance's* captain arrived in mid-afternoon to take charge. As this account shows, the lifesavers' mission extended to cargoes as well as persons aboard wrecked vessels, and Matthews and his men would do whatever the circumstances required to complete their duty.

❧

OWING TO THEIR STATION'S PROXIMITY, MATTHEWS AND HIS MEN WERE ALWAYS ALERT TO THE OPERATIONS OF POINT BETSIE LIGHT. They would call its keeper's attention to problems with the light of which they became aware. As we have seen, reflecting the rivalry between the respective agencies from bottom to top, they were not averse to reporting the problems to their *own* agency's superior officers. A week after the *Advance* episode, when the lookouts on May 20th would record twenty-six schooners, twenty-nine steamers, and four tugs passing the station, Matthews recorded a complaint from two of his patrolmen that "Point Betsey Light smoked up so that the light could not be seen from 3 a.m. until daylight. The Keeper was away for twenty-four hours and two small boys were left in charge of the lighthouse property." This may have been one of those occasions when Keeper Slyfield's medical services were urgently required elsewhere in the county.

Matthews was still concerned about the point's light later that summer. On July 30th he wrote that "In consequence of Point Betsey Light burning very dim and having stopped flashing" a schooner out of Toledo had run "...right in on the beach near this station and would have grounded if not warned of his danger by Patrolman Kaarvand hollering, the Captain mistook the light on Point Betsey for a steamer's head light—weather was quite smoky & thick at the time. Captain swore he would report the Keeper of Betsey Light."

At this time, Slyfield, age fifty-six, had begun his twenty-first year at Point Betsie following his rather lengthy service at South Manitou Light. While Matthews may or may not have known about it, his companion at the light was exploring, through his own channels, the possibility of resignation. In a September 23rd letter, Slyfield asked his superiors if his twenty-two-year-old son, born during his service on South Manitou Island, could be named his successor.[2] The Keeper emphasized that the young man had assisted him for about a dozen years or "since his age would permit." The son was of "good habits," Alonzo wrote, adding that he "understands this Light well" and could keep the books and manage the supply inventory. Alonzo reminded his bosses:

> Twenty-eight years I have been Keeper of the Manitou and this Light. I have as far as I know given good satisfaction. I would like to make the change if it could be done. But if not, I would not like to resign. I know it is not according to the rules to apoint those who are not assistant. But he is as well posted in Light Keeping as the best of assistants for the reason he has been my only help in bad weather to assist in running the machinery & cleaning the aparatus & taking apart...the watch in bad weather.

Slyfield's reasoning served as a reminder of his devotion to duty:

> Seems to me officers of 28 years' Service who have been faithful to the government and attentive to duty ought to have the privilege of making the change which I desire. [I]n 21 years I have only been to Chicago twice & then to get supplies for my family. My duty has tied me here as I have had no assistant allowed me which in my opinion is required at this Light as much as at many others less important. This Light is a very important one, as it shows all the mariners the Straights of Mackinac....[W]ill you carefully consider this matter & inform me at your earliest convenience. Respectfully yours, A. J. Slyfield, Keeper of Point Betsey Light.

There is no record of an immediate reply, but the appeal did receive attention early in the next navigation season. On April 20, 1882, Inspector Watson of the 11th Light-House District in Detroit wrote to Rear Admiral John Rodgers, chairman of the Board, affirming his personal support of Alonzo's rather unusual request.[3] It is also clear that the several criticisms voiced by the lifesavers—within the confines of their own bureaucratic channel during Alonzo's later years at Point Betsie—apparently had no sway upon his reputation in the lighthouse community. "I have to say that in my opinion," Watson explained, "Mr. Slyfield deserves this reward for his long and faithful services, he having been Keeper of the same light for twenty-one years, and having generally given satisfaction. I would therefore recommend that if possible his request be granted, more especially as he has been failing in health for some time and his son appears to have assisted him in his duties."

Thus, the way was opened for young Edwin Slyfield to succeed his father as keeper at Point Betsie Light; there being no raises reflecting one's length of service, he would receive the same annual salary of $560. Giving up his fishing partnership with brother Charles, Edwin received an interim appointment on May 23, 1882; the appointment became permanent on July 14th. Edwin would serve as Point Betsie keeper until July, 1888, when, having requested a transfer to a pier-head light, he was assigned to the light at Ludington harbor, about sixty miles south of Frankfort. In taking this post, he and Keeper Peter Dues, who had served at the Ludington for almost six years, would exchange positions.

That Edwin Slyfield would be more than a merely convenient successor to his father is shown both by his service at Point Betsie and by his subsequent career at Ludington, where he served for twenty-one years while coping with two noteworthy difficulties. First, despite numerous appeals, Congress had provided no funds for construction of a keeper's dwelling at the Ludington light site. Nor would there be until the late 1890s, the task of erecting the building not being completed until the summer of 1900. Meanwhile, Edwin and his family, provided with a meager stipend, rented quarters in town. In addition, the keeper's job presented unusual physical challenges; for a number of years, he had two lights to maintain on the south pier as well as one on the north one, thus requiring him to make perilous treks, amidst waves often smashing against the narrow structures from the northwest or southwest, to service them.

His father finally was freed to enjoy an active retirement in Frankfort, surrounded by family and friends in a community with which he had long been associated. When he eventually succumbed to pneumonia on October 14, 1896, the weekly *Benzie Banner* described him the next day as simply "…one of the oldest and best known residents of Frankfort." Then, making the common mistake of saying that he was the first keeper of Point Betsie Light (he had served so long there that probably few people remembered his predecessors), the news bulletin concluded with the succinct understatement, "He had also gained considerable reputation as a doctor."

Looking back at Alonzo Slyfield's life and work, we today might describe him as a dedicated "multi-tasker" who, like other such able persons, had to balance diverse, and sometimes competing, professional and personal responsibilities. He can be rightly described as a hero of his time and place, having spent most of his own lifesaving the lives of others through both medicine and his distinguished service as keeper of two vitally important Lake Michigan lights. A comparable tribute is doubtless due his Alice, who with him bore the rigors of pioneer life and who dealt with the periodic conflicts between her husband's dual responsibilities.

Alice was to survive Alonzo by more than seven years. According to son Charles' account, in late January, 1904 "…she had been ailing for a number of days but we did not expect anything serious. She was setting on the edge of the bed when all at once she laid down and died right then and there. She had been bothered some with her heart and I suppose it was heart failure." With the couple's passing, the Frankfort community lost much respected members. They have many descendants, some of whom still reside in the area, who are justifiably proud of their ancestors' historic role in northwest Michigan and within the annals of Great Lakes lightkeeping.

∽

THE POINT BETSIE LIFESAVING CREW CONFRONTED A BIT OF MYSTERY IN MID-SEPTEMBER, 1881, when they spotted wreckage "…in the shape of pieces of hurricane deck" as well as bedding and other materials "…judged to be the upperworks of a steamer, drifting to the north." They were launching the surfboat to retrieve the flotsam when they heard that the British steamer *Columbia* had foundered six miles due west of Frankfort on the night of Sept. 10th. The station was ordered to "maintain a patrol of the beach day and night to look for dead bodies and property." Matthews would report:

> *Dispatched a patrolman north to follow the wreckage thinking that bodies might be entangled therein. Launched surf boat and pulled out about a mile off-shore abreast of station and picked up two trunks, locked, also half an office desk…One empty trunk, four chairs and two stools. Returning to the beach the surfmen on patrol south picked up out of the surf one empty trunk, several feather pillows and 15 cork life belts. No bodies found by us up to date.*

The following day's patrols headed north and south as usual, but no bodies were found. Lieutenant Walton, who was to produce a sketch of the *J.H. Hartzell* rescue of the previous fall, came to Point Betsie to learn more about the wreck and the lifesavers' response to it. He advised that four bodies, presumably from the *Columbia*, had been found by citizens of Frankfort on the beach north of the piers, and a female victim had been found south of the harbor. The next day, Matthews recorded that his night patrols had found three bodies in the water, and the coroner in town had been notified. An inquest was scheduled the next day in Frankfort; Matthews ordered four surfmen to assist the coroner with loading and handling these victims. Meanwhile, he reported, "Patrol was maintained and a vigilant lookout kept for other bodies [and] also property."

That crisis over, the crew had turned to routine maintenance and other chores to enhance the station's effectiveness. Writing on October 18, 1881, Matthews reported, "Myself and five of the surfmen took axes and crosscut saw [and] went and cleared a foot path over the hills along the lake shore so that the patrol could get along. For one mile the beach is cut away up to the hills and it is impossible when the surf is high. We now have a road over the hills and can keep a [lookout to] the limits of our patrol."

The patrol's southern trek along the beach brought the Frankfort pier light within sight. Any anomaly a patrol encountered during the trek was to be reported. Such was the case on a night in mid-November, when Point Betsie patrols twice reported that Frankfort harbor's pier light was not burning. Some months later, on June 20, 1882, Matthews recorded that during the previous night he and his crew had experienced

Slyfield family monument in Crystal Lake (North) Cemetery
Photo by author

something quite memorable: "An unusual light lighting up the whole hevens so that for half a minute a pin could be picked up, and…changing from a very bright to a greenish, and then to a deep red. Was really startling to behold. This occurred 10:30 p.m. We are at a loss to account for so strange a light…all who saw it are as mystified as myself. Hope to get an explanation in the newspapers." There is, unfortunately, no record that his curiosity was satisfied, but perhaps he had witnessed an extraordinarily vivid display of the aurora borealis.

❧

THE LIFESAVING COMMAND OCCASIONALLY HAD NEW EQUIPMENT TO EVALUATE, AND WOULD SOMETIMES SEND IT OUT TO A STATION FOR TRIAL. That must have been the case at Point Betsie in the fall of 1882, when Matthews reported that the crew had launched a craft known as the "Long Branch Surf-boat" and rowed her through the surf. "She behaved well," he opined, but "she is a heavier boat to pull to windward than a five-ored Buffalo boat." He speculated that if the "Buffalo" boat had six oars she could cut through the surf in a heavier wind and take as much surf as the Long Branch boat could function in, but a five-oared boat "...is not balanced as to power or trim."

That fall, Matthews was yet conscious of the huge ordeal his crew had faced in hauling the beach cart through the tangled woods before they could reach the dirt road that led to the distant location of the *Hartzell* rescue. Determined to ease this burden, on September 18, 1882, he reported in his log, "Myself and crew opening up a waggon road from this station to the State road, distance one and half mile. This is only way from here to Frankfort with apparatus." The record indicates the crew spent four days hacking out this wagon track, the first cleared land route, albeit a very primitive one, from Point Betsie to the outside world.

∽

THE HIGH VOLUME OF TRAFFIC PASSING POINT BETSIE was sustained in the mid-1880s. Increased lake commerce meant, of course, money in the bank for vessel owners, who were always eager to get underway in the spring, and for lenders and shippers. On March 13, 1883, Matthews reported Lake Michigan as "full of ice as far as the eye can see..." and he judged that the prospects of navigation opening by the first of April were poor. But anyone who knows Lake Michigan is aware that conditions can change quickly, as they apparently did on that occasion; just one week later he reported the lake "clear of ice off this port." The point continued to be a busy place during the long navigation season. The 1883 lifesaving journal entries often reported nearly a hundred vessels—primarily schooners and steamers—passing on a single day. That probably made for some nervous moments in circumstances such as those of July 5, when Matthews recorded, "Weather is so thick that we cannot see twenty rods out on the lake. Can hear vessels' horns, and steamers' whistles, but cannot see them."

The "brass" from the Life-Saving Service showed up that summer to inspect the station and put its crew through their paces. Senior officers and politicians from Washington typically scheduled their field site visits in pleasant weather, July and August being favorite times of the year for lake cruises! Thus, under clear conditions on August 8th, the Cutter *Andrew Johnson* arrived off the lifesaving station at 5 a.m. Matthews launched his surfboat and brought ashore General Superintendent Kimball, the service's legendary leader, and a senior associate as well as a district officer and legislator. The station personnel went through the beach apparatus drill, performed the resuscitation of those apparently drowned, and demonstrated use of signal flags and other equipment for the distinguished visitors. Matthews was obviously delighted at the outcome: "Mr. Kimball pronounced himself pleased with our proficiency in all the above drills. Senator Conger was highly gratified with the workings of the Service. The whole inspection passed off to the entire satisfaction of all concerned. The cutter left here at 8:20 a.m. for Manistee." A collective "whew!" was likely heard around the station as the visitors' vessel pulled away.

෴

BY MID-NOVEMBER, 1883, THE POTENTIAL FOR SUCH SUPERVISORY VISITS HAD PASSED FOR THE YEAR, YET A SUBSTANTIAL NUMBER OF VESSELS WERE STILL PASSING THE POINT. Fourteen schooners and twenty-two steamers were tallied by the lifesavers on the 11th of the month, a day on which clear conditions, moderate wind and low surf would give way to gale-force winds, squalls of snow and hail, and pounding surf. It became a day that would freshen the crew's memory for what fall could bring, and present a real challenge for them. Wrote Keeper Matthews:

> Today we have the heaviest gale of the Season...at 12:30 p.m. sighted a three-masted schooner to the S.S.W. under short canvas and running....2 p.m. wind veered to the westward and continued to haul until it got into the W.N.W. It was evident by this time the vessel could not clear Point Betsy, at 2:40 p.m. she [headed] for Frankfort. I sent Surfman Larson along the beach south to see if the vessel succeeded in getting into Frankfort, and, if she grounded outside to return with horses, to transfer apparatus to the scene of the wreck. At 4:40 p.m. Wm. Woodward came to the station with a team and said we were wanted as a three-masted schooner lumber laden was ashore just north of the piers at Frankfort. I secured the services of the team that brought Woodward and was on our way to Frankfort inside of ten minutes; same road that we passed over in going to the wreck of the **Hartzell** in 1880.

> When we had reached within one mile of Frankfort (or cemetery hill) we met Surfman Larson (on his way back) who reported that the crew had got ashore from the wreck. We turned and retraced our steps to the station. It appears that the wind [had] veered to the N.W....heavy snow and wind squall drove the vessel in alongside of the north pier or near enough to let the crew reach the pier by jumping from the mizzen boom. But for the wind changing so suddenly to the N.W. we would have had quite an interesting job as our work would have to be done in the night. The team of horses left us half a mile from the station as they could not haul the apparatus cart up the steep hill. We accomplished it with a tackle and arrived back to the station at 9 p.m.; pretty well blown.

The harsh wintry weather continued for several days, featuring snow squalls and high surf that kept the crewmen on their toes, watching for vessels in trouble. They didn't have to wait long for an episode recorded by Keeper Matthews on November 15, 1883:

> At 3:20 p.m. sighted a three-masted schooner in the NW and about three miles from shore. She was standing to the southward under reefed fore-sail and fore stasail, it was blowing a heavy gale from the NW and very heavy sea running, and blinding snow squalls, could not see the vessel only between squall, at 4:30 p.m. she appeared to be heading in for this station and trying to beach her, at 5 p.m. darkness was coming on and they began burning torches. I concluded she would strike the beach between this point. I dispatched Surfman Rohr to procure a team of Farmer Lockhart his place is one mile NE of this station. The team arrived at 6:20 p.m. and in ten minutes we got started for Frankfort by way of the State road. The only way to get south is by this road; it is impossible [to] go [by] the beach. A team and some places even a man cannot get along without going back in the woods to skirt deep and steep gullies cut into the hillside. When we started it was snowing hard and about six inches on the ground. We didn't see anything of the vessel for a long time before we started. I sent No. 1 and 4 other Surfmen with the apparatus cart and myself and 2 Surfmen went south along the beach to look after the vessel. No.1 with the apparatus was to meet us at Norwegian creek where there is road leading out to the beach and is half way from the station to Frankfort called the old Stone road. From this point to Frankfort there is no possibility of getting along the beach. At this place I burned a Coston Signal [a red flare] to see if I could get a Signal from the vessel but did not. We now pushed on for the creak where we found the others with the apparatus. We all struck out for Frankfort where we arrived at 9 o'clock.

> Mr. Burmeister said she drifted past Frankfort about an hour before our arrival and while passing they burned their torch several times he could not get the tug to go out to her they insisting the light was a steamers. The wind...and sea had moderated very considerable since we left the Station. I telegraphed Keeper Finch to be on the look out for a disabled vessel as one had passed here between 7 and 8 o'clock. We then started back for the station where arived at 12:20 all of us pretty well whipped after our tramp of 12 to 14 miles through the snow. Perhaps I have been too zelous and should have waited but with such a heavy surf running and freezing weather if anything was [done] it must be done with dispatch. The use of the team will be about $4.00. I will forward bills for the horse hire to Supt. as soon as I get them.

Just a dozen days later, on November 27th, Matthews reported they had discovered a three-masted schooner northwest of the station and about five miles out flying a distress signal. He sent a surfman to Frankfort for a tug, which came past the station at 9 a.m. He sent three men out to the tug to see if its master would need additional help; if so, they were to go aboard. The tug took the vessel to safety in South Manitou harbor. Matthews went on to record that at noon "...it commenced blowing another terrible gale from the south, steamers running back [to Frankfort] for shelter." He also noted that the Point Betsie station was closing for the inactive season, and he had placed at Frankfort harbor "...at Fred Kerns' sawmill free of charge, and not to be used unless in case of a wreck, one 5 oared Surf boat, 6 cork vests, 5 pulling ores and one steering ore." Having shuttered his Point Betsie station on November 30th, he would thus be in a position to respond to an emergency in the immediate vicinity of the harbor, where boat traffic would continue as long as conditions permitted.

⋘

THE FOLLOWING SPRING, SURFMAN ROHR LEFT THE STATION FOR THE SOUTH PATROL after midnight on May 2nd. Seasonal lake traffic was underway; that day thirty-one vessels passed the station, twelve of them schooners, seventeen steamers and two tugs. Matthews would report:

*"The weather was very dark and hazy, and looked like bad weather coming on...about 1/4 mile from the Station and right abreast of him, he thought he saw a light. Just then a snow squall burst upon him, he went a few rods and turned to take another look for the light when he discovered something coming right onto the beach [and] sails began to flap. Rohr hailed the vessel, the Capt. jumped off the bow and came ashore, Rohr conducted him to the Station, he was so wet and cold that he needed assistance to get along; we gave him dry cloths and warm drinks, we then returned to the vessel and secured her sails and booms. She proved to be the small schooner **Hope** of Grand Haven, Capt. Frank Smith, with rags and scrap iron...bound to Milwaukee. This morning Surfman Heater went to Frankfort to notify a tug to be on hand as soon as the sea ran down. Tug **Hall** arrived soon after dinner. This crew run all the lines and hawsers to the tug, and unloaded...about 5 tons of rags and scrap iron and in 4 hours we had the vessel afloat. Myself and Surfman Larson went to Frankfort with the schooner to look after our lines which was used in getting the vessel off. **Hope** is 14 tons measurement."*

⋘

MEANWHILE, LIFE CONTINUED AS EXPECTED AT THE LIGHTHOUSE, Keeper Edwin Slyfield following the prescribed routine of fueling the light, cleaning the plate glass and lens, servicing the clockwork that produced the light's characteristic flash, and painting the dwelling's woodwork, the tower steps and other interior and exterior parts under his care. Now and then, the light would fail in some regard, most commonly, it seems, in its flash components. If the keeper was asleep at the time, he would be alerted by a lifesaving patrolman or lookout. The problem was usually a mechanical breakdown, but now and then it would be something else—as on June 25, 1885, when Slyfield recorded, "clock stopped 'cause a spider [was] on the track."

∽

A PROBLEM AROSE AT THE LIFESAVING STATION THAT MID-SUMMER, 1885, THAT WOULD BEDEVIL BOTH POINT BETSIE STATIONS AND OTHERS ON THE LAKES FROM TIME TO TIME. On July 17th, Keeper Matthews wrote that the crew was busy putting in a platform in front of the boat house because the old one had washed away during the night. "I fear the station house will have to be moved back at least 100 feet…150 feet would be better," he noted. A bank in front of the station "…cut away last night 8 feet; surf approached within 12 feet of the house. I think there is no doubt but the surf will reach the house in the fall blows." Matthews recommended that the station be moved promptly; the cost would be from $100 to $150, he estimated, assuming that his crew would assist Frankfort people who had equipment for moving buildings. "I will be obliged to move beach apparatus, surf boat, etc., out of the house every time a gale of wind springs up, as there is but 12 feet of a platform in front and that is liable to be swept away the first gale that comes up," he emphasized.

Matthews' concerns registered at the service's district level and in Washington, and the lifesaving station was pulled back about one hundred feet from its original location. Subsequently, an exchange of letters between General Superintendent Kimball and the Lighthouse Board gave the Life-Saving Service permission to permanently occupy the new site, which the officers presumably thought would adequately protect the station from the seas' encroachment.

Not all the station's needs were as significant as surviving Lake Michigan's rising levels. Of more mundane, bureaucratic nature, yet important to station operations, Matthews would record having received by mail, "2 hasps, 4 staples, and 2 tin painted notices [to mark] U.S. Government property, for posts to secure keys of time detectors."

∽

1886 WOULD PROVE TO BE THOMAS MATTHEWS' LAST FULL YEAR AS KEEPER OF POINT BETSIE LIFESAVING STATION. His journal again includes reports of malfunctions at the light; the lifesavers who were standing watch throughout the night would be immediately aware of any such problems and pass the word. Matthews once allowed as how "a little too much" was being asked of his lifesaving crew by the lightkeeper, but with the latter having no relief, they seem to have achieved a cooperative relationship.

On June 14, 1886, Keeper Matthews reported he had dealt with a discipline problem:

Called the men together and directed their attention to the rules relative to watch from top of the station house and that getting to leeward of the lookout house and sitting on the railing and laying their heads down on their arms was contrary to rules. Rohr said he would sit down when he got tired, and was insolent and insubordinately inclined and as it was not the first offence on his part I concluded it was necessary to make an example of him. I informed him that he was discharged and in presence of the rest of the crew he defied me to discharge him. I gave orders that he would not be called for watch duty in the morning. But before his watch he came to my bed and asked me to let him take his watch, that he was sorry for his conduct. I said no, not in that way would the matter be settled, but after breakfast I would muster the crew and in their presence if he would apologize for what he said and ask to be reinstated I would overlook the offence this time and give him back his place. He made the [apology] as desired and was reinstated.

So that crisis passed, but it would prove suggestive of difficulties in employment relations that Matthews—and doubtless other keepers—would be apt to encounter in their station commands. The tasks involved in leading locally chosen crew members, under the disciplinary standards and performance requirements of the U.S. Life-Saving Service that were likely a sharp shift from most recruits' typical experience, would surely present some formidable challenges to keepers. It was not unusual for there to be some turnover within crews from season to season, which necessitated integrating new members into a team whose effectiveness depended on every member's cooperation and collaboration.

As already noted, beach apparatus drills and the practice of other rescue routines were an unending reality of life for the crews, and the Keeper's journals were filled with detailed performance reports. On June 3, 1886, Matthews, having that day recorded the passage of five barks, three brigs, sixty-eight schooners, forty-one steamers and thirteen tugs, also reported the results of the beach drill. "Drill with beach apparatus with 2 oz. powder, elevation 15 degrees, No. 7 shot line, wind light and favorable. Range 165 yards, distance from drill post to sand anchor 75 yards. Time from word 'action' until man was landed at the crotch 5 and ½ minutes," and he added that ½ minute had been lost by some slippage caused by the "carelessness of [Surfman] No. 5". Three months later, after many more drills, the crew—such carelessness presumably having been remedied—would have this vital exercise down to a more respectable four minutes and ten seconds.

A few days later, he reported thick fog conditions in which the 1,115-gross ton steamer *Iron Duke* , home-ported in Detroit but en route from Milwaukee to Buffalo, had come ashore a half-mile south of the station. It was carrying 50,000 bushels of wheat, valued at $35,000 and the vessel itself was valued similarly. The station crew from Point Betsie had boarded it just ten minutes after it grounded, and its captain had asked Matthews to find a good tug as quickly as possible. As Matthews described the incident:

> *We manned the surf boat and pulled to Frankfort four and half miles, but the only tug fit to do the work went to Manistee early this morning. I had her owners to telegraph for her to return at once. We then returned to the steamer, arriving at 12:30 p.m. (W)ith the assistance of three fish tugs which came along and four hours' hard work shifting cargo from forward aft and dropping anchors at forefoot we succeeded in getting her afloat. We staid until all was in good shape to resume the voyage. The Captain was very hearty in his thanks for the prompt assistance rendered by the crew of Point Betsy Station.*

On July 12, Matthews, who was required to report the receipt of all supplies, advised that he had received by mail from the District superintendent "...for use at this station 17 envelopes, 14 steel pens and 3 lead pencils." A couple of months later, the in-coming supplies included one bottle of black ink, one bottle of mucilage, seventy-two rubber bands, thirteen steel pens and three lead pencils. The "green eye shade" folks in Washington were ever alert to signs of wastefulness or misuse of equipment and supplies in the field.

The equipment was not always as good as the crew might hope. For example, on September 25th Matthews was notably frank in his assessment of a type of light's ineffectiveness:

> *This night very dark and rainy and the patrol have much difficulty in getting along the beach from station to key post. The Buckeye lantern is a failure so far as burning in a gail of wind: in fact they will not burn in a moderate gale. Such a night as last night it is no joke to be left in total darkness while patrolling the beach. It is impossible to relight a lantern out on the beach when blowing and raining even in ordinary gale. If men are expected to [go] through their patrol they must have a light. In the very worst weather is the time that a patrolman has no light and must grope his way among fallen timber and drift-wood, sometimes on his hands and knees. We had no falt to find when we were allowed mineral, sperm or lard oil. We have good brass railroad lanterns and all that is needed to give us a first class light at all times in all weather is about 3 gallons of mineral oil per year.* (One can only hope the oil was forthcoming.)

Keeping the clocks in working order was always a challenge for a lifesaving station keeper. They were essential to station record-keeping and its evaluation by district officers. In late October that year, Surfman Ross was held accountable for "dropping or knocking" the lookout clock. The clock was taken to Frankfort for repair, at a cost of thirty-five cents—a not insignificant impact on a surfman's wage. Matthews reported that because the damage was "...either maliciously or carelessly done by Ross I requested him to pay for the repairs which he refused to do. I told him he would pay or get out of the Service; he preferred the latter. I am satisfied that the interests of the Service demanded his dismissal," Matthews wrote.

Matthews again wintered in Frankfort, but fulfilled his responsibilities of station maintenance. On January 19, 1887, he reported visiting the station that day and finding everything in good condition. He continued periodically to report the weather, as on February 27, when he reported the heaviest gale of the season with about two feet of new snowfall and roads blocked with drifts four to five feet deep.

≪⑥

BUT CHANGE WAS COMING, IN BOTH WEATHER AND THE LEADERSHIP OF POINT BETSIE'S LIFESAVING STATION. On March 10, Matthews reported that two steamers had passed that day, and that a local boat had made a round-trip voyage from Frankfort to Manistee—the year's first departure and arrival at the local port—encountering no ice of consequence on Lake Michigan. And just four days later, Harrison "Tip" Miller recorded that he had signed the oath of office as the new lifesaving station keeper at Point Betsie; he was to open the station for the season at noon on April first. Matthews would be staying in Frankfort, having been named keeper of the newly constructed station on the south side of the harbor, in the community known then as South Frankfort and now as Elberta.

The new station would provide on-site, enhanced protection for mariners entering or leaving the harbor. More significant from Point Betsie's standpoint, it would reduce the physically exhausting and time-consuming overland trips to shipwrecks in the immediate Frankfort area and farther southward, such as the one Matthews and his crew had endured in accomplishing the memorable *Hartzell* rescue. It would also be possible to maintain routine foot patrols south of the harbor, along beach too distant and isolated for Point Betsie's surfmen to reach.

Presumably, Matthews welcomed the opportunity to serve at a facility in the town he knew so well. Having served at Point Betsie for eleven years, he was to hold his new town post for a half-decade until he was suddenly discharged from the service on January 16, 1892. The unfortunate end to Matthews' notable career stemmed from a dispute he had with some of his South Frankfort crewmen in the final days of the 1891 season. Though these facts have no bearing on his record at Point Betsie, it is only appropriate to include them in reviewing Matthews' long career in lifesaving.

Recording the key events of December, 1891, Matthews said he had been busy in the wee hours of the morning checking on a steamer that had run aground several hundred feet beyond the harbor's south pier and had returned to the station at about 4:30 a.m. His journal account then indicates that one of his surfmen, while out on south patrol, had found a bag of flags on the beach. His account does not disclose the nature of the flags, but presumably they could have come off a vessel or, more likely, be from the station's equipment inventory, left on the beach by a careless crewman. In any event, a finding of such a noteworthy item would be regarded as important; failure to immediately report such a discovery would be expected to prompt an investigation.

Matthews wrote that when he had first encountered this surfman after they had both returned to the station, the man had said nothing of this discovery. Only later, when the surfman was going to breakfast did he advise Matthews of his find. "I demanded to know why he didn't report the matter as soon as he returned to the station," Matthews recorded, adding, "he said he didn't have to and other insolent words which led to a controversy and finally to blows" in which three crewmen, including the one who had failed to report the discovery, were "on one side and the Keeper on the other." Matthews' account continued, "The result of which was that the Keeper had two ribs on the right side broken and otherwise badly beaten, and Geo. Sogge received a pistol wound in fleshy part of upper left arm." Sogge, who as the station's No. 1 would have been expected to have a close working relationship with the Keeper, swore out a warrant charging Matthews with intent to kill, and the keeper was arrested and placed under a $500 bond pending a court appearance. A telegram advised the district superintendent of these sordid events, which had resulted in the station's two senior men being rendered unavailable for duty by virtue of their disability.

Charles Rogers from the service's Chicago office soon arrived to investigate this matter; he interrogated the crew, Matthews' wife Mary, and others who had witnessed some or all aspects of the altercation or could shed light upon it. The proceedings in the criminal case, officially known as "The People of the State of Michigan vs. Thomas E. Matthews," continued for many months and doubtless gave rise to much anxiety for both the Keeper and his wife.[4]

At the close of 1891, a petition was filed in the circuit court by numerous Frankfort area residents, respectfully asking the judge "...in view of the fact that Capt. Thomas E. Matthews has during his life been a quiet, orderly and law abiding citizen, to consider this in passing sentence and to impose the lowest possible punishment that Your Honor can...." Many of the approximately one hundred signers of this petition were prominent community people; they included Capt. George Morency, who had come north from the Point Au Sable lifesaving station to take over for the fired keeper at the harbor station; Captain Harrison Miller, who had succeeded Matthews at Point Betsie, and Edwin Bedford, a key member of Miller's crew.

The wording of their appeal, implying that the case against Matthews was not without foundation, was an affirmation of his otherwise fine character and a plea for the court's mercy. But, given the U.S. Life-Saving Service's own high standards and its dedication to positive public relations, the community's support of Matthews would have no bearing upon the agency's disposition of the matter. Certainly, the fight and shooting were unacceptably bad form. Hence, on January 16, 1892, Matthews found himself sadly writing in the journal, "My Services as Keeper of This Station came to a Close at noon this day." Interestingly, when the Frankfort station closed late that fall, the men who had been involved had retained their jobs under his successor.

Court records indicate that legal proceedings against Matthews were delayed throughout much of 1892 at the request of his attorneys. A local physician, Dr. Isaac Voorheis, filed a statement with the Circuit Court in April saying that he had examined Mrs. Matthews and found her "...suffering from a relapse of the 'Lagrippe' and 'nervous prostration.'" He advised that "...she is totally unfit to leave her house, much less to go any distance" and if she was compelled to do so "...it would be liable to greatly injure her general health, and possibly cause her death." Matthews' counsel obtained continuances owing to their inability to bring Mrs. Matthews, a key witness, as well as Charles Rogers of the Life-Saving Service, to the court. The case finally came to trial in late 1892. Matthews stood mute when asked to enter a plea, so a pro forma plea of "not guilty" was entered for him.

After the twelve-man jury had heard the case, they immediately found Matthews guilty as charged. Requiring him to pay $275 in court costs, he was placed under the court's jurisdiction for a year, after which he was to reappear before the judge. However, there is no further trace in Benzie County's records of Matthews or his case, and he and his wife apparently left the area following the distressing circumstances that had so abruptly terminated his distinguished lifesaving days. An entry in the 1900 U.S. Census raises the possibility that they settled in distant Long Beach, California, where sixty-eight year old Thomas Matthews, residing with his wife Mary, identified himself simply as "sailor (ret.)"

CHAPTER SIX

NEW LEADERS, NEW TOOLS AND NEW CHALLENGES

Matthews' talented replacement, Captain Harrison "Tip" Miller, would initiate another illustrious era for Point Betsie's lifesaving station. Destined to become one of northwest Michigan's most notable men of his time, Miller was born in 1838 in Westchester County, New York. As a feature writer of a 1929 story summed up Harrison's eventful life at a still vigorous ninety-one years of age: "Probably no one living today has been in such intimate touch with so many dramatic and colorful bits of American history as has Capt. Miller."[1]

The characterization is far from baseless, for the story of his life finds him roaming the country from New York to Illinois, the Great Plains and the Southwest as a boy, and culminates as an adult on the Great Lakes, where his long career would be one of unsurpassed distinction. His wide-ranging experiences placed him in intimate contact with many people—with a tightly knit religious community and its zealous leaders; with nineteenth century Native Americans of both the West and the Great Lakes region; and, finally, with countless mariners and colleagues who shared his lifesaving experience.

When Harrison was a young boy, his parents, who had been drawn to the emerging Mormon faith and its leader Joseph Smith, followed the latter to the church's settlement in Nauvoo, Illinois. There he was baptized by being immersed in a hole chopped in an icy river; later in life, he was known to quip that because one shoulder had stayed dry, it probably accounted for the bit of the devil that was left in him.

To greatly abbreviate an important but only partly relevant event, not long before Harrison's baptism, Joseph Smith, who had been jailed in the nearby town of Carthage,

Captain "Tip" Miller in his later years.
Courtesy of Claudia Lewis

was killed there in a battle with a mob. Subsequently, several men claimed to be Smith's rightful heir at the helm of the infant religious denomination. As this jockeying for leadership went forward, Harrison's family—his father a "general" in the religious ranks—initially migrated west by wagon caravan. The family headed first for the Utah settlement that Brigham Young was creating, but somewhere in Nebraska, his father soured on Young's claim to the church's mantle and he re-routed the family to Texas. There they joined followers of Lyman White, another leadership claimant. But after reaching this destination by a long, arduous journey, his father then became convinced that a third man, Jesse James Strang, who had led a flock of followers eventually to Lake Michigan's Beaver Island, was Smith's proper successor. That judgment precipitated another long wagon trek. The family finally arrived at the island in 1850, where Strang was asserting his power not only among his followers but over the German, Swedish and Irish residents who previously had come to that "Emerald Isle" and were living among the descendants of its original Ottawa and Chippewa residents.

CERTAIN FACTS OF THE STRANG STORY HAD AN IMPACT ON HARRISON MILLER'S LIFE and should be noted, though they had no direct bearing upon his lightkeeping and lifesaving exploits. Strang, who was elected to the Michigan State Legislature but ruled his island with an iron hand, eventually proclaiming himself Beaver's king, ultimately offended many islanders—not only residents he termed "Gentiles" for not sharing his convictions and living according to his dictates, but some of his own people who increasingly resented his dictatorial ways.

Retribution was finally planned and carried out by two islanders, Thomas Bedford, who had married Harrison's sister Ruth, and Alexander Wentworth. These men, who had vociferously defended their wives against Strang's excessive edicts, were castigated by him as trouble makers. He ordered them to be publicly whipped—humiliated—by his henchmen. Having had enough of Strang's domineering leadership, and having endured this final straw, the men plotted to kill him. Gunning him down, the two assailants boarded the *U.S. Michigan*, which was docked at the island's wharf, and were delivered to Mackinac Island. They were subjected to a brief legal proceeding, then promptly released and treated as heroes by the local populace that had despised Strang—some of them having fled the island in the wake of his takeover and rule. The severely wounded ruler, taken by loyalists to a former place of residence in Wisconsin, soon died.

Harrison was not on Beaver Island at the time of the "liberation" which followed these events. He lived at Mackinac Island and nearby Harbor Springs for several years, visiting the island briefly, and in 1859 married Bridget Harkins, a native of County Donegal, Ireland, whose family had come to the island the previous year. They initially resided in Harbor Springs but in the early 1860s Miller was placed in charge of Beaver Head Light, a tall lighthouse at the island's south end, and he and Bridget took up residence there with their first two children. Through the years, eight more children would expand their family. Harrison tended that important light for eleven years and had the benefit of steady, if modestly compensated employment at a time when the nation's economy was under the stress of the Civil War.

It is noteworthy that toward the end of that assignment, he was sometimes helped by a young nephew, Edwin Bedford, son of his sister Ruth. The two men would enjoy a lifelong association that eventually included service together as lifesavers at Point Betsie and as Frankfort neighbors in retirement. Year after year, however, it was Bridget who was Harrison's essential partner in the island's lightkeeping duties. She would later recollect, "I worked for Uncle Sam 11 years and never got a cent for my service…I watched the light when the captain had to go for supplies, and never a cent did I get because I wasn't duly appointed. Every time an inspector called he'd say, 'You must have an assistant here.' So I was the assistant, but with never a commission and so I got no pay."[2]

Millers' portraits in the Print Shop Museum, Beaver Island.
Photo by author

Going from the lighthouse for the mail, groceries and other supplies, incidentally, was no easy stroll. It meant hiking several miles through much of the island to the harbor-side village of St. James. Harrison's trek took him near a quiet pond in a two-hundred-thirty-acre wetland now known as "Miller's Marsh Natural Area" which, under the present stewardship of Central Michigan University, commemorates Miller's faithful island service. As this recognition indicates, even though Harrison and Bridget

Beaver Head Light.
Photo by author

left the island to reside on the Michigan mainland for many decades, they kept in touch with Beaver Islanders and others living close by, and remain very notable figures in its rich history.

∽

LIKE POINT BETSIE'S "DOC" SLYFIELD, MILLER SOMETIMES SUPPLEMENTED HIS MEAGER EARNINGS OF $350 PER YEAR WITH OTHER TALENTS, SUCH AS BARREL-MAKING AND FISHING, TO SUPPORT HIS LARGE FAMILY. Most notably, during the winter when the boats that regularly stopped at the island were no longer running, he was its mail carrier. In this capacity he made two trips weekly to Mackinac Island, the mail in a backpack, each time walking some fifty miles across the often wind-swept Lake Michigan ice, over and back. Relatively speaking, it wasn't cheap then to feed a family of twelve, as prices had been pushed up by the Civil War. Bridget would recall that a barrel of flour cost twenty dollars, which was just about what a barrel of fish would be worth; a barrel of salt pork was ninety-five dollars, and calico material was a dollar a yard. The Millers had to be very frugal to survive, sometimes taking boarders into their already crowded quarters to meet expenses.

Eventually giving up his lighthouse duties in 1874, Miller supported his family by building boats, fishing, and other pursuits for a couple of years and then returned to government service in a different, but quite compatible line of work. On December 7, 1876, this skilled boatman was chosen to be the first keeper of the new Beaver Island Life Boat Station. He was to hold hold this post for an eleven-year, adventure-filled stint, during which he was also the elected sheriff of Manitou County, before being transferred to the Point Betsie lifesaving station when Captain Matthews was assigned to Frankfort.

Given Miller's extensive experience in both lightkeeping and lifesaving at the time he came to Point Betsie, it should be borne in mind that he was destined to hold his new post for an amazing twenty-one years. Considering the character of his career as hereafter depicted, it should be kept in mind that his employment ended only because—to his real frustration—age and length of service regulations mandated his retirement. He seems to have been unimpressed by intimations that some deterioration in his vision justified his departure from the service. Sadly, lifesavers—even one, as Miller's career poignantly reveals, of about forty-three years' federal service—had no pension benefits. Only years later, and then without retroactive application, was General Superintendent Kimball of the U.S. Life-Saving Service able to persuade Congress to grant pensions to lifesavers qualifying by length of service. Nor would his annual compensation have given him the opportunity to squirrel away appreciable savings. Having started his lifesaving work on the island at $200 annually, this father of ten children eventually got a raise to $400, then went to Point Betsie at $700 and after ten years there earned only two hundred dollars more. His highest salary was $1,000 annually, but he received pay at that rate for only a portion of his final year as a federal employee.

❧

CERTAIN EVENTS THAT OCCURRED ON BEAVER ISLAND DURING HIS LIFESAVING TENURE DOUBTLESS CONTRIBUTED TO THE SERVICE'S DECISION TO GIVE HIM THE MAINLAND APPOINTMENT AT POINT BETSIE. Two rescues under his command of that station—personnel from the schooners *J.I. Case* and *Chandler J. Wells*—particularly stand out. Each also illustrates the nature of operations at stations having volunteer crews, each member being paid just three dollars for undertaking life-threatening rescues.

It should be remembered that part of Miller's task at the Beaver Island station was to recruit a crew. Miller was not alone in having difficulty getting men to commit to the discipline and dictates of the Life-Saving Service. In what appears to be a draft of a letter to the service's Cleveland, Ohio, office that Miller penned in a journal, he pled, "I have done my best to get a crew but am sorry to say have not succeeded—the men around here as I have said before are most all fishermen and fish on other islands and some of them fish on the North Shore." They wouldn't sign up, Miller explained, as "they could not be here when called on...." He added, however, that "...if they were again to be here all the time they would volunteer readily—or if any of them are here they will go with me at any time in case of a wreck." For the most part, however, he seems to have met the station's crew requirements when emergencies arose, and he was confident of the abilities of those men who agreed to serve. As he later recounted:

> I had as good backing as any lifesaving captain.... The Beaver Islanders were all fishermen and expert sailors: you might say they were born on the water. They didn't know fear where the lake and storms were concerned, and thought no more of sailing up to a reef in a blinding storm with the surf beating over it and them than you'd think of walking up to a dinner table. I wouldn't be afraid to go out to any wreck with a bunch of such sailors as I had in those days.

The three-masted *Case*, out of Racine, Wisconsin, was hauling corn from Chicago to Buffalo, N.Y. when in the midst of a major snowstorm it stranded on Hog Island Reef, roughly nine miles northeast of Beaver Island, on the afternoon of November 13, 1883. The wreck wasn't discovered until the following morning, after the storm had passed and the volunteer crewmen of the Beaver Island station, virtually all of whom made their living by fishing, were out on the lake. When the stranding was reported to

Miller by a man who had sighted the vessel, the Captain asked him to sail out to the wreck and see if a tug was needed. The sailor did so, and as he arrived at the vessel he found that its own captain was departing the scene on a government steamer to procure a tug. The captain returned two days later with a tug and a crew, who began to dump the cargo, whose estimated value of $17,000 was quite significant in those days, in preparation for hauling the schooner off the shoal. However, a severe windstorm set in, forcing the tug to seek shelter at Beaver Island while crewmen of both the *Case* and tug, nineteen in all, were left aboard the beleaguered vessel.

Soon, however, those on board the *Case* were seen to hoist a distress signal, but under conditions that did not permit an immediate rescue attempt; fishermen who knew these waters recognized that even if they would reach the wreck, they likely would be unable to return to the island. On the 17th, Miller succeeded in persuading the tug captain to take him out, with the station's surfboat having been put on board the tug. But as the party approached the stricken ship, it became clear that sea conditions were too severe to mount a rescue effort; as the Keeper recounted, "No lifeboat could have lived in it."

Not to be dissuaded, Miller decided to attempt to reach the *Case* with a larger thirty-two-foot sailboat, filled with life preservers, a heaving stick, grapple and lines, and seven volunteer crewmen. Quickly blown out to the schooner, they found they couldn't come alongside without being swamped and broken apart in the surf. After one unsuccessful attempt to throw a line to someone on board the stricken vessel, they faced the harrowing prospect of backing away from the reef in the wild sea. They somehow managed to accomplish this and then get a line to one of the men on the *Case*, who had climbed out on its jib boom. This line was used to get a stronger cable to the schooner for the rescue, all nineteen men quickly sliding down it and into the sailboat.

Having to cut the hawser because it was still tied to the schooner, the crowded boat then had to beat its way back in wild waves. Miller said later that the men off the schooner apparently didn't know much about sailing, at least in a smaller craft, as "... every time the boat lay over they would clamor up the other side. I asked them once or twice to sit still, and after they nearly swamped us, I picked up a pike pole and promised to brain the next man that moved. After that they kept their seats, and we finally got back safely."

The 1884 annual report of the U.S. Life-Saving Service described the scene this way:

> *Indeed, so anxious were the poor fellows to leave the half-submerged craft that as soon as a life-line could be attached to the jib-boom and the other end caught by the life-savers, they swarmed down it one after the other, as the keeper graphically describes it, "like a lot of rats." It was a great risk,*

taking so many into the boat, but the idea of leaving some of them behind and trusting to the chances of a second trip was not for a moment to be entertained. As soon, therefore, as they were all snugly ensconced wherever shelter could be found, the reefed sails were hoisted, the lines were cut, and the boat's head hauled to the westward. It was a dead beat against an almost overpowering sea, but by half past 6 in the evening they reached the harbor in safety, every man of them heartily thankful to reach the shore again. The schooner was subsequently taken off the reef in a damaged condition, with the loss of nearly all her cargo.

An anecdote Miller shared from the *Case* rescue is that he had loaded the sailboat with barrels of salt for ballast when preparing to go to the wreck. Each time a sailor slid into the boat, a barrel was tossed overboard. Having sent the bill for the purchased ballast to headquarters, he got back an inquiry as to why lifesaving required so much salt! Much correspondence was required to settle the account reflecting his resourcefulness.

At least equally compelling is the account of the midnight stranding of the three-master *Chandler J. Wells* about a year later on a reef off Whiskey Island, seven miles west of the Beaver Island station. Like many old schooners, she was operating under tow at the time, hauling lumber from Manistique, Michigan, to Tonawanda, New York, crewed by eight men. Having tossed much of the steam-powered barge's own cargo overboard, the men got the barge got off the reef, but had to cast the schooner off and left her to fend for itself. Weather prevented any rescue attempts by Miller and his volunteer crew for a couple of days, but eventually they were towed out in their surfboat with the intent of transferring crew onto the schooner and attempting to free it. After they were aboard, however, a frightful turn in the weather caused all but two of the men to return to shore on the tug.

A snowstorm ensued and it became impossible to get back to the schooner, but nearly five days after the stranding a distress signal was observed from it. Miller and his volunteers were again towed out by the tug to a point about a mile to the windward of the schooner, where they were released to drop back down to it. The 1885 annual report concludes:

The two men, who were almost perished, were soon taken off. The schooner was so covered with ice that its weight, in conjunction with the seas breaking on board, had crushed the cabin in and compelled the two men to remain on deck all the previous night. Besides this, they had no means of making a fire to warm themselves or to cook anything. They certainly could not have withstood the hardship much longer. As soon as the boat cleared the reef to the leeward, it was taken in tow again by the tug safely back to the harbor. The men in the boat suffered intensely with the cold, and, in their ice-covered garments, presented a sorry sight upon getting ashore. They also narrowly escaped a capsize on the way back by the breaking of the towing strap on the stem, which caused the boat to take a broad sheer, and it was only by quickly cutting the tow-line that she was saved from going over. The vessel became a total wreck, and only a small portion of her cargo was saved.

෴

THESE TWO RESCUE EFFORTS ARE CLEAR EVIDENCE THAT POINT BETSIE'S NEW LIFESAVING KEEPER WAS A HIGHLY RESPECTED, COURAGEOUS BOATMAN, VIRTUALLY AN IDEAL "FIND" FOR THE IMPORTANT POST. Yet, he was also something else—an experienced lighthouse man from his lengthy tenure at Beaver Island Light. These operations being the responsibility of two separate agencies, this likely had no influence upon his selection, but it increased his understanding of all facets of marine protection. His appointment at Point Betsie thus began a unique, if brief, period when both the lighthouse and the adjacent lifesaving station were under the charge of experienced lightkeepers. Miller and Edwin Slyfield served side-by-side for about a year and a half until the latter was transferred in mid-1888 to the Ludington harbor light; Edwin's departure closed the Slyfield family's twenty-seven-year reign as Point Betsie Light's respected and faithful keepers.

෴

THE YEAR 1888 SAW THE FIRST MAJOR WORK AT THE LIGHTHOUSE IN MANY YEARS. Special appropriations' estimates for rebuilding the structure amounted to $35,000, as its future continued to be debated. In October of that year, an additional weight was sent to "...improve the working of the revolving machinery of the illuminating apparatus, and a spare pane of plate-glass was also sent." Again, the argument was made that the tower and dwelling "...are poorly-built brick structures, which were erected by contract in 1858. They are now in poor condition," the Board added, and situated "...dangerously near the bank of the lake. They do not satisfy the requirements of this station, which is one of the most important on Lake Michigan." There was a renewed call for the tower's replacement by a taller one that would create a focal plane for the light not less than one hundred feet above the lake, and for the installation of a third-order lens. The recommendations went unheeded.

෴

TRAGEDY STRUCK MILLER'S FAMILY DURING THEIR FIRST YEAR AT THE POINT when their dear son William, known as Willie, was drowned there. Harrison later wrote to a friend, "...(T)he world is still going round and round and every year brings a change, to some pleasure and others sorrow and grief. The first fall I was here I had my cup of it in the death of my son William and I never will get over it. I feel sometimes like following the advice of Job's wife, curse God and die. If it were not for the little girls depending on me for support, God only knows what would become of me, a sinner." He added, "Mrs. Miller is better off than I. She has her religion to console her."

Pond boat built by Miller's crewmen for Willie.
Gift to the Friends of Point Betsie Lighthouse, Inc. by Ted Hansen.
Photo by author

Only a few years later, grief again came to the Millers when another son, Charlie, succumbed after a long illness. Writing to a friend in Boston only four days prior to his death, the discouraged Captain wrote, "I don't think he will ever get well, have done everything a father could do but nothing seems to do him any good." Two months later, Harrison would lament to that friend, "He would have been 30 years of age…. The loss of our boy to whom we were all much attached nothing but time can heal."

❧

As already noted, certainly Captain Miller's light-tending years would have given him firsthand insight into the tasks a solo lighthouse keeper constantly faced, and perhaps made him especially sensitive to those demands. His cooperative spirit is reflected in several lifesaving journal entries in which Miller simply noted that he had asked his crew to notify Slyfield when the light had stopped working during the previous night so the latter could address the problem; if daylight was imminent and the need for the beam was not pressing, Miller had taken no other action. His sensitivity also would be revealed in a journal entry of September 15, 1888: "Omitted practice with the beach apparatus this week on account of the Light House Keeper's son being very sick. Our drill pole is just back of the House and the report of the gun makes the sick boy nervous."

The Millers were well regarded, not only by the crew he led, but within the community. Two artifacts of their era at Point Betsie reflect his standing among his men: surfmen not only built a handsome toy sailboat for Willie, but they also constructed a beautiful chest of drawers for Bridget to use in their residence. She cooked for the crew and treated them well. The same was true of the public, as suggested in this story:[3] A party of young Benzonians had crossed Crystal Lake to Point Betsie on a summer day, sailing the length of the lake and then hiking through the woods to the lifesaving station "...where Captain Miller and his good wife made it very pleasant for them. There was an abundance of 'good things' provided." The party had rowed back in the evening—a distance of nine miles.

Point Betsie's lifesaving crew and original station.
Courtesy of Benzie Area Historical Museum

❧

EVEN AS THE LIGHT STATION'S FUTURE CONTINUED TO BE DISCUSSED AT THE SENIOR ADMINISTRATIVE LEVEL, a new keeper, Peter Dues, arrived in early August of 1888 to succeed Edwin Slyfield. Born in Copenhagen in 1832, Dues was one of many of his country's native sons who went to sea at an early age, sailing all over the world. He ultimately brought that skill to America, owning a sailing ship on Lake Huron with his eldest son serving as crew. A true sailor at heart, Captain Dues reportedly had little use for the steam-powered vessels that gradually displaced the schooners and other tall ships, calling them "smoke boat workhouses." And when his ship could no longer compete with the newer technology, he left the lake trade and took up lightkeeping.

Dues' career record shows that he was a worthy successor at Point Betsie to the legendary Slyfields. He had entered the lighthouse service in 1878, serving as first assistant keeper at Harbor Beach Light on Lake Huron. About four years later, he was transferred to the Ludington pier head light as acting keeper, and soon thereafter received the appointment as keeper. After he had served for about six years in Ludington, the lighthouse leadership facilitated a job switch, Edwin Slyfield going to Ludington and Peter Dues coming north to Point Betsie. Dues would command the point's light for over five years, until 1893; during that important time in the station's history, many changes were made in its structures and its services were expanded.

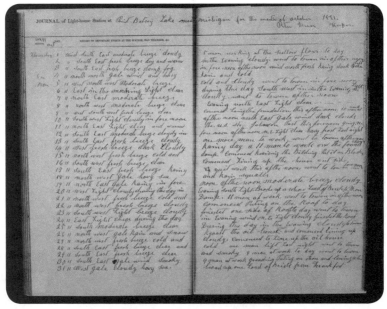

Dues' Point Betsie log for October, 1891, in bold and beautiful penmanship.
Log is property of National Archives.
Photo by author

✍

THE OFT-DISCUSSED TOTAL REBUILD AT POINT BETSIE LIGHT STATION WAS NOT TO BE. Perhaps the idea had been talked to death, or simply that priorities within the agency may have shifted over time. But whatever the reason, the Board had changed its mind as to the most appropriate investment at this site. The panel reported in 1889 that hardware for repairing the shutters and materials for re-shingling the dwelling roof and laying floor in the kitchen had been purchased, the labor being done by the Keeper. And recalling its own previous calls for abandoning the structure and erecting a new station with a substantially more elevated light, the Board reasoned:

> *After careful consideration, however, the Board is of the opinion that if the repairs indicated are made, and particularly if a new lens and revolving apparatus be provided, the station will fully answer the requirements. It is true that the elevation of the focal plane, 53 feet, is moderate, but the range, 13 and ¾ miles, is but 4 miles less than that of South Manitou, which is 104 feet high, and with which the range of Point Betsey overlaps nearly 8 miles. In any case, it could not be made to intersect with Grand Pointe au Sable [later known as Big Sable Light] which is 45 miles up the coast to the southward. If a new light is built the Board is persuaded it should be erected...18 or 20 miles to the southward, to cover an unlighted stretch of coast and to mark the projection of the only rocky piece of shore south of Point Betsey. What this station really needs is a third-order lens flashing alternatively red and white at intervals of ten seconds and a steam fog-signal.*

No such additional coastal light was ever built, nor would Point Betsie Lighthouse be replaced, a third-order lens be installed in its tower, or the light changed to include a red beam. The light would remain for a time as it had been—white, varied every ninety seconds by a white flash over the lake.

✍

HOWEVER, POINT BETSIE LIGHTHOUSE WOULD RECEIVE MAJOR ATTENTION THROUGHOUT THE PERIOD OF PETER DUES' SERVICE AS KEEPER; substantial enhancements were made that yet shape the station's character. The process began when Dues was keeper. The Board reported in 1890, "...this station was entirely renovated and put in good order." Thus, the possibility that a new facility would be built had been eliminated, once and for all; instead, a significant investment was made in the existing building, designed to fortify it so as to ensure its survival from pounding seas and shifting sands. The Board's description reveals the job's extent:

> *An examination was made of the tower and its foundations in April, 1890. The walls were found to be sound, though damp from solidity and the absence*

of air-spaces, but the foundation was insecure owing to insufficient depth below the surface of the sand. This was strengthened by an underpinning of concrete 4 feet deep, in the form of a ring measuring 16 feet external diameter at the base, 12 feet external diameter at the top, and 4 feet internal diameter. This was placed in radial sections between the blocking which was inserted to support the tower temporarily. The inside of the tower was afterwards filled in from the bottom of the new footing to the floor level with concrete containing a large quantity of large stone and was finished with a brick floor. The concrete apron surrounding the base of the tower, laid some seventeen years ago, was broken out to make the foundation and was replaced with new work. The shore immediately in front of the tower was protected by a revetment flanked by short jetties at each end. The revetment is 210 feet long, with a slight curve approximating to the curve of the shore, and consists of two rows of piles 14 feet apart, driven from 10 to 12 feet into the sand, the outer row at a distance of 18 inches from centres with the tops cut at a uniform level with the water. The inner row at distances of 6 feet from centres has the tops cut 1 foot above the water. Above this there is a crib construction of timber a foot square, four courses in height, with cross pieces every 12 feet. The interior is filled with broken stone ballast, and the top is planked with 3 by 12 inch timber with 2 inch spaces. The jetties are of similar construction, 14 by 50 feet at a distance of 75 feet from each end of the revetment. The timber used here was the surplus material purchased for repairs at Spectacle Reef. An attempt was made to begin the work of driving the piles in the fall, but it was abandoned by the contractor owing to rough weather and breakage of a portion of his plant. In the spring the work was re-advertised by poster and circular letter. The contractor commenced the pile driving on April 17 and finished it during May. At the close of the year the work was completed with the exception of about 50 to 60 cords of stone filling and the laying of a small portion of the deck planking. The work thus summarized obviates the construction of a new station which heretofore was deemed necessary.

⊸

"POINT BETSEY LIGHT MARKS AN IMPORTANT HEADLAND, AND THE TRAFFIC WITHIN RANGE OF THE LIGHT-STATION IS LARGE," the Board's 1890 report noted, adding, "Numerous casualties have occurred to vessels in the vicinity, and a life-saving station is established there." These remarks presumably were intended not only to justify a requested modification in the light's "characteristic," from flashing every ninety seconds to flashing every ten seconds, but also—and perhaps more significantly—to again press for funds to add a fog signal at the light station. This time, the Board's case proved persuasive; the $5000 for the fog signal was appropriated in March, 1891, and a contract was soon signed for the construction of a duplicate set of boilers and machinery. (Dual sets of machinery were always installed, as loss of a fog signal could be fatal for a vessel.)

Also, a new lens was ordered for Point Betsie at this time—not the third-order model that had been suggested earlier, but an improved fourth-order with six bull's eyes, estimated to extend the light's visibility by nearly two miles. Mr. Crump, as he is generally known to history, who was the district's official "lampist," directed the installation of the lens and modification of the light's characteristic the following spring. His job required him to travel throughout the district, not only overseeing the installation and adjustment of lighting equipment, but also teaching keepers and their crews—who in those days often began lighthouse management with little relevant experience or training—how to operate and care for it properly.

The fog signal would consist of two, ten-inch steam whistles similar to those on a locomotive. The boilers and associated equipment were soon finished, delivered to the site and installed in a new, twenty-two by forty-foot separate frame structure, built with corrugated iron siding and roof on the exterior, and a smooth iron lining inside to survive the intense heat that would be generated. A brick well was also constructed to supply the boilers. On December 12, 1891, the Board issued a "Notice to Mariners" to inform them of the new fog signal, which was in operation during storms that arose at year's end. In the first six months of the whistles' availability, they were operated about one hundred and thirty-nine hours and consumed about thirty-three cords of wood— not "face cords" but true cords comprising a stack eight feet long, four feet high and four feet deep.

Getting up steam to power the whistle, and keeping it going during long periods of inclement weather, greatly added to the station's work, necessitating the appointment of an assistant keeper to help the keeper operate a twenty-four-hour duty station. There being no other housing for lighthouse crew at the time, the first such assistant (with an "acting" appointment for two months starting in late February, 1892), was Charles W. Butler, who lived with the keeper's family.[4] His successor, George Chamberlin who served about a year and a half, likely did the same.

The usefulness of the fog signal became quickly apparent. Although the prevalence of fog would vary greatly through the years, according to the 1894 Annual Report the steam whistles had been used during the previous year for a total of four hundred eighteen and one-half hours, consuming eleven and one-half tons of coal and nineteen and one-half cords of wood. (The boilers were generally fueled with wood initially, but coal was also used extensively until a subsequent modernization led to the use of diesel fuel.)

In addition to the new lens and characteristic that were installed in the spring of 1892, there was another notable addition at that time—the round, iron-sided "oil house" built on a concrete foundation between the lighthouse and the fog signal building, equipped with a series of shelves capable of holding three hundred and sixty gallons of kerosene for the light. The hut's presence constituting evidence that the light had been switched to this new, more volatile fuel by this date, a separate structure was desirable to minimize the chances of an accidental fire or explosion that could demolish the tower, lens and other valuable equipment. Years later, after the light was electrified in 1921, the oil structure—no longer being needed for its intended purpose—was moved to the far side of the fog signal building, where it was used to store paint and other flammables. Other improvements in 1892 included the laying of a concrete floor in the residence's cellar, and building more than five hundred feet of plank walkways between the station's principal structures.

✑

DUES' SERVICE AT POINT BETSIE ENDED WITH HIS TRANSFER, IN 1893, ACROSS LAKE MICHIGAN TO WISCONSIN'S GREEN ISLAND LIGHT. Four years later, he was moved down the shore to Little Fort Light in Waukegan, Illinois, and when that facility was discontinued on December 31, 1898, he took over that city's new harbor light. Finally wearying of such repetitive transfers, Dues retired from the Lighthouse Service after his service there, during which his son, Peter, Jr., served as his first assistant during the final three years of his twenty-four-year lightkeeping career. Having apparently become Michiganders at heart, Peter and his Canadian-born wife, Mary, retired in the Wolverine state.

The couple lived on two Michigan farms before finally returning to Ludington, where he had also served as keeper. Mrs. Dues died six years before Peter's own death in March, 1924, at age 92; three Michigan-resident sons and their families survived him. Wrote *The Ludington Daily News* upon his passing, "Thus is written 'finis' to a long and adventurous life, a life of which much might be written of interest and inspiration, for of Peter Dues it is said, 'He was straight.' He never intentionally wronged any man and as long as strength was given him he did his duty as he saw it." It would be hard to write a more apt tribute to a veteran lighthouse man.

Point Betsie *circa* 1893, looking toward Lake Michigan from the east, with the new fog signal building on the right. Its steam whistles, one of which is largely hidden by the left stack, top two thin protrusions from the roof. A privy can be seen in the photo's center, as well as the then-new round oil hut on its original site between the two buildings. The picture conveys a sense of the openness, and isolation, of Point Betsie Light Station shortly before the turn of the 20th century.

Courtesy of National Archives
College Park, MD.

CHAPTER SEVEN

ACCOMPLISHING MISSIONS THROUGH PREPARATION AND COURAGE

By the latter 1880s and early '90s, observers could readily spot a notable change in the powering of new commercial vessels on the Great Lakes. No longer the vagaries of Nature's wind, but steam was becoming the power source of choice, facilitating the construction of vessels with larger cargo capacities, greater certainties of scheduling and other benefits. The Lake Carriers' Association, which yet represents the owners and operators of the laker fleet, reported in 1893—the organization's second year of existence—that its membership, encompassing nearly all the vessels of significant size sailing the inland seas, included 612 vessels, 384 of which were steamers and the others either schooners or barges. The transition in the fleet occurred remarkably quickly, as the group noted that "...more than one-half the tonnage on the Great Lakes at the present time is less than seven years old, and as all vessel owners know, the character of vessels built during the past seven years is very different from that which prevailed at an earlier day."[1]

Accompanying this trend, with implications for insurers and the agencies responsible for aids to navigation, was a gradual lengthening of the shipping season. The new vessels were sailing deep into December rather than laying up by the traditional date of December 1; some owners would continue to haul cargo until ice had actually blocked their courses or ports. With the lengthening shipping season, owners were pressing lighthouse authorities to delay the seasonal removal of buoys on important channels throughout the region.

∽

RENOVATION PROJECTS AND ENHANCEMENTS AT POINT BETSIE LIGHTHOUSE continued in the mid-1890s, the major investment—prompted by the need for additional personnel—featuring the expansion of its residential quarters. The required authorization for an assistant keeper had finally been approved in 1892, after the installation of the steam fog signals had made the position essential. The first appointee, Charles Butler, served in a temporary role under Keeper Peter Dues for only a couple of months. He was succeeded by George W. Chamberlin, who held the assistant's post on a permanent basis until Dues' transfer brought Soren Christenson to Point Betsie as keeper.

∽

NORWEGIAN-BORN IN MID-1852, SOREN CHRISTENSON CAME TO AMERICA WITH HIS PARENTS IN 1872, the family settling in Chicago. It was there that Soren eventually entered the lightkeeping profession, serving as the harbor light's 2nd assistant keeper. He was apparently well regarded, for after just a few years' experience he was named keeper at Point Betsie. His wife, a Norwegian girl named Hannah, was more than twenty years younger; they had a baby girl, Grace, born just before their transfer from Point Betsie, across Lake Michigan to Wisconsin's Chambers Island Light, in the fall of 1895. Christenson's dedicated service at that Door County light ran for five years. Then, stricken with cancer, he was forced to give up his post in mid-August of 1900; apparently he took his wife and two children, five-year-old Grace and one-year-old Horace, to Chicago where he died just weeks after his resignation.

While at Point Betsie, Christianson was assisted briefly by Thomas Hart, then by Medad Spencer, who served for a decade under the direction of both Christianson and his successor as keeper, Philip Sheridan. Spencer's tenure as assistant keeper was one of the longest in Point Betsie's history. His lighthouse career culminated with a promotion as keeper of the important light at the south end of Beaver Island, the same light that Harrison Miller had tended from 1863 to 1874 and Charles Butler, Point Betsie's initial assistant, had run from 1897 to 1904. Spencer would serve at Beaver's light for five years, until mid-summer of 1909, when he resigned at about age 72.

Picking up his story, the New York-born Spencer had come to Michigan's Ottawa County, about one hundred and fifty miles south of the point, from Lancaster, Pennsylvania, as a homesteader shortly after the Civil War. His grandson recalled that Medad's only crop was wood, to be sold as fuel for lake steamers. Presumably, that represented an adequate financial opportunity for a time, but as steamships shifted from wood to coal as their primary fuel, the market for wood gradually dried up and Spencer was compelled to seek other work.

Spencer learned that there was an assistant's opening at Point Betsie Lighthouse, and at about age fifty seven he found himself embarking upon a new career, moving north in the spring of 1894 with his fifty-year-old wife, Julia Williams Spencer (a descendant of Rhode Island's founder, Roger Williams) and the youngest of their children, teen-aged Louis Martin Spencer.

Julia and Medad Spencer.
Courtesy of Christina Spencer-Fidler & the Spencer Family

Young Louis apparently enjoyed his years at the Point; Dr. John Spencer, his son, would later recall his father's telling of hiking several miles daily through the back country, carrying a five-shot Winchester rifle and a sack which on a good day would be filled with partridge by the time he arrived home from the Frankfort school. Another story Louis related to his son centered on windrows of shelled corn and casks of butter that littered Point Betsie's beach after a ship had wrecked just offshore. "Ducks and other waterfowl were soon on the scene. Duck hunting was very good for a time, as long as the corn lasted. Many a duck dinner with generously buttered bread to accompany was enjoyed by Frankfort and Point Betsie area residents that winter."[2]

Point Betsie's steam fog signals continued to prove their worth, and probably exhausted the crew in the process. During Soren Christianson's final year at Point Betsie, he and Medad Spencer were required by unusually poor weather to operate them for an extraordinary 1,312 hours—equivalent to nearly fifty-five, twenty-four-hour days, or about fifteen percent of an entire year—during which the boilers consumed approximately sixty-three cords of wood. One can easily imagine not only their aching backs, but also the effect such recurring blasts would have had on the nerves of persons residing within ear-shot of the whistle. That said, those incessant sounds were doubtless much welcomed by ship captains groping their way along the shore.

❧

AIMED AT BETTER ACCOMMODATING POINT BETSIE LIGHT'S CREW AND THEIR FAMILIES, THE 1894-95 ADDITION TO THE DWELLING consisted of six rooms and an attached back building. The original twenty-eight-foot square dwelling evolved into today's basic footprint, twenty-eight by forty-eight-feet, with the interior configured into two entirely separate residences under a single but reshaped, gambrel roof. Two new dormers on the north and south sides allowed more daylight into the upstairs. The wood kitchen, which had run across the back of the original building, was swung around to the north side. An outside door to the tower was added at ground level, along with new tower stairs and altered landings to enable the assistant keeper to enter and climb to the lantern without going through the keeper's own quarters. During the mid-1890s' overhaul, a sewer was built along with new walks around the station, an old structure serving as a barn was reconstructed, and the existing fog signal machinery was overhauled, tested and approved. Two years later, storm shelters were provided at the tower, keeper's residence and kitchen entrances.

Late in 1897, authorization came through the bureaucracy for a second assistant's position, which the expanded residence—perhaps with some re-partitioning—accommodated. With three men serving at the busy lighthouse, a more desirable schedule could be set up, using balanced shifts that allowed the men adequate time for rest and for completing the numerous tasks about the station.

This era's last major structural change at the lighthouse came in 1900, when the tower and dwelling, built of yellow "Milwaukee" brick that tended to blend into the surrounding sand dunes when viewed from the lake, were painted white with red roofing, thereby increasing the structure's visibility in daylight. The original color posed a common problem at lighthouses on the Great Lakes, and one could wonder why it took so long for the administrators to get around to this particular change at Point Betsie; as early as 1876, the *Light List* had described the tower and residence on South Manitou Island as whitewashed brick.

Each annual edition of the *Light List* informed mariners how to spot Point Betsie from the lake in daytime, at night and in fog. Subsequent to the above modifications of the structure, the 1901 issue specified the light as a white beam, situated fifty-three feet above Lake Michigan's level, flashing every ten seconds and visible for fourteen and three-quarters miles under good conditions. The tower and connected dwelling were described as painted white with red roofs, and the corrugated fog-signal house, situated about one hundred seventy-five feet northeast of the tower, was described as brown. The lifesaving station could be seen from the lake just to the south of the lighthouse. In fog, the light station would be identifiable by the distinct pattern of its ten-inch steam whistle: a five-second blast; ten seconds of silence; another five-second blast, then forty peaceful seconds—that sequence unceasing until the fog lifted.

Point Betsie Lighthouse *circa* 1900, after its expansion and painting.
Courtesy of Michigan Maritime Museum

WHILE THE LIGHTHOUSE WAS GOING THROUGH ITS EXPANSION IN SERVICES, FACILITIES AND STAFF, THE ADJACENT LIFESAVING STATION REMAINED BUSY, UNDER THE SKILLFUL LEADERSHIP OF CAPTAIN "TIP" MILLER. He and his wife Bridget, whose services were always a vital part of station life, provided meals for surfmen living at the station. The Millers kept careful account of the meals they ate and the reimbursements they were to make. As always, days were taken up with the service's mandatory drills, the beach patrols, the reporting of the weather and the vessels passing, and assisting lake travelers. Miller recorded one such event of not unusual nature in his journal on October 24, 1888:

> *At 2-5 a.m. [Miller generally wrote hours and minutes, e.g., 2:05, in this matter], the watch called my attention to a Steamer blowing four whistles. She was abreast of the station about one mile off. Called the crew up. Launched the surfboat and went out to her. It proved to be the Steamer Lawrence from Cheboygan, Michigan, bound for Chicago. They had two passengers to land at the Port of Frankfort. And as she was drawing too much water to go in there the Captain requested me to land the passengers ashore [which] I did, arriving at the station at 2-45 a.m. That is the reason the card on the detector is not punched at 2-30 a.m. It gave us an early boat practice for today. Every man was on his taps in a very short time after I wrung the alarm bell.*

As already indicated, one of the challenges any keeper faced, essential as it was to a station's success, was to achieve and retain the respect of his crew. Being a leader was a balancing act; without finding the key balance point, leadership would be extremely difficult to provide and the crew's effectiveness would be compromised. Miller expressed this truth in a letter to a friend in which he said that he had a "...forecastle lawyer in my crew" who had "preferred charges against me." While the charges were ultimately dismissed, Miller said he had learned something in this episode: "It was all because I was to good to them and to easy." He added, "I tell you after this I will draw the lines close. It won't do to be to good to the men, if you do some of them will try and run on you."[3]

Miller informed his district supervisor of a "breach of discipline" on the part of Surfman Mead, whom he had permitted to go to Frankfort in late November, along with another crewman, to rent housing in town for the winter.[4] Having departed the point at morning light, they were expected back in the afternoon, but returned not only two hours after sundown, but "a little under the influence of liquor." When he had reprimanded Mead, Miller reported, "...he got mad, pulled off his coat and talked very loud, thinking perhaps to scare me." Miller made it clear to the surfman that this behavior was a disciplinary breach, but asked the district to overlook it, this being the first offense on the part of a "good man in the crew;" the Keeper said Mead had assured him that such behavior would not be repeated.

On another occasion, when one of his men, Surfman Anderson, had been discharged for failure to mark the dial during his watch, Miller voiced his own regret over this offense; in other respects, Miller wrote the district superintendent, "...he is a <u>Good</u> strong active surfman, and a fair boatsman."[5] Some months later, still troubled by the Anderson situation, he decided to go to the top, apparently writing directly to the General Superintendent, Sumner Kimball, in Washington to endorse the man's possible reinstatement. "Surfman Anderson was with me three seasons and I can safely say he was one of my best men," Miller wrote, continuing that "he is of good moral character, a good boatman and was always ready and willing to do what was asked of him. If a vacancy should occur in my crew I would not hesitate to engage Anderson with your permission to do so."[6]

Maintaining a sense of discipline within the crew presented keepers with an unending challenge, a reality that Miller confronted at Point Betsie in the spring of 1893, when he needed replacements for three men who had been terminated in the prior year. One had been fired by order of the General Superintendent for failing to punch the time detector, one for failing to handle the beach apparatus and lines at the expected level of proficiency, and the third for filthiness—it having been determined that he had urinated on the station's kitchen floor, presumably in a fit of anger and resentment. This resulted in several of Miller's key appointments to his crew—Edwin Bedford, who had six years' experience in lifesaving, and two other men whom he warmly and favorably described as "...old fishermen's sons brought up on a boat and don't know anything else."

In light of their rigorous duties, lifesavers had to be certified by a physician as physically fit for their job. In Miller's time, this was done by a doctor in Manistee, thirty-some miles south of the point, to whom Miller was not reluctant to assert himself. On one occasion, Miller wrote the doctor that he was sending seven potential crewmen for examination. "The object of this examination is to get sound healthy men for the Service," he explained to the physician, saying, "I think the men will all pass—at least they look as though they would—except Christian Jacobson. He was with me last season—but was ailing most of the season. Every little cold he got he would shit blood quite freely—I had to excuse him from boat drill once or twice. I understand he has been same way all winter—when you come to examine him, if you find him not a No. 1, state it on the certificate and I will send another for examination."[7]

A couple of years later, Miller wrote the same doctor, apologizing for having written him numerous times that spring but nonetheless making his views unmistakably clear:

I was never so much surprised in my life as I was last night when Kolph Kern returned from Manistee with his certificate filled out as a sound man. I know to my own certain knowledge he has been taking medicine more or less all winter and men don't usually do that unless they are ailing. But the most surprising is that he should present himself for examination on the 22nd and fail to pass on account of some heart trouble, and then present himself again on the 28th and get a good sound certificate. I don't want you to think, Dr. that I am finding fault with your examination for I am not. What I would like to know is this—is not this the same heart trouble as liable to come back in a short time as it went away.[8]

❧

THE YEAR 1888 BEING A PRESIDENTIAL ELECTION YEAR (Benjamin Harrison defeated Grover Cleveland), Miller omitted boat practice on November 6, reporting that the surfmen had requested to "...go to the election at Frankfort to vote. They say it has always been customary with the Keepers to let them go when the weather would permit. As this was a very nice day I let four of them go in the forenoon and three in the afternoon."

❧

BY MID-1889, THE POINT BETSIE LIFESAVING STATION HAD BOTH A "MONOMOY" SURFBOAT AND A "DOBBINS" LIFEBOAT, constituting the station's primary means of rescue. The name of the former model, a self-bailing but not self-righting hull that could be sailed as well as rowed, came from its having been designed in the Monomoy area of Cape Cod; the latter was known by the name of its designer, Captain David Dobbins, a Great Lakes ship captain, who in 1876 was appointed superintendent of the Ninth Lifesaving District (Lakes Ontario and Huron, and the Ohio River). Both models were of small draft. The relatively light (approximately seven hundred pounds) surfboat, some twenty-three feet in length, was intended to be launched straight into the waves by the men themselves, whereas the twenty-six-foot lifeboat was designed for use where it could be launched off a "car" that would ferry it on rails into the water.

Practicing with the Monomoy surfboat.
Courtesy of Claudia Lewis

Bringing in Life Boat.

Returning a heavier boat to its launch car.
Courtesy of Michigan Maritime Museum

Even though the Dobbins' craft weighed between 1,500 and 2,000 pounds, it was considerably lighter than the well-known "English" lifeboat that the Life-Saving Service also employed for many years. Promoters of the Dobbins boat stressed that it was self-righting, self-bailing and unsinkable. However, such was not the experience at the Point Betsie station, whose own Dobbins failed to live up to the claims. As Miller wrote on July 23rd, "Practice with the Dobbins….Capsized her but as before she would not right herself. There was some sea not very heavy but enough to right her if she was what she has been recommended to be. The boys all stood on one gunwal with the water up to their necks and held the boat on her beam end and still she would not come up." A month later a practice with the Dobbins yielded the same result; it "...would not right with the crew in her," Miller complained, and he later said he had sent Surfman No. 2 to Frankfort to get some "rudder iron" made for the craft.

The Dobbins problem didn't go away; in 1890 the assistant inspector replied rather bureaucratically to Miller's continuing concerns, "We must look into that and find the cause." That wasn't the only boat problem the station was then facing, however. Miller received a letter early that fall, approving his request to obtain materials to build a boat house, eighteen feet wide and thirty feet long, to protect their boats before winter. The district superintendent told Miller he was to "...purchase in open market at the lowest cost obtainable not to exceed $79.00, including freight and all other cost, and put up such a building as in your opinion will answer the best purpose." None of that sum was to be used for labor; "...it is supposed that the crew will do all the work." The boss advised that he would be visiting the station in a month, and hoped the structure would be ready for inspection at that time.

The boat building was completed, but four years later, surviving correspondence indicates, the problem with the Dobbins still persisted. Finally, an assistant inspector sought to be more responsive to Captain Miller, who apparently had suggested that additional weight might be added to the keel. He directed Miller to purchase, at the lowest cost, strips of iron weighing not more than one hundred pounds; as usual, the installation work was to be done by the crew.[9] (The boat on which they were working may have been the station's second Dobbins, for in that same month of September, 1904, Miller reported in his log that the men "...broke up the <u>old</u> Dobbins boat and burnt her to save the old iron.") Iron was a valuable commodity, and nothing of value was to be discarded, but rather re-used whenever possible.

An extraordinarily capable boatman, Miller once went so far as to remind General Superintendent Kimball of this ability. Kimball apparently knew of Miller's reputation, and had asked him about a particular boat's suitability. Miller replied that its design was flawed, its deck being too low. He also said it takes on water somewhere and is susceptible to rot because the water, once in, can't get out. "You asked for my opinion, I will give it to you honestly," Miller stressed:

> *Perhaps I am wrong, but time will tell. Some one will be caught and the qualities of the boat will then be shown. This is the 18th season I have been in the L.S.S. [and] before that I was in the Lt. H. Service 11 years, during that time I built boats and fished and before I went into that Service I fished from the time I was large enough to get in and out of a boat....If I ever get money enough I will build a life boat—I don't write to make a brag of myself, but to show you that if there is any one thing I should know it should be about a boat.*

At another time, Miller brought up his boating skills as a way of supporting a transfer to a less isolated station so that his daughters would be nearer a school. He wrote to Lieutenant Henry Rogers in Chicago that his eldest daughter was about to graduate, but the other girls were not old enough to drive a pony to town. "I am desirous in giving them an education as that is all I shall ever be able to give them," Miller said, adding, "Don't think, friend Rogers, that I want to get away from the Point on my own account for such is not the case." Then came the boating angle, for Miller was aware that the superintendent intended to erect an exhibition station at the up-coming Colombian Exposition in Chicago and apparently decided to do some trolling for the assignment. Miller noted that he presumed "...the man [heading that station] would have to be a collage bred" for that post, yet in this letter to the district despaired as to whether there would be any point in making application for that assignment "...if I was the best man in the district as far as handling the boats.... I have been in small boats all my life and if there is any one thing I know it is how to manage a small boat," Miller again insisted.

Miller's concern for his children's education, incidentally, never slackened. In late November, 1893, he wrote for permission to reside during the winter at his cabin on the north side of Frankfort so his younger children could attend school. He would care for the isolated station by regularly visiting it as he had in the past. "If you can consistently grant me this privilege, you will confer an everlasting favor on your humble servant," he appealed.

"SCRUBBED HOUSE AND CLEANED THE COTS OF BEDBUGS." That was one of the more telling journal entries in the summer of 1889; Point Betsie Life-Saving Station, though a beautiful site, was not a "cushy" assignment. And there were the point's incessantly blowing sands. On the 24th of August, Miller reported that a steam barge, the *S. Neff* of Detroit, had unloaded square timber for the construction of a breakwater around the lighthouse; the erosive winds and waves were taking their persistent toll.

Yet, the station unfailingly kept up its practice routines. The keeper described firing the Lyle gun in an exercise on September 12th:

> *Practice with Service cart as directed by Assistant Inspector, by anchoring Surfboat out 250 or 275 yards from shore. The first Shot I fired fell about 15 feet from the Boat, but before the men in the Boat could get it it sunk. The Gun was fired with 6 oz. Powder, 20-degree elevation, No. 9 line. I then fired another Shot with 5 oz. Powder, 20- degree elevation, No. 7 line. The line parted at the Shank of the Shot as soon as it left the Gun. I loaded again with 5 oz. Powder, same line (No. 7) after cutting off three or four feet of the end. It parted again 8 or 10 fathoms from the Shot. I then faked the No. 9 first line, fired loaded the Gun with 6 oz. Powder, 20-degree elevation. The line fell close to the Boat and we Soon had the Life car out to the Boat and ashore again with one of the men in her. The car leaks Badly where she has been jammed and soldered over. Our Whip and Hawser worked well. Not a kink in them. The lines I used were not our two best Service lines. They were lines that have been used...by firing long range Shots, but they were supposed to be good.*

The beautifully restored Glen Haven Life-Saving Station in Sleeping Bear
Dunes National Lakeshore includes two boats and life car suspended overhead.
Photo by author

A RECURRING DISCIPLINARY DILEMMA DOUBTLESS TESTED
MILLER'S PATIENCE throughout the fall of 1889, ending with the inevitable
consequence of losing the Keeper's trust. Based on the journal entries, Surfman Wallis
first interfered with the Keeper's reprimand of another surfman during the unloading
of lumber. On several occasions Wallis failed to punch the time detector, leading
Miller to report that he would have fired him on the spot had not the payroll for the
quarter already been signed. But when the offender again failed to punch and either
inadvertently fouled or sabotaged the crew's execution of a nighttime breeches buoy
drill by putting a double knot in a hawser, Miller had had enough of Wallis. He soon
received a telegram from the service's acting general superintendent telling him to
discharge the wayward Wallis immediately, irrespective of the fact that only a month
of the station's active season remained.

That November, a southbound patrolman discovered a body in the water; the crew retrieved it and the victim turned out to be a surfman from the Frankfort station who had been lost from his small skiff several weeks previously. Another drowning victim, never identified, was found by the Keeper's two little girls several weeks later when they were walking the beach to Frankfort. Lake Michigan never seemed to cease claiming victims, some of whom were simply careless and others who proved themselves helpless before its forces.

As was typical, the late fall's weather also presented problems. On November 18, Miller reported drifts of snow from two to six feet deep around the station, a "fearful gale" underway from which the "...station building sways with the force of it. One of the surfmen said it made him seasick when on watch." And, on November 27, Miller reported "...the worse day I have ever seen at Point Betsey for wind and snow...part of the time the watchman is unable to see the Lake. At 9-5 a.m. I sent Surfman Ellis on the beach north to see if he could discover any vessel that wanted assistance. He returned at 1-15 p.m. without seeing anything in distress. Sent Surfman Bedford over the same beat at 3-5 p.m. He returned at 5-15 without seeing anything."

CORRESPONDENCE IN 1890 INDICATES THAT THE STATION THEN LACKED AN ADEQUATE LAUNCH CAR FOR ITS DOBBINS BOAT. Trucks and axles were needed to construct a car that would carry the boat on rails into the water (the crew had already hauled and spliced long timbers to build the launch-way), and in early fall the district superintendent gave Keeper Miller authority to purchase, for up to twelve dollars, the materials needed to construct the vehicle. The crew members were to do the work. Storage for the boat was an issue at the same time, and the superintendent gave Miller authority to spend as much as $74 for supplies that the lifesavers were to turn into an eighteen by thirty-foot boathouse "before inclement weather arrives."

A year later, Miller sent the Life-Saving Service's assistant inspector a purchase request for a sail for the Dobbins boat, similar to that with which a Monomoy was typically equipped: "I think it is essential the boat should have one," he wrote, noting "...if I had one last fall I could of went to the dismasted vessel that was about ten miles N.W. of the station. You remember it cost thirty dollars for teams hired to transport the surfboat and apparatus down the beach, and the former Inspector was in favor of a sail for this boat and had promised to get me one but for some reason he never got around to it."

The crisis to which Miller referred is apparently the rescue attempt he recorded on September 14, 1890, when, with a gale roaring from the west, the lookout reported a vessel flying a distress flag about ten miles off the station. From the tower and using glasses, they could tell the ship was a three-master whose main and mizzen masts had been carried away, the distress signal being fastened to the foremast. Having reckoned that the ship would be driven ashore about sixteen miles north of the station, Miller, using a relatively new piece of equipment, telephoned to Frankfort for teams of horses to haul the beach apparatus and lifeboat to the likely grounding site. Even with those teams and the aid of yet another they commandeered along the way, it took the party about nine hours to make the journey to Platte Bay, where they launched the boat and started rowing six miles across to towering Empire Bluff. With dawn approaching, Miller wrote that he had climbed the six hundred-foot bluff to get a good view of the coast. Not finding any sign of the expected wreck on shore, he concluded that some captain had towed the stricken schooner to South Manitou Island harbor where, with the aid of his glasses, he could see numerous sailing ships and steamers lying for protection.

With no rescue to be mounted from the mainland, the crew started its long return trip to the station, arriving "...worn out, hungry and disappointed. I don't believe there has been a crew in the Life-Saving Service that ever worked harder," he recorded in his journal, "every man being very anxious to render assistance." Complaining of the route they had had to take for this rescue attempt, he wrote, "I don't believe there is a worse road in the State of Michigan, or the United States, that is [any] worse than the one we traveled last night. Nothing but sand hills and sand plains the whole distance – a continual drag on the teams. The men charged two dollars apiece for their teams, and I think they have well earned it."

On August 8, 1891, Miller recorded assistance to a figure having special significance at the point:

At 8-30 p.m. the watch rang the alarm and cried out that there was a small boat trying to land. The men had just gone to bed, but in less time than it takes to write it they were all on the beach. Some in their drawers, some barefooted and others with their stockings on. They got to the boat just as she struck the beach and before the man knew where he was himself and boat were hauled up high and dry on the beach. The man [turned] out to be William Dues, the Light-House Keeper's Son, returning from Edgewater where he had been to work. If the men had not of been there the boat would of swamped and broken to pieces as the beach is strewn with logs and the man might have been crippled for life.

Of course, practices didn't always go well, as was—to considerable embarrassment, no doubt—the case on July 24, 1892, when fifteen visitors had come to the station. Because they had never seen the beach apparatus work, Miller had the crew practice it for them. Apparently the sand anchor, which keeps the hawser taut so the breeches buoy can ride along it above the water, had not been buried deeply enough to hold it; the fact that no one was hurt in the ensuing collapse was attributed by Miller simply to luck. "But it made a bad exhibit for the spectators," he wrote, adding, "I reprimanded the men for their carelessness in burying the anchor. I don't think it will ever happen again with us."

To Miller's credit, the typical public performance was more like that of a day in August, 1896, when about fifty people from Benzonia and the surrounding country came to the station. Leading his crew through the breeches buoy drill for the visitors, Miller said, "They were astonished when we took the man from the drill pole in four minutes."

Women try the breeches buoy drill.
Courtesy of Claudia Lewis

By the early '90s, Miller was keeping a pony at the lifesaving station, allowing him to more quickly investigate circumstances to which he had been alerted. So, too, did he and his crew sometimes learn of emergencies by someone riding a horse to the station. They also relied on teams to haul the beach cart and boat wagon substantial distances. In mid-September, 1893, the men rescued the three-man crew and two paying passengers of the *Three Bells* near Empire; the vessel's foremast and bow sprit had been torn away during a squall at night, and the following morning the mainmast and much of her rudder were lost. This rescue led to Miller's asking the district to compensate the owners of teams used to haul the surfboat, beach cart and crew to the distant rescue site. He explained that he thought the man who had notified him of the grounding should be paid, as well: "I should not want a horse of mine rode as that one was for $4.50." Miller added that it was necessary in order to alert the station quickly enough to allow the equipment to be hauled to the site. "Some teams that I tried to get would not hitch on the boat for any price," he noted, "as it is about 16 inches wider than the road waggons."

September 24, 1893, was yet another interesting day of work for Miller and his crew. Shortly after a wind shift, a man arrived at the station from Otter Creek, north of Point Betsie, to report that a dismasted small ship had come ashore. Wrote Miller:

> *The wind being fair I immediately launched the Monomoy boat, taking five of the men with me and started for the Scene of disaster. Launched at 1-15 p.m., arrived at the wreck at 3-35 p.m., distance 14 miles. The crew were taken off and the vessel anchored by some fishermen just before we got there. The wreck proved to be a Small Sloop owned and Sailed by C. Marshall named* **Two Brothers** *bound for Frankfort after a load of fruit. Thinking there was to much sea to make Frankfort Harbor, they thought to make the Manitou Island Harbor when about 10 miles north of the Station the mast broke and left them helpless. The crew consisted of one man and a Boy. We made him a mast during the afternoon and evening, but there was to much wind and sea to step it. As the wind and sea was ahead we were unable to return with the boat. At about 12-30 a.m. the wind howled into the N.W. and blew a gale. As the Capt. could get no help to step the mast and rig it I left two of my men with the boat to help him and the rest of us returned to station on foot...We left the Creek at 1-15 a.m. and arrived at the station at 5-45 a.m. distance 14 miles.*

An entry two days later wrapped up that story with a nice touch: "Surfmen Hendrickson and Guilbault returned to Station from Otter Creek. They stept the mast. Set up the rigging. Weighed the anchor. Set Sail, and Capt. C. Marshall of the little Sloop *Two Brother*s sailed for Manitou Island Harbor rejoicing. The Capt. thanked them kindly and offered to pay them for their Services but they declined to take anything."

෨

ANOTHER ISSUE ASSOCIATED WITH THE DOBBINS BOAT AROSE IN THE FORM OF A LETTER FROM GENERAL SUPERINTENDENT KIMBALL in September, 1894. Kimball, addressing all keepers of stations equipped with a Dobbins boat, wished to make clear that "...this pattern of boat is designed for effecting rescues from schooners and other vessels carrying comparatively small crews...where the distance intervening between the wreck and the station is considerable, and where tugs are not available for towing the larger and heavier English lifeboat."[10] The Dobbins boat wasn't intended for heavy loads, he said, warning against ever taking aboard more than eleven persons, including the boat's crew. If a stranded vessel had more than seven people on board and it seemed as though there would be time for just one rescue attempt, Kimball advised that the crew should be reduced in size—even to five lifesavers, if necessary—to avoid exceeding the lifeboat's maximum load.

Kimball's long leadership at the U.S. Life-Saving Service is known for his unfailingly high standards and expectations. It was the responsibility of district superintendents to ensure that the requirements were met by the individual stations and crews. In what was an annual procedure, Keeper Miller received a March 21, 1894 letter from the district superintendent, directing him to hire seven surfmen "under the same terms" [sixty-five dollars per month] as prevailed the prior year. The letter also advised the Keeper that crewmen would be paid three dollars for rescuing life or property during the "inactive" season preceding the station's opening on April 2. "Any neglect of patrol, or watch duty, shown by the time detector, should be carefully noted in red ink on the dial card, and the reason, if any, why it was neglected, explained by a letter to this office, accompanying the transcript of Journal." Not only did the letter so advise the Keeper, it insisted that "...hereafter all official correspondence should be properly folded and endorsed before forwarding. In conclusion I will say that the good name of the Service is largely in your keeping, and having this in view, I trust that nothing that is in peril in your vicinity will escape observation."[11]

The service's good name was certainly in diligent hands under Miller's leadership at Point Betsie. Little escaped his observation and note-taking, as seen in the journal entry of May 12, 1888: "The watch called my attention to something floating in the Lake about 2 and 1/2 miles S.W. from the Station. I could not make out what it was with the Glasses—Launched the surfboat and after one hour...found it to be a large pine tree with large limbs out of the water, which made it look like some kind of a wreck from the shore."

❧

ALWAYS REQUIRED TO BE A CONSCIENTIOUS STEWARD OF HIS STATION'S EQUIPMENT, a keeper even had to record how donated clothing was used. Miller once wrote the superintendent to say that "two of the men that I took off the waterlogged schooner *Ebeneezer* [on November 27, 1891] were destitute of socks. I gave each a pair from the supplies furnished by the Women's National Relief Association." The socks came from the inventory of clothing for "the succor and use of destitute shipwrecked persons" regularly shipped to lifesaving stations by the Women's National Relief Association. The keeper was to inform the general superintendent's office whenever shipwrecked persons were furnished items from this relief box.

The details of the schooner *Ebeneezer* are a riveting example of many vessels' fate in the storm-filled fall of the year. Having departed Manistee a few days before Thanksgiving, 1891, the ship sprung a leak when only two hours out of port and filled with water so quickly that the seamen had no time to get any clothes on other than what they were wearing at the moment. Though the ship's captain believed he was just a few miles off Point Au Sable Station, he had no way of making a signal as all his equipment was under water. Drifting more than forty miles before gale-force winds during two days without food or shelter, they were finally spotted by Point Betsie crew member Christian Jacobson at daylight. Miller wrote of this perilous event:[12]

> As soon as it was light enough I could see by the aid of the glasses that something was wrong with her and called all hands to launch the surf boat. We launched about 6-30, when going over the...bar we got one sea that threw No. 5 and 6 off their thwarts and filled the boat half full of water. When a half mile out I could see the yawl had left the vessel and was drifting towards us. The men were trying to make headway by paddling with short pieces of boards, their oars having been washed away. I took them into the surfboat. Some of them being unable to help themselves on account of being frozen and famished with hunger. They had been without anything to eat from the time the vessel water logged 36 hours.

Miller wrote that he met a tug while coming ashore, and got the tug's captain to take the schooner in tow and haul her into Frankfort, with Surfmen Kaarvand and Anderson climbing aboard the water-logged schooner to steer her. Meanwhile, the Keeper and the rest of his crew took the schooner's men to the station, where they found some of the victims had frozen limbs. "Put their feet and hands in cold ice water and rubbed them with snow to draw out the frost," he wrote; "After the frost was out put on Dog Oil, having nothing better and it worked like magic." He went on to recommend this treatment for frostbite.[13]

Miller wrapped up this account by noting that his wife had a "...smoking hot breakfast ready and the men went to work with a relish. They also took dinner, then they thought they could walk to Frankfort. They left the station at 1-20 p.m., well satisfied with the reception and thanking the Lord they were once more on shore." The men were grateful of their rescue, having had no way of signaling the station and presuming that it was already closed for the season. As earlier noted, having given each crewman a pair of socks from the Women's Aid association inventory, the men having only thirty-five cents among them, Miller gave the captain five dollars, trusting that he would get it back from the owners of the saved vessel.

PERSONNEL ISSUES WERE AN INESCAPABLE PART OF THE KEEPER'S COMMAND OF HIS STATION. It was his job to manage the crew whose services he had chosen to retain. The keeper's superiors had clear expectations in this regard, as indicated in an 1899 letter to Miller from General Superintendent Kimball.[14] He wrote to him on October 14, in reference to two surfmen whom Miller had reported for failing to properly mark the dial of their patrol clocks. The instruction was customarily clear and firm:

> *You will obtain an affidavit from each of these delinquents stating all the circumstances pertinent to their failure of duty as stated, especially where they were at the time they were to mark the dial and whether they had been asleep at any time while on the patrol during which the failure occurred, and forward them to this office with any recommendation you may be pleased to make.*

A keeper had to be sure his crew complement was filled at all times. He looked to the surfmen to obtain substitutes if they had to be away, and juggled the workload if necessary. One November night in 1890, the No. 1, Ed Bedford received word that his wife was seriously ill in Charlevoix. Bedford left immediately in the morning; Miller found a substitute and did what he had to do to keep the station operating smoothly. Apart from an emergency such as this, surfmen were required by federal law and regulation to reside at their station during the active season. They were not allowed to sleep or dine away from the station except when on authorized leave. In other words, in contrast to the old days when volunteers manned the rescue stations, these were full-time employees who, except when on authorized liberty, spent their time at the station either working and relaxing on-site:

One couldn't be expected to work all the time!
Courtesy of Claudia Lewis

Surfboating.
Courtesy of Claudia Lewis

Now and then there were major maintenance jobs to be completed on the station's structures, as on a spring day when District Superintendent Robbins told Miller that paint was being sent to him, freight pre-paid, from the service's warehouse. The Keeper was told in the usual detail to "see to it that the paint is spread on evenly;" if there were no suitable brushes on hand, Miller could purchase good flat ones, four inches wide, for about seventy-five cents each. Robbins' final advice was that "...the job should be finished before flies are plenty." With such direction, there was little room for misunderstanding.

Fall brought other tasks, as in late November, 1892, when Miller wrote that the men were busy sawing firewood "to keep themselves warm" and that he had omitted scrubbing the house as "water freezes in the rooms when there is no fire." Of course, there was always the possibility of the unexpected. Whatever need was brought to their attention, the Keeper and crew, consistent with the service's tradition, tried to be responsive. For example, there was the memorable call for the station's help on November 17, 1896, Miller reporting as follows:

> *A man living about one mile south of the station came to get help to get his horse out of a well that she had fallen into. Four of the crew and the Keeper went over with tackle and shovels and got the horse out. The well was about 14 feet deep. Nothing but the horse's nose was out. Had to shovel the earth away in order to get the horse out.*

IN THE LATE 19TH CENTURY, POINT BETSIE LIFE-SAVING STATION SECURED THE USE OF TELEPHONE SERVICE TO FRANKFORT OVER A LINE THAT SERVED A LUMBER COMPANY SEVERAL MILES FARTHER NORTH. Captain Miller had been a vigorous advocate for telephone service at the station, as in a letter to the assistant inspector, Lieutenant Rogers, in Chicago in late 1892. He pointed out the necessity of communication to the "...north so that we could hear of disasters and to Frankfort for teams [of horses] to transport our apparatus as that is the nearest place teams can be got. Another disaster occurred Saturday, October 29th, which will illustrate the necessity again," he pled:

> *The vessel is flying a flag of distress and dragging her anchors ashore off of Empire 17 miles north. The Postmaster, Marvin LaCore, an old Surfman that was in this station with Capt. Matthews, starts for help. The nearest station is this one. In coming this way he meets with falling trees that have blown down in the Gale. When abreast of our road [actually a primitive pathway at the time] he thinks perhaps it is full of falling trees and knowing we would have to go to Frankfort after teams he concluded to go to Frankfort at once and get help from there. The above is what LaCore told one of my men yesterday.*

Miller was obviously embarrassed that LaCore didn't bother to alert the Point Betsie station to the emergency, but chose to go miles further; a phone connection would have kept his station fully apprised of the situation and permitted the crew closest to the grounded vessel [i.e., Miller's] to respond in timely fashion.

With so much value placed upon the telephone connection, keeping the fragile line in service was a constant challenge given the harsh weather at Point Betsie. Conducting one of their periodic line inspections over its fourteen-mile length in the summer of 1894, Miller and several surfmen found that a half-mile of wire was missing, as well as about one hundred and fifty insulators. Troubles of that nature arose frequently, and whenever the line was out of commission the Keeper lamented its lack of availability, especially vociferously if he had been prevented from quickly summoning a tug or other assistance. The time-consuming alternative to the phone link was, as in earlier times, to send a man to Frankfort by rowboat, or on foot or horseback for whatever was needed.

On the morning of November 2, 1892, a steam barge, the *Robert Holland*, blew four whistles off the station. Miller launched the surfboat and went out to her, learning that the ship had been damaged and was taking on water. The vessel's captain requested Miller to return to the station and call Frankfort for a tug. "Was surprised when I told him we had no communications," Miller wrote; "I offered to go to Frankfort for a tug with my boat, but he said he could whistle for one. This is another case where the telephone would have been useful to the Service".

When the line worked, it was a great convenience and a potential life-saver. As Miller had recorded on June 22, 1888:

> *Steamer Cuba from Chicago bound for Buffalo ran ashore at 6-45 p.m. in thick fogg about 80 rods southwest of the station. Manned the surfboat and went out to her. Rendered assistance by coming ashore, telephoned to*

Frankfort for a tug. Went out to her the second time at 8-25, arriving at 9-20 p.m. Crew arrived at Station at 10-15. Left the tug drudging as she was unable to pull the steamer off.

Loaded with 60,000 bushels of corn, the steamer was released by the tug the following day, with no damage to the vessel or her valuable cargo.

❧

THE APPROACH OF THE CENTURY'S TURN found the shipping community generally pleased at the progress that had been made in improving the system of navigational aids on the lakes. The Lake Carriers' Association reported in 1898 that the federal government had been responsive to their pleas, and that the coasts had been equipped adequately with lights and fog signals. The group remained interested in securing more gas-lighted buoys, despite the Lighthouse Board's concern that the agency's tenders were too taxed to permit them to handle additional seasonal buoy installations and removals.[15]

❧

THERE COULD BE NO MORE FITTING WAY OF CLOSING THIS ACCOUNT OF POINT BETSIE LIGHT AND LIFESAVING SERVICES IN THE LATTER NINETEENTH CENTURY THAN BY RECOUNTING THE COURAGEOUS RESCUE OF CREWMEN FROM THE STEAMER *ST. LAWRENCE* in late November of 1898. Laden with corn, the steamship was bound from Chicago to Prescott, Ontario, on the St. Lawrence River. Her course would require her to travel through much of the Great Lakes system—through Lakes Michigan, Huron, Erie and Ontario and the great river whose name the vessel bore.

The U.S. Life-Saving Service prefaces its account of this great achievement, published in its 1899 annual report[16], by noting, "The usual course of vessels bound that way is said to be to make Point Betsy on the starboard bow, and then haul around to the eastward of the Manitou Islands, passing between them and Sleeping Bear Point, and this is the course the steamer appears to have been following." This is the classic Manitou Passage course described earlier. "Snow was falling in the afternoon, and it would seem that the master must have reckoned his vessel considerably farther to the westward than she really was, for at about 5:30 p.m. she suddenly took bottom and held fast." The vessel was about two miles south of Point Betsie, and at that season of the year darkness rapidly enveloped the shoreline and lake.

This magnificent story is best told through the words of the Life-Saving Service's own comprehensive account as presented in that annual report, which was based upon the journal entries Captain Miller penned after the episode and from additional information gathered during the service's subsequent investigation. A story such as this was exactly what the service's legendary general superintendent was eager to share with Congress and the country:

The sea was running high, although there was no immediate danger to the steamer, and the captain began blowing the steam whistle at short intervals, the sounds of which were heard at the Life-Saving Station, and not being distress signals were supposed to come from a car ferry bound into Frankfort. However, Keeper Miller thought that she was too near the beach for safety, and therefore sent Surfman Bedford down the shore with instructions to warn her off with Coston signals.

The falling snow was so thick that Bedford could not see the lights of the steamer until he was abreast of her, when he burned two Coston signals, and became satisfied that she was already stranded, which was in fact the case, no signals of any kind having been made by her until after she struck. In response, as Bedford supposed, to the second Coston, the steamer blew three short blasts, whereupon he began hastily to retrace his way to the station, where he stated the facts, estimating the distance of the vessel from the shore as somewhere near three hundred and fifty yards.

A surfman was at once sent off to procure a team of horses, while the rest ran out the wagon with the surfboat on it, and prepared to set out along the shore to the place of the disaster. Within twenty or thirty minutes the team came, and all hands started down the beach, arriving opposite the steamer in less than three quarters of an hour. With reference to this arduous journey, the investigating officer, Captain G. W. Moore, one of the most experienced officers of the Revenue-Cutter Service, states that he drove over the same beach the day he made the investigation, when at times the snow was falling quite thickly, and it seemed wonderful that the wagon was not wrecked soon after starting—in the night, amid heavy winds, and seas dashing on the shore, and blinding snow and over a beach strewn with drift logs and dangerous debris.

As soon as the life-savers were abreast of the steamer they launched the surfboat, but the weather was so thick that their vision could penetrate only the little space close about them, and while crossing the second bar an unseen breaker dashed into the boat, nearly filling it, and compelling Keeper Miller, in the exercise of sound judgment for the safety of his crew, to return to the beach. The snow was then falling so fast, and the boat and oars were so encumbered with ice, that he concluded it would be foolhardy to try it again, and he therefore sent the crew back to the station with the team for the purpose of bringing up the beach apparatus.

On account of the severity of the storm, the obstructed condition of the beach, and the weight of the apparatus, two trips became necessary to haul it abreast of the vessel. On the second trip, when returning to the wreck, Surfman Jeffs stopped to trim a lantern, and when he had done so and resumed his way, was surprised to see a man rise up from the beach and stagger toward him. As the two men met, Jeffs saw that the stranger was wet and weak and scarcely able to stand. In a feeble whisper he told the surfman that he and four others had left the steamer in a yawl boat and had been capsized. Then he charged Jeffs to leave him and look out for the others, who, he supposed, had reached the shore farther southward, and might be in greater distress.

Following this pathetic injunction, Jeffs proceeded, and soon stumbled on two more men, alive but very much exhausted, one being the first mate of the steamer. Still pressing on to the southward, he made no further discovery, and arriving at the scene of operations reported finding three shipwrecked men and imparted the information he had received from the first one.

Neither the vessel nor the crew on board were then in great danger, and Keeper Miller wisely resolved to give his attention to those already on the beach, lest they should perish at once. The apparatus cart was cleared of its contents with a view of placing the shipwrecked men in it and transporting them to the station as speedily as possible after they could be found again. While some of the surfmen hauled the cart, the keeper followed after it.

Four living men were picked up and hurried on to the station. Meantime the keeper discovered the fifth of the unfortunate number lying just in the edge of the water, whom he drew father up on the beach and tried to resuscitate. Four or five minutes later three of the surfmen who had been to the station came back and joined in every sort of effort to restore the apparently lifeless form to animation but without avail. As a matter of fact, what they had done was more for the purpose of leaving "no stone unturned" than with expectation of success, for as soon as the man was examined by the light of the lantern it was revealed that his head was severely bruised, and there were wounds about the temples, ears, and nose. That he was gone past all possibility of restoration was clear to the eye, and was confirmed by the fact that the hand, laid upon his chest, could detect neither warmth nor the slightest suggestion of life. Whether he was drowned or battered to death by the capsized boat could not be absolutely determined, but his general appearance, and the fact that the lifesaving men could get no water from his stomach while practicing the resuscitation methods, satisfied them that he perished from the blows of which his wounds bore ghastly evidence.

That this man was needlessly sacrificed, and the others almost lost, is shown by the fact that all on board the wreck were subsequently saved by the life-saving crew, as they would have been had they stood by their ship. The testimony discloses that the attempt to land was initiated and directed by the mate, who is said to have declared that he could land without wetting his feet. As it turned out, however, the boat had scarcely cleared the steamer when it was upset, with the miserable result already narrated. Referring to this matter, the keeper says: "None of the four men we helped to the station could ever have reached there alive alone, and if we had not had to make the second load for the apparatus we never should have known anything about them until 4 o'clock in the morning, when we took off the balance of the crew, and there would have been five dead men within one mile of the station." Twenty-two inches of snow fell that night.

As soon as the four living men were placed in the station and the fifth had been proved beyond the possibility of doubt to be dead, the life-saving crew began vigorous operations for the succor of the men still on board the steamer. The Lyle gun was placed in position, and the first shot laid its line across the wreck, but in the confusion and darkness, nobody saw it, and after a few moments another was sent out. This, too, seemed to be undiscovered, and the disappointed surfmen began to haul it back to the shore. Then the whistle on the wreck began to blow—why, the surfmen could not understand and did not learn until after the rescue was effected, when they were informed that the ship-wrecked people knew nothing of the life lines until they were startled to hear their own whistle blowing without any agency of theirs. Proceeding to discover the cause, they found the life line lying across the whistle cord and causing a blast of the whistle at every pull on the line.

As soon as the sailors began to haul out the shot line, the whip line and then the hawser were bent on, but when they reached the vessel the sailors got them foul, and the disheartening fact that they would not work was soon apparent. Then the keeper resolved to man the surfboat again, and instead of trying to use the oars to pull her out by means of the whip line. This the life-savers doggedly accomplished under adverse conditions of almost insurmountable proportions. The sea was furious, the lines, the boat, and the men were incrusted in ice, and the night was so dark that one could hardly see his neighbor. Twice the brave men made the perilous trip, each time carrying to the shore five of the steamer's chilled and almost disconsolate crew.

Mr. Warner, the prosecuting attorney of Benzie County, who conducted the inquiry as to the cause of the death of the lost engineer, testifies that he had a conversation with all the survivors in the presence of one another, and especially with the mate, and they all related to him the circumstances of the wreck, and told him in grateful and enthusiastic words of the work of *the life-saving crew. They declared that their conduct in going out to the steamer in such a blinding storm and fearful sea was "simply one of the most heroic acts that any of them ever knew," that they did more than could be expected under the circumstances, and that the only ones to blame for the loss of life were the sailors themselves. On a later occasion, says Mr. Warner, the captain of the St. Lawrence reiterated what his crew had said, and spoke in "glowing terms" of Keeper Miller and the wonderful rescue he and his men performed.*

St. Lawrence or similar rescue scene, with cart and life car on snowy beach.
Courtesy of Claudia Lewis[17]

To conclude, the 1898 *St. Lawrence* rescue by Point Betsie's life-savers is one of the great accomplishments in Benzie County's history and, like the station's rescue from the stricken *J. H. Hartzell* eighteen years earlier, holds a distinctive place in the annals of the honorable U.S. Life-Saving Service. Some persons thought providence played a role in the rescue, wrote the agency, especially given two key elements of the story. First, that it was only during the second trip to the station, necessitated because of the weather, the cluttered beach and weight of the wagon, that the men from the swamped yawl were discovered and could be saved; and second, the sailors on the wrecked steamer were made aware of their opportunity for rescue only through the fortuitous crossing of their ship's whistle cord by the amazingly accurate Lyle gun shot.

"Whether these incidents are viewed as merely fortunate accidents or in a higher light, it is certain that they resulted in saving many lives which there is reason to believe might otherwise have been lost," the service concluded. And summing up the long night's labors in more earthy terms, Keeper Harrison Miller raised another vexing issue: "Some of the [steamer's] crew say they saw our patrol signal. Why any of the crew should leave the wreck in their yawl in such a sea is more than I can comprehend."

CHAPTER EIGHT

POINT BETSIE AT THE DAWN OF THE 20TH CENTURY

At the outset of the new century, the navigational season saw a substantial volume of traffic sailing past Point Betsie. Southbound cargo and passenger vessels, having come through the Manitou Passage, were heading to major Lake Michigan ports; vessels sailing north were on course toward the Straits of Mackinac. Other commercial vessels were serving the nearby harbor towns. The 1899 edition of *Beeson's Marine Directory*[1], a prominent annual guide, extolled Frankfort's assets, saying this port of entry had "...a magnificent harbor with 18 feet of water in the channel" as well as a lighthouse, a lifesaving station and a weather signal station.

The guide presented an attractive description of Frankfort at the century's turn, its population, including the residents of the village of South Frankfort just across the harbor, totaling about 2,000. "The town boasts of water works, electric lights, etc.," the description emphasized. Commerce being of keen interest to companies in shipping-related businesses, the publication described Frankfort as having two saw mills, one of them owned and operated by the local collector of customs, a shingle mill and a machine shop with iron and brass foundry. There were two newspapers in town, one bank and three hotels.

Frankfort's harbor, yet labeled in this guide as Aux bec Scies Lake, was also identified as the home of the Ann Arbor Railroad's ferries *No. 1, 2 and 3,* sailing year-around to cross-lake ports. Throughout that pioneering line's nine decades-long history, the vessels' officers and crew, sailing day and night throughout the year within easy sight and hearing of Point Betsie's sweeping beam and piercing fog signal, sensed a kinship with the storied landmark.

View from Frankfort bluff of departing Ann Arbor ferry circa 1920.
Courtesy of Claudia Lewis

Beeson's added that "...during the summer season numerous lines connect Frankfort with Manistee, Ludington, Milwaukee and Chicago on the south, and Charlevoix, Petoskey, Harbor Springs, Cheboygan and Mackinaw on the north." It also identified ten resident owners of sail and steam vessels, among them Charles B. Slyfield and the Slyfield Tug Line.

THE FIRST U.S. CENSUS OF THE 20TH CENTURY, taken in the spring of 1900, sheds light on the small community of lightkeepers, lifesavers and their families who resided at Point Betsie. Keeper of the light station was thirty-five-year-old, Michigan-born Philip Sheridan, who had arrived there in 1895 from South Manitou Island. As a teenager on the island, he had assisted his lightkeeping father, Lyman Sheridan, and nearly a decade later had served officially as assistant to Keeper Thomas Armstrong. At the century mark, Sheridan and his Ohio-born wife, Mary Elizabeth, had been married four years and had no children; in the spring of 1902, Mary Sheridan succumbed to tuberculosis. About two years later, the widowed keeper married Grace Oliver, daughter of Frankfort area pioneers. The couple, who were to have two children, Lyman and Elizabeth, retained strong ties to the local community.

View from Elberta bluff, with AA Ferry, schooner and passenger vessel in the harbor.
Courtesy of Claudia Lewis

Phil Sheridan in later years.
Courtesy of Stephen Sheridan

They stood watch over a steadily increasing "laker" fleet, especially in terms of its tonnage. The Lake Carriers' Association reported in 1903 that its vessels' tonnage had increased from 590,000 tons in 1894 to 874,203 in 1901 and 1,014,066 in 1902—that most recent annual increase being the largest in the organization's history.

Assisting Sheridan at Point Betsie Light was Medad Spencer, age sixty. A number of men briefly held the 2nd assistant's position over the next several years, including Frank H. Glover, whose daughter was born at the lighthouse, and Charles Stibitz, who served there for about five years, during which he earned promotion to the 1st assistant's spot. Edward L. Gray, who started as 2nd assistant in 1906, served until 1910, having also been promoted to the 1st assistant's position. A descendant has said that Gray and his wife Dora had seven children living with them at Point Betsie, four from her previous marriage. One can only presume that their living quarters must have been stretched to capacity.

Substantial improvements were undertaken at the lighthouse in the spring of 1907. Seven hundred fifty dollars was the estimated cost for repairing 234 feet of revetment, renewing 384 feet of sidewalk with concrete, re-plastering the walls in the keeper's dwelling and providing a new "drive well" at the station. Three hundred twenty-three dollars of the estimate was for materials, and the balance, just over four hundred twenty-six dollars, was for labor, which included the services of a superintendent, mason, carpenter and a laborer whose services were needed for seventy-four days. As was generally the case, the materials were to be purchased in the Great Lakes area and delivered by the lighthouse tender *Hyacinth.*[2]

The importance of Great Lakes trade and the navigational duties of the Lighthouse Establishment was made clear in the Lake Carriers' 1907 annual report, which stated that there were then 415 lighthouses and beacons on the lakes as well as eighty-four steam fog signals, twenty-one mechanical fog signals, eighty gas buoys and ten lightships. These were two-sevenths of the lights, close to half the steam fog signals and more than one-half the gas buoys under the agency's entire jurisdiction. And the Association proudly added, "While our Government places no tax whatever upon vessels for furnishing aids to navigation, this is by no means the case in foreign countries. In Great Britain, light dues on voyages between New York and the United Kingdom vary from 8 to 26 cents per ton for entering, as well as an equal charge for departing."

≈

AT THE ADJACENT LIFESAVING STATION, Captain "Tip" Miller and Bridget had two daughters in their early twenties who were living on their own; four of this education-minded couple's children were recorded as students. At least two of their brood were young enough to still be residing with their parents. Among the crew at the lifesaving station, two other well known figures were Miller's nephew, No. 1 surfman Bedford, and German-born surfman Charles Gaul who also resided there with his Wisconsin-native wife, Cora, and infant son, Goldie.

Mid-summer in 1902, Keeper Miller received a letter from the district office regarding a "Lake Service" lifeboat that had been transferred from the Frankfort station to Point Betsie.[3] Replying to a previous inquiry from Miller, the letter, from Assistant Inspector Reynolds, said the boat would come fully equipped, including all its gear and outfits, as well as materials that had been removed when the boat's deck had been taken off in preparation for repairs. Miller was told to follow up with Keeper Morency in Frankfort to get the oars, boat hooks, spars, rowlocks and other items that belonged with the boat, as well as cork that had been taken from the craft. Miller and his men were to undertake major work on the boat in their boathouse, installing new air chambers. In the meantime, they were to store their other boats temporarily on the beach, covered by sails of condemned boats, or floated in the lake in good weather. "I believe you are quite capable to do the work, or to properly direct its performance," Reynolds said to the highly respected boatman, adding, "I have no doubt you can get the boat ready for service before the fall gales commence."

The Lake Carriers' Association put its political weight behind a growing movement to provide retirement benefits for lifesavers. Its 1907 annual report emphasized, "Such legislation is not only an act of simple justice to the lifesaving crews, but a matter of sound public policy in making the service more efficient. It is unnecessary to add the very deep interest that every member of this Association should take in assisting in the passage of these bills and I suggest that each member write the Member of Congress from his district asking his assistance in the passage of the bill." This was not merely a matter of treating long-serving lifesavers equitably with other federal works, but also of sustaining the agency's effectiveness. As the Carriers' report noted, "It appears that during the last five years rapid and constant decline has taken place both in the number and qualifications of the men who offer themselves as recruits...." The shippers were concerned that "Men were leaving the stations for less hazardous and better compensated positions" and replacements were getting harder to find, leaving "...scarcely a station with its full complement of surfmen."

Another step to help lifesavers was the agency's initiative at this time to bring book collections to its stations, as was the practice of the Lighthouse Establishment. The aim, reported the Carriers in 1907, was to provide "...good, wholesome reading material made up of well-selected books of fiction, travel, history, biography, newspapers and magazines." The plan was to initiate this service using surplus books from the Treasury Department's library. Congressional and presidential approval was required for this new program, which was underway about a year later.

The Lake Carriers Association also passed along to its members a statistical breakdown of the lifesaving agency's performance, nation-wide, in responding to maritime emergencies during the prior year. Summing up the data, the lifesavers had responded to a total of 347 disasters involving "documented" vessels carrying 3,936 persons, only twenty-two of whom lost their lives. Fifty-five of the ships were reported as totally lost. An additional 491 "undocumented" vessels—ships of less than five tons burden—also incurred emergencies. Of the 1,176 aboard them, twenty-three were lost.

Also important is the fact that 204 vessels had been spotted as they approached danger and had been warned of their imminent peril by signals from lifesavers. In close to 200 of these cases, the signals had been fired at night; the other instances occurred during thick daytime weather.

❧

MOST GOOD THINGS EVENTUALLY COMING TO AN END, CAPTAIN MILLER ULTIMATELY WAS COMPELLED TO SURRENDER HIS POINT BETSIE LIFE-SAVING STATION POST, A BITTER PILL FOR THIS VETERAN TO ACCEPT. It was in the summer of 1908 that "physical disability," justified on the basis of deteriorating eyesight (a claim with which Miller didn't agree), brought to a close an extraordinary career that exemplified the best in U.S. lifesaving—not only at Point Betsie but throughout the inland seas.

Miller had said of himself when in his thirtieth year of service and soon to be sixty-seven years old, "I am getting a little too old to be frogging about on the beach, but am still able to get around as lively as any of them." The Charlevoix spirited keeper added that he might "linger along for 80 or 90 years more," to which the *Charlevoix Sentinel* had simply rejoined, "We wish it were possible." In fact, this much-respected leader had managed thereafter to continue his physically demanding lifesaving command for more than a decade.

Captain Miller's journal entry on July 9, 1908, records his retirement preparations. The crew omitted flag drill that day to assist Miller in packing his household goods, preparing to vacate the station after twenty-one years' service. These mundane activities continued the next day, but the crew then returned to its customary exercise with the beach apparatus—the last time the surfmen would be performing for Tip Miller.

By mid-morning on the eleventh of July, the station's crew was under the leadership of Captain Edwin E. Bedford, Miller's nephew and former No. 1, who had just arrived from his White River post. There is no doubt that Miller was greatly proud of his successor; after Bedford had been promoted to his White River command, Miller had observed, "No better man ever held an oar or guided a life boat."

Bedford had joined the U.S. Life-Saving Service at Milwaukee, Wisconsin, in 1882 and in that year married Alice O'Neill of Green Bay. After two years, he and Alice moved to Charlevoix, Michigan, where many former Beaver Island families or their relatives resided, and he worked as a fisherman and lifesaver. He and Alice had two children, Ruth (Garvin) and Alvin. In the early 1890s, the Bedfords spent two years in the South on account of Alice's health, then went north again and in 1893 he became a key member of Captain Miller's lifesaving crew. Her death in 1897 left Ed a widower with two adolescent children; at the close of 1900, he married Anna Swanston in Frankfort. After a few years' faithful service as Miller's top surfman, he had been appointed to lead the White River crew.

Captain Bedford promptly assumed the responsibility for all operations and swung into the Point Betsie station's routine. He was soon off to Frankfort in the Monomoy for supplies and administrative needs, later dutifully recording receipt, by mail, of fifty-five sheets of writing paper, fifty-six envelopes of nine-inch length and ten six-inch ones.

The Bedford logs recorded the usual required routines, including the never-ending wood-cutting, white-washing and occasional assistance to neighbors. On August 27, 1908, Bedford would write, "A boy came to the station from the Crystal Lake Resort and told me that the woods were all afire around the cottages and that they needed help. I took part of the station crew and went to the fire one mile away and we helped to put the fire out." Helping the public, as always, was part of the daily job for the men of Point Betsie.

As Bedford assumed command, Point Betsie's historic prominence was undiminished, as was well illustrated by the 1908 edition of *Scott's New Coast Pilot for the Lakes.*[4] The volume not only described the station's structures, light characteristics and fog signal in detail, but identified seven courses from a location four miles offshore Point Betsie to major destinations on Lake Michigan, including the distant port of Chicago.

Bedford's ten years of leadership at Point Betsie proved to be an active time in the station's history. His long experience had certainly prepared him well for the serious duties and challenges of running a Great Lakes lifesaving station.

What he could not have anticipated was that he would be leading his crew at the time of a major administrative change, the 1915 merger of the Revenue-Cutter Service (successor to the Revenue-Marine) and the storied U.S. Life-Saving Service. The reorganization created a new agency, the U.S. Coast Guard, (in the Treasury Department, with transfer to the Navy in wartime) but also cost the nation's lifesavers a significant measure of their valued and well-earned identity. Hence, during Bedford's years, as in subsequent less active times, separate federal agencies continued to be responsible for the operations on Point Betsie. Answering to different bosses and functioning under different regulations, compensation schedules, etc., the crews were both rivals and partners in their daily mission of ensuring the safety of mariners coursing this section of Lake Michigan's coast. In fact, the two roles were never administratively united at Point Betsie, for by the time lightkeepers had donned Coast Guard uniforms, the Point Betsie lifesaving station had been closed.

Keeper Bedford on right.
Courtesy of Claudia Lewis

INTERRUPTIONS OF TELEPHONE SERVICE ON ACCOUNT OF HARSH WEATHER POSED SERIOUS OPERATIONAL PROBLEMS AT THE STATION DURING THE MILLER AND BEDFORD YEARS. The line's significance was underscored when the car ferry Ann Arbor *No. 3* arrived in the harbor on the morning of September 29, 1908, its captain promptly notifying Keeper Morency of the Frankfort Life-Saving Station that a vessel had sprung a leak and capsized about ten miles out from Point Betsie. Bedford recounted that Morency had "...telephoned over to Harmon's store (a local grocery which supplied the station), asking the clerks to notify us that a crew of 6 men was in the yawl boat coming a shore and to keep a lookout for them." As Bedford continued in the log, "The message we received was that their was a wreck 10 miles from Point Betsie. And I sent Surfman No. 1 north to see if he could locate it and the rest of the crew was at the Station. We knew nothing of the crew in the yawl until after they had landed and Keeper Morency came up the beach with a team looking for them." Bedford promptly pointed out, "If we had been connected by telephone with the Frankfort station we would have been there to help them a shore. I took part of the crew from the Station and found the sailors in a farm house all well. We pulled the yawl boat out of the surf on the beach. The schooner drifted a shore 2 and 1/2 miles south of the Station at 5 p.m.; it was the Schooner Ida…loaded with hardwood lumber."

❧

IN ADDITION TO THE ADMINISTRATIVE CHANGES BEDFORD AND POINT BETSIE WOULD EVENTUALLY EXPERIENCE, HE WOULD ALSO ENCOUNTER CHANGES IN THE LAKE MICHIGAN FLEET THAT WOULD IMPACT UPON HIS STATION AND ITS SERVICES. When Bedford had entered the Life-Saving Service, schooners were seen everywhere on the Lakes and regularly transited the Manitou Passage. Throughout his career, he saw the aging fleet of tall ships fading from the scene, their cargoes being borne by swifter steamers. On a late August day in his first year in command at the Point, he recorded thirty-three vessels passing, twenty-three of them steamers, seven of them tugs, and just three schooners. The trend was unmistakable; as he served there, he could also see the early steamers— the "propellers"—gradually giving way to even larger, more powerful vessels built to maximize the efficiency of Great Lakes shipping.

The already noted increasing capacities and seaworthiness of the "laker" fleet gradually led to some reduction in the number of cargo ships sailing along these shores. But at the same time, the lifesavers found themselves called upon to protect crews of fish tugs, barges and other smaller commercial craft, as well as yachts and other pleasure craft whose gasoline engines weren't especially reliable. Additionally, he experienced innovations in the rescue fleet, as motorized boats that could cover larger areas of open water emerged as the craft of choice for potentially dangerous search-and-rescue operations. In that regard, the Lake Carriers' Association advised its members in 1909 that the Life-Saving Service had determined power boats to be "so indispensable" that they were being introduced as quickly as possible at all stations where they could be used effectively. The organization's annual report stressed, "Official reports show that in the performance of wreck duty in the worst of weather they have repeatedly accomplished hazardous enterprises, taking crews far beyond the former limits of their field of work. In no instance has it been shown that they have failed to withstand the severest test."

❧

NOW AND THEN THE "DAILY GRIND" AT POINT BETSIE WOULD BE RELIEVED BY AN UNUSUAL DEVELOPMENT. One such memorable event occurred in early December, 1914, when a canoe bearing two men landed on the beach, the paddlers saying they had come from Montreal, Canada, and were heading to Chicago. These extraordinarily ambitious canoeists said their ultimate destination, once they cleared Lake Michigan, was the Panama Canal! "Better you than me," perhaps the crewmen thought, since the modern voyageurs faced more than two hundred miles of paddling down Lake Michigan amidst winter winds and surf upon them, not to speak of the subsequent ocean journey the intrepid pair was anticipating!

Given the hazards that came with work on Lake Michigan, on some days the lifesavers' activities were more somber. That was doubtless the case just after Christmas, 1908, when, Bedford reported that a local gasoline fish boat, the *Rhine*, had foundered near the Frankfort piers with the loss of four men, including its master. The men spent several days scanning the shore and nearby waters for bodies; one was found a mile north of the station and another was recovered by Lightkeeper Sheridan. One more body from this sinking was found weeks later, miles up the shore.

One night about a month later, when the crew was presumably tired from the task of cutting wood for the station's use, the watchman reported at 11:40 p.m. that he had spotted, southwest of Point Betsie, a boat shining a torch. Bedford recorded, "We launched the Beebe-McClellan surfboat and went to her. It was the gasoline yacht *Willow H.* and her engine was broken and was 2 and ½ miles from the Station and her owner said he wanted a tug to tow him to Frankfort." Bedford continued, "We rowed ashore and sent a man to Frankfort on foot after the tug. The surfboat returned to the launch and we towed her into shoal water and let go of our anchor and waited for the tug, who towed the same to Frankfort. We returned to the Station at 2:45 a.m." As required for the Life-Saving Service's tally of the value of rescued vessels, Bedford recorded the value of the rescued boat as eight hundred dollars.

By this time the Great Lakes commercial fleet was nearly fully converted from wind power to steam propulsion; on August 24, 1909, for example, the station's count of passing vessels included twenty-four steamers and three tugs, but just a single schooner. Certainly, however, the few remaining sailing ships were of great interest to seamen and other coastal observers. And as these impressive old vessels acquired the scars of age, they and the big storms with which they had to contend were likely to compel surfmen to test their skills.

Any vessel, of course, could find itself in serious difficulty. On one summer day when the telephone connection to the station was functioning, Bedford recorded that after the crew had completed surfboat drill, the station had received a call that a steamer was aground on a reef at the mouth of the Platte River, about ten miles north. "We arrived at 11 a.m. and run a kedge anchor for them and tried to heave her off and could not. The tug *E.D. Holton* came and the Frankfort Life-Saving crew. We run a towline to the tug and then we helped to throw overboard one hundred thousand [feet] of lumber and 60 thousand shingles before the boat got off…" Recognizing that his journal would receive the customarily careful scrutiny, Bedford also explained that the lookout dial had not been marked for twelve hours that day on account of the crew's attending to the wreck.

One duty that keepers at both lighthouses and lifesaving stations faced, each to his own superior officers, was managing their facilities' supply inventory. As already noted, this meant that arriving items had to be accounted for in detail and worn-out ones could only be disposed of according to regulations and with proper recording. Thus, on June 14, 1910, the 12th district superintendent informed Keeper Bedford that the following articles at his station were "condemned" and should be disposed of: "2 soup bowls, 1 whitewash brush, 2 paint brushes, 1 galvanized bucket, 1 bull's eye and strop, 1 signal book, 1 paper bucket, 4 cups, 1 Seth Thomas clock, 1 dipper, 3 saw files, 8 flat files, 1 chopping knife, 8 table knives, 8 table forks, 1 force pump, 2 china plates, 2 tin plates, 1 tin pan, 5 saucers, 1 flour sieve, 4 table spoons, 16 tea spoons, 1 steamer, 1 shovel, 2 padlocks, 1 oilcloth table cover, 2 time detector cases, 1 tin signal case, 1 tumbler, 2 mop sticks, 2 wheel barrows, all broken or worn out and all to be destroyed; 18 blankets, worn out, to be sold for not less than 25 cents a pair."[5]

The litany didn't stop there, but continued: "1 glass, binocular marine, to be forwarded to the Inspector of Life-Saving Stations, 379 Washington St., New York City, by the most feasible and economical means; 100 feet hose, worn out, to be used for miscellaneous station purposes; 12 mattresses, 10 pillows, worn out, covers to be used for cleaning rags, contents burned; 2 pillow covers, 8 pillow cases, 9 sheets, and 4 yards toweling, worn out, to be used for cleaning rags." All these items were to be "expended on your next inventory as condemned," Superintendent Morton wrote of this thorough spring house-cleaning.

On another occasion several years later, Bedford was ordered to dispose of some household items that a board of survey had determined should be condemned. A kitchen chair was to be used for firewood, but most items, including one spittoon, were simply to be destroyed. There were other sorts of regulations, too, such as an order President Woodrow Wilson issued in the fall of 1913, presumably for health reasons, prohibiting the use of towels by more than one person in all public buildings of the United States.

In August of 1911, Bedford was advised by his superintendent that "Charles Fairchild, Frankfort, Mich., having purchased the condemned Monomoy model boat at your station, I would thank you to turn it over to him when he calls for it. No outfit is to go with the boat."[6] A replacement craft would soon arrive; that December, Bedford recorded receipt of a Beebe-McLellan surfboat, oars, sails and manila line. His station being closed for the season by that time, Bedford called upon the Frankfort harbor crew to help him unload the boat, tow it to Point Betsie, and put it in the boathouse. The old boat, actually named the "Monomoy" for its design, apparently was later owned by a man who used her to ferry passengers to resorts and other destinations around nearby Crystal Lake.

On September 6, 1912, Bedford said he had cancelled the customary Friday resuscitation drill and taken part of his crew to Frankfort to obtain lumber and other construction materials for enlarging the boathouse so that it would accommodate a new power surfboat. This was not a small job. His purchase included thirty-five two-by-sixes, each ten feet long, and thirty two-by-sixes, sixteen feet long; forty fourteen-foot two-by-fours, thirty-two one-by-twelves, each sixteen feet long, and thirty one-by-fours of the same length. Also, more than fifteen hundred feet of two-inch maple flooring. The Keeper had to call upon his counterpart at the Frankfort Life-Saving Station to tow the materials to Point Betsie because his own station's power boat wouldn't run.

This assistance proved to be just the first of the day's adventures. Late that morning, the man in the lookout told the No. 1 that he saw a small "gasoline boat" a mile and a half south of the station, near shore, and that the boat's occupant had sought assistance by hoisting a distress flag. The crew took a towline to the boat and pulled it to the station and onto the shore. The rescued boater turned out to be their neighbor, the first assistant lightkeeper!

Such references in the station logs suggest that Bedford and Sheridan had a good working relationship despite the historic rivalry between their respective agencies. Each had his own bureaucracy with which to deal but also a job to do, and each found himself occasionally reaching out to his neighbor for assistance.

The following year, Bedford was instructed to "...sell to the best advantage what it will bring, 1 boat wagon, old style, for Long Branch boat, recently condemned at your Station. Try to get as much as possible for it and send the money here. Attend to this at once," the district superintendent ordered.[7]

The 1910 U.S. Census records that Bedford, then fifty-six, had a full crew on hand; six surfmen, the oldest of whom was fifty, were recorded then as "boarders" with the Captain and Anna, taking meals with the couple. One day that fall, the crew spotted a gasoline launch coming from the north but drifting toward shore. The men responded, eventually finding the craft against the beach, with a man, his wife and their two children aboard. "We took them to the station and gave them shelter for the night and gave them their breakfast," he recorded, adding that the boat was worth three hundred dollars.

❧

Keeper Bedford and crew, motorized boat on right.
Courtesy of Claudia Lewis

WITHIN THE LIGHTHOUSE'S OWN BUREAUCRACY, THE CENTURY'S SECOND DECADE OPENED WITH A MAJOR ADMINISTRATIVE CHANGE. The Lighthouse Board ceased to exist, being succeeded on July 1, 1910, by a Bureau of Lighthouses in the Department of Commerce, and headed by a commissioner in whom were vested all the powers of the predecessor authority. Selected by the president of the United States, the initial appointment went to Mr. George R. Putnam, who would prove to be an outstanding, long-serving choice. Other key appointive positions were a deputy commissioner, a chief constructing engineer and a superintendent of naval construction signifying lighthouses' major importance to business, the department's official seal featured a massive light tower and beam.

An important task for the agency's new leadership team was reorganizing the nation's coasts and navigable rivers into nineteen districts, each to be headed by a lighthouse inspector. This was a civilian function; with rare exceptions, only for a transitional period of three years could the president assign military officers in lieu of appointing civilians as lighthouse inspectors. The goal was to place the nation's entire lighthouse operations under civilian leadership. As characterized by the Lake Carriers' Association, "This reorganization will doubtless secure a more direct, simple and economical method of administration, but let us hope that it will be kept free from political influence and that these important offices will not be used to pay political debts."[8]

This point in time also marks a significant technological innovation at lighthouses, the introduction of the incandescent oil vapor system. In the first half of 1910, oil vapor lamps replaced traditional oil lamps at a number of Great Lakes lights, including Grand Traverse Light, South Manitou Island, Big Sable Light and Cana Island, across Lake Michigan. The new system was regarded as far superior to the predecessor lamps, and even comparable in effectiveness to electricity and acetylene gas systems that were starting to be installed at about the same time.

Both to enhance lights' power and achieve greater operating efficiency, the Lighthouse Bureau was determined to install the improved system elsewhere as it became available. That program would soon reach Point Betsie; on October 1, 1913, the candle power of its light was raised to 55,000 by use of the incandescent oil vapor system.[9]

&

THE VETERAN PHILIP SHERIDAN REMAINED IN CHARGE AT POINT BETSIE LIGHTHOUSE AS THE NEW CENTURY BEGAN. His first assistant was twenty-nine-year-old Raymond Grant; he and his wife Mildred were there for about eight years. Frederick W. Ferguson, who had held the second assistant position for a brief time, was being promoted; in 1910, he turned the second assistant slot over to Howard A. Kimball, who held that job for about six years before moving on to the pier light at Michigan City, Indiana, a station which Sheridan himself would ultimately join.

Another assistant to Sheridan at this time was Fred Bennett, who came to Point Betsie from adjacent Leelanau County early in that decade. Bennett worked at the light until May, 1916, when he, his wife Mary and their large family moved to Kenosha, Wisconsin, where he assisted at its pier light. While the Bennetts lived at Point Betsie, their daughter Mary gave birth to a son at the lighthouse's quarters on February 22, 1914, George Washington's birthday.

A novel event occurred the next year in the wee hours of a morning when the lookout called Bedford to alert him that a sailboat some eight miles south of the station had hoisted a distress signal. The Keeper recorded, "We launched the Monomoy boat and went to them. And I asked them what we could do for them. They said their spar was broken and they wanted to be towed a shore. We towed them to the Station and put a new spar in for them…they got away from the Station at 11:30 a.m." Bedford continued, "The boat was the English life boat that was bought from the government from Frankfort Life Saving Station and was bound to Beaver Island." Even then, "buyer beware" apparently was to be kept in mind when purchasing surplus items!

&

WEATHER DURING THE WINTER OF 1912 POSED CHALLENGES FOR THE POINT BETSIE CREWS, ESPECIALLY AT THE LIGHT STATION WHERE SOME NEW EQUIPMENT WAS BEING INSTALLED. On February 12 at 3 a.m., the thermometer read twenty-two degrees below zero, the low for the year. Amidst the frightfully cold temperatures whose "bite" was intensified by winds off Lake Michigan, workers were replacing the aged, locomotive-type steam whistles with new fog signaling equipment that could be blasted much more quickly when fog arose on the lake. The Lighthouse Bureau hoped to have more melodic ten-inch chime whistles—whistles with several openings that were presumably powered by diesel-driven air compressors linked to five storage tanks—in operation for the start of that year's navigation season.[10]

Headquarters' impatience over what senior administrators apparently thought was undue delay of this project prompted a letter from the district to the commissioner of lighthouses to clarify the situation: "Point Betsie is about six miles from the nearest freight depot, no roads lead to Point Betsie and present winter conditions make hauling impractical unless at great expense; in the lake off Point Betsie ice is 20 or more inches thick; the steam plant will have to be moved out of [the] building and temporarily operated while [the] air system is being installed, the living conditions for workmen would be too severe during the winter with a five-mile walk to [the] nearest point of supply." Furthermore, if Mother Nature alone weren't enough of an explanation, the district pointed to a more conventional problem: "The air tanks for the system have not been delivered."[11]

WINTER 1912

Courtesy of Michigan Maritime Museum

The conversion turned into a major construction project that consumed much of the year. The fog signal building's walls had to be removed in order to get the new engines inside, then the building had to be repaired. After the old apparatus had been removed from the building its concrete floor had to be renewed. Additional footings were needed to support the new machinery, and the fog signal well had to be deepened by ten feet to secure adequate water flow at all times; an old water tank was also installed and piped by gravity and pumps to the engine cylinders and air compressors for cooling purposes. Because the new engines would require more oil, provision for its storage had to be made, and the existing coal bins needed to be rearranged so that they would also support the heating system. The "bottom line" was that the full cost was exceeding the estimated total of $5896.88. Part of the over-run was due to the fact that one old boiler and signal had to be temporarily re-installed in a shed that the workers put up next to the fog signal building so a whistle would be available throughout the shipping season, while the new works were being assembled.

Indications are that the new signal was operational by the middle of October. When fog arose, the chime whistle, powered by compressed air, sounded two five-second blasts every sixty seconds, one followed by ten seconds of silence, and the next by forty seconds. While Washington was soon assured that all was in order, there was still considerable work to be done at the site. Not until the spring of 1915 were funds approved for tearing down the temporary building as well as an old woodshed, which a new three-section shed [which still stands] would replace, and for relocating privies, putting a new shingle roof on the dwelling, repairing and adding to concrete walkways, installing a storm sash at the keeper's dwelling, and other repairs.

Inside Point Betsie's fog signal building.
Courtesy of Michigan Maritime Museum

❧

"OH, NO!" On October 30, 1914, the district lighthouse inspector wrote the commissioner to request authority for an additional position of "temporary laborer" at Point Betsie Light Station for three months, and indicated that an extension for three additional months would likely be required.[12] The reason for this request, the officer explained, was that Keeper Phil Sheridan had fallen while whitewashing the lighthouse tower on October 14, 1914, breaking both his legs! The "temp's" compensation was not to exceed an annual rate of four hundred and eighty dollars, or forty dollars per month, said to be the minimum amount for which a laborer could be obtained in this district. Reflecting on Sheridan's nineteen years of diligent work since entering the Lighthouse Service, as well as the fact that he had been seriously injured on the job, the inspector urged that the government—not Sheridan himself—should pay the substitute's wages. This was an uncommonly generous step, as keepers who were injured on the job typically received no aid, nor were they entitled to retirement benefits until the adoption of a reform measure several years later.

CHAPTER NINE

LIFESAVING'S TRANSITIONAL
YEARS AT POINT BETSIE

Federal policy-makers reached out to isolated Point Betsie and all other lifesaving stations on January 29, 1915, with the announcement, "The official name of the Service is now the 'United States Coast Guard'."[1] Known far and wide for its vital accomplishments throughout nearly five decades, the extraordinary U.S. Life-Saving Service was relegated to history.

Point Betsie's Edwin Bedford officially received a warrant officer's appointment in the new agency but continued to be addressed with the legendary title of "Keeper" as well as Captain. Surfmen were now enlisted men with station's No. 1 being a petty officer. Bedford and his colleagues would be leading their respective stations at the pleasure of the secretary of the treasury. Two weeks later, a notary public attested to Bedford's having taken the oath of office, which began with a promise to "use my best endeavors to prevent and detect frauds against the laws of the United States imposing duties upon imports" (a keeper's duty as a Coast Guard officer), and closed with the same promises intoned by American presidents at their inaugurations.

District officers advised Bedford and other keepers, "All official telegrams and correspondence will in the future be addressed Coast Guard Station, or Superintendent, together with name of station and town. (Nothing personal was to be used in the address; this was a new, more military-like entity whose bureaucratic character was quickly established.) You will officially notify the postal and telegraph authorities in your city in accordance with the foregoing, so that official correspondence and dispatches will reach you without delay."

Subsequently, there came a letter to Captain Bedford telling him that the station's name was to be changed to the "United States Coast Guard Station" and that this terminology should be placed not only on the station building, but on its boats. The superintendent instructed Bedford, "Materials on hand will be used for this purpose and no expense should be incurred in making this change."[2] Accustomed to the Life-Saving Service command's "sharp pencils," Bedford would have presumed nothing else.

In another directive, Bedford was told how to activate his station for the coming season. Among the tasks were those his crewmen were to perform on the station's boats: "All the boats should be scraped and varnished and painted as may be necessary to have the boats in the best possible condition. The engine compartment of your power Surfboat should be thoroughly cleaned and painted, using white lead and zinc paint to do the work. Clean out the boat under deck, and paint as far as possible, using a light gray color. Scrape and <u>oil</u> all oars and boat hooks. This to include all spare oars fit for use. Oars not fit for use have ready for survey. Scrape and varnish all spars, stretchers and other boat gear that comes under brightwood work."[3]

Bedford might not have been too surprised when, two months after the start of the Coast Guard's creation, all personnel in charge of stations or vessels were informed that "hereafter any person of the Coast Guard below the rank of warrant officer will be required to furnish his own bedding." And one more thing: "The top cover of beds of the Coast Guard will be of plain white material."[4]

That's <u>his</u> own bedding, mind you. In these early times the Coast Guard was far from gender-blind. Instructions also were issued on September 7, 1915, not only that the keeper was to answer all telephone calls when he was present or, in his absence, that a surfman was to take all calls, but that any woman who was allowed to reside at the station was not permitted to answer the telephone except when the entire crew was absent. As in the military, a specific pattern was to be followed to ensure clarity and accountability. Keepers were to answer, "Coast Guard Station, keeper speaking;" surfmen were to say, "Coast Guard Station, Surfman (followed not by name, but by his crew position number) speaking." Presumably, it was feared that the use of names could invite confusion or erode accountability.

❧

NOW AND THEN, SOME EVENT OFFERED RELIEF FROM THE STATION'S ROUTINES. One day in August, 1915, the steamer *J.H. Crouse,* was passing; she blew four whistles, alerting the crew to a need for assistance. Bedford and his men promptly launched their power surfboat and ran out to her, only to learn that her captain had an improbable request. He had a package that he wanted to mail to a resident of the nearby village of Empire, and he wanted the recipient to be advised by phone that the package was en route. "Anything to oblige," the Keeper likely replied. On another day that summer, Bedford wrote that "...a woman weighing about 200 pounds came over the sand hills to the station and on account of the heat and a weak heart had a bad spell and was not able to return. We took the boat and landed her 2 miles south of the station where she could get back to camp, for which she thanked us very kindly for it."

But most of the time, there presumably was little escape for the crew from the daily dose of duties, their performance being recorded and evaluated by Bedford and the superior officers to whom he was responsible for all station operations. A March 28, 1917, letter to Bedford from the District Superintendent Lofberg offers yet another example of the continued attention to details that marked both the Coast Guard and its predecessor. Referring to a station log that had been transmitted to the district office in Grand Haven for review, Lofberg observed that the specific time that crewmen left the station on liberty was recorded as the last entry in the 8 a.m. to 4 p.m. watch. "This is incorrect," he advised, "for if a man leaves the station at 8 a.m. it should be so entered in the log, and anything recorded in the log as having occurred after that hour, should therefore be entered in the regular order of time as per paragraph 7(d) in the instructions for keeping the log (on fly page of the log book), that is anything occurring at 8 a.m. should be entered in the log before an entry of something that occurred at 8:20 a.m., etc."

Lofberg apparently had discovered that Point Betsie's procedure in this regard was not unique, for on May 11 he issued instructions to all keepers in the 11th District that logs be kept "in regular order of time." A mid-level officer in the order of command, Lofberg was making sure that reports from his stations were submitted in correct form. Otherwise, he noted, "considerable unnecessary work is experienced by this office in getting the transcripts in proper shape before submitting them to Headquarters."

Effective September 1, 1915, the Coast Guard also imposed new reporting forms. Bedford would enter disciplinary matters (most often, failure to mark a dial) in red pencil. Weather reporting requirements also seem to have become more rigorous, with station conditions classified and reported every few hours of the day.

◆

IT WOULD BE HARD TO OVERSTATE THE RIGOROUSNESS OF THE COAST GUARD'S RECORD-KEEPING REQUIREMENTS. The instruction page at the beginning of a logbook started off simply enough, mandating that "The Keeper, or surfman in charge, shall write the log daily, and shall make all entries as soon as possible after the occurrences to which they relate happened. Should any change or addition be made in the log after the keeper, or surfman in charge, has signed it, or after a period of twenty-four hours has elapsed since the incident to which such change or addition refers took place, there also shall be entered a note showing the day and hour of the day that such change or addition was made. No erasures shall be made. A single line shall be drawn through any part of the log it is desired to change." The books were to be retained at the station as its official record and the keeper was instructed to "...be particular to see that they are stored in a safe place and carefully preserved."

Coast Guard logs of this period consisted of two side-by-side, legal-length pages covering each day's activities at and about the station. The general instructions required the keeper to "...enter in the log daily the required data on the left-hand page concerning the state of the weather, surf, vessels sighted, lookouts and patrols stood, absences, substitutes, vessels boarded and reported, assistance rendered, lives saved, cases of resuscitation, and drills held." To be written in "civil time", meaning ordinary, non-military time, the entries were to be made in ink or with indelible pencil, and the day's events were to be recorded in plain language in the order in which they occurred—not within a single twenty-four hour watch, but within each of three periods: from midnight to 8 a.m., from 8 a.m. to 4 p.m., and from 4 p.m. to midnight.

Following that general instruction, the requirements became more complex. A "SYNOPSIS OF ENTRIES THAT ARE TO BE MADE IN THE LOG BOOK" next included seventy-five specific items, seemingly embracing every event that could have occurred at or within sight of a Coast Guard station. The instruction page closed with a twelve-category scheme for reporting wind conditions, from calm air to hurricane blasts, and eighteen symbols for recording general weather conditions and seven more for classifying the state of the surf. There could be no mistaking the significance of this task; log-keeping was a serious practice, and it was a daily ritual for the officer-in-charge.

Like its famed predecessor, the Coast Guard had a "nose" for spotting public relations opportunities. Keepers were advised by Superintendent Lofberg in August, 1917, that "...at stations located in the vicinity of sea-side resorts where there are visitors, the drills for restoring the apparently drowned be held out of doors, on the station premises, in suitable weather during the summer season, in order that they may be witnessed by spectators in the interest of public information and instruction." Keepers or others in charge of the drills were to "...courteously answer such inquiries regarding the drills as may be made of them...."

Point Betsie crews generally followed this routine on weekends during the summer season, when the station and adjacent lighthouse were popular attractions. For decades, resorters and local residents came on foot, by boat and eventually in automobiles to watch the drills, climb the lighthouse tower, and see the fog signal and other apparatus.

With the new agency's leaders came redefined regulations and enforcement mechanisms. In the fall of 1915, the Coast Guard Commandant issued a "Circular Letter" to the keepers, instructing them to advise potential Coast Guard applicants that they should not pursue required physical examinations if they have obvious physical defects: have more than three teeth missing that had not been replaced or capped, weighed less than one hundred thirty-five pounds or more than two hundred and five pounds, were less than five feet, four inches tall; spoke with a stammer; apparently lacked good vision, or were color-blind. They were also to be advised to take a bath on the day of examination!

On September 16, 1915, Bedford and the other district keepers were informed of the punishments they were to impose on crewmen committing specific offenses. For a crewman's first failure to mark the dial of the lookout clock during the night, he was to be confined to the station's premises for eight days, losing one precious liberty day; a second such offense would add five hours of duty time to the above punishment.

Surfman Michael J. Barr must have pushed the Captain Bedford's patience to the limit two years later, but because his services were otherwise valued, he nonetheless managed to survive as a crewman. A November 12, 1917, letter from the District instructed Bedford that he was to impose a punishment of eighteen days' quarantine, including two liberty days, on Barr for having failed to mark his watch on three occasions. The directive added, "This man will also be informed that a like neglect of duty in the future will not be so leniently dealt with."[5]

A soiled or ragged uniform would lead to four hours of extra duty. The extra hours of duty were to be imposed at times when other members of the crew were enjoying leisure time. All punishments were to be recorded in the station's "conduct book" and reported to the district superintendent's office.

Bedford dutifully implemented all such regulations, which were intended to assist the officer-in-charge of a station to run a "tight ship." A letter from District Superintendent Lofberg, dated March 30, 1916, referred to the Captain's report that Surfman Millgard had failed to properly mark the dial on the lookout clock. It being Millgard's first offense, Bedford was told to quarantine him for eight days, including one liberty day. As Lofberg explained, "As the use of the time clock is the only method by which this office can tell that the men are properly attending to their duties, no excuse, unless of grave character, will be accepted."[6]

Interestingly, this matter didn't end there. The Superintendent instructed Bedford to have Surfman Millgard submit a notarized statement as to whether he was, or was not, asleep at one a.m. A subsequent letter indicates that Millgard insisted that he had not been asleep during his watch; with that testimony, and whatever comments Bedford had made on the matter, Lofberg confirmed that the appropriate penalty would be eight days of quarantine, including loss of an off-duty day.

Even that didn't conclude the issue. An April 29, 1916, letter from District Superintendent Lofberg referred to a "telephonic" conversation with Surfman Millgard regarding the illness of the latter's wife. Bedford was told to postpone the punishment and that further action would reflect "...the surfman's attention to his lookout duty in the future." It can be presumed that Surfman Millgard's services were usually satisfactory for at the end of the year, his request for a leave of absence during the inactive season was approved along with those of his six colleagues; they all could return the next season. Captain Bedford's crews, it seems, were well regarded by superior officers who respected his station leadership.

⤸

SURFMAN MILLGARD MUST HAVE BEEN ONE OF THOSE PEOPLE WHOM TROUBLE SEEMS TO FOLLOW AROUND. Bedford received a letter in March, 1917, from Superintendent Lofberg, replying to the Keeper's having reported that this surfman had failed to mark the dial during that year's enlistment. Because this transgression had occurred at the time of a watch change, Lofberg said no punishment was due for that instance. But, he added, "It is noticed that Surfman Millgard's record shows several failures to mark the dial during his last enlistment, and it is suggested that you direct him to be more careful in the future regarding the matter of properly marking the dials when on watch duty."

But that wasn't the only crisis Millgard would face. That October, Lofberg advised Bedford that two of his men, No. 1 Surfman Hendricksen and Surfman Bernier, would not be discharged immediately for failure to qualify as good swimmers, because of their long service. Rather, they were to be required to practice at every favorable opportunity in order to qualify for tests that would be held the following summer. Millgard and Surfman Wallis, on the other hand, were only to be allowed to re-enlist with the understanding that "...if they fail to qualify next summer in the tests in which they failed this summer they will then be discharged for inaptitude." Millgard's days at Point Betsie were numbered; a Lofberg letter on December 19, 1917, states that Surfman Millgard would be ordinarily discharged at year's end.[7]

As motor boating became subject to increased government regulation, Keeper Bedford found his station had new duties, among them that his crew was to assist the Chicago-based Supervisor of Anchorages in enforcing boating law in the vicinity of

Point Betsie. He was authorized to use his boats and personnel for this task, but it was not to interfere with the station's regular duties. Included in this task was an order directing Bedford to report to the Frankfort Coast Guard Station, by telephone, all motor boats, sail boats and other vessels passing the station after sunset without lights.

In November, 1915, Bedford received a letter from Superintendent Lofberg commenting on the "Report of Inspection" that an assistant inspector had filed regarding Point Betsie Station. It seems that there were no lifelines on the station's surfboats. Bedford had said that he had no cordage for this feature. The roping subsequently being supplied, Lofberg ordered him to install lifelines at once and to report when the job had been completed.

The year's "active" season was to close at midnight on Christmas Day. Bedford was instructed that "...great care should be taken to see that the engine of the power surfboat at your station is thoroughly drained and taken care of during freezing weather."

✎

THIS "INACTIVE SEASON" WAS TO BE JUST TWO AND ONE-HALF MONTHS LONG. Bedford received notice to reopen the station on March 15, 1916, with the customary seven surfmen. They faced the usual initial tasks, including putting the boats into the best possible condition. A circular dated March 29, 1916, from the Grand Haven office instructed him that any outside painting ought to be completed before flies would interfere with proper performance of this maintenance duty.

At this time the Point Betsie lifesavers had three rescue craft, likely the station's largest fleet ever. These were described as a twenty-five-foot Beebe-McLellan motor-powered lifeboat and two sail and oar-powered surfboats, one known as a twenty-five-foot Beebe and the other a twenty-six-foot Beebe-McLellan. Maintaining all of them in first-class shape and keeping up the crew's skill levels in operating each one, was vital to the crew's own well-being and that of those aboard any stricken vessel. Boat drills were promptly resumed in the spring, the Captain reporting that he occasionally switched places with his No. 1 so that this surfman gained experience at the helm. In the event of an accident involving the Keeper's loss or injury, the crew's survival might depend upon the No. 1's proficiency on the steering oar.

Records show that beach drills were expanded that spring to include semaphore signaling, and each month beach apparatus drills were conducted at night so that the crew could perform well in darkness.

Original U.S. Life-Saving/Coast Guard Station at Point Betsie.
Courtesy of Michigan Maritime Museum

MAJOR NEWS REACHED CAPTAIN BEDFORD IN APRIL, 1916, from Superintendent Lofberg, who reported that a new station building was to be erected at Point Betsie. The classic structure of mid-1870s "stick" design, by Treasury Department architect Francis W. Chandler, pictured above, was to be replaced by a handsome "Chatham" building drawn by Victor Mendleheff, who was destined to become the Coast Guard's longest-serving and most productive architect.

On May 5, Bedford recorded receipt of six complete sets of plans, along with advertisements and other forms relating to contracting for the construction of the new building. Instructed to deliver them to "any reputable contractor" who wanted to examine them, he noted giving them to Frankfort builders Charles Collier, Charles Chilsen and J.W. Park; the latter two declined to bid, Park saying he did not have sufficient funds to undertake the project. The job was soon awarded to the firm of Nelson and Mysen of Muskegon, about 125 miles south of Point Betsie; with the site being staked and excavated by mid-summer, construction was soon underway under the supervision of Coast Guard Field Assistant D.C. Wickham.

Several other notable events were to occur that year, Captain Bedford's final fall season at the station. He recorded that there had been no night watch kept on October 29 because "all hands was working on wreck." At 6:30 p.m. the man on watch in the lookout had observed a gasoline fish boat ashore a half mile south of the station. The Keeper and crew went to find out if assistance was needed. He reported, "The captain of the boat wanted us to run a anchor for him…we launched the Beebe McLellan Power Surfboat and went to him [but] on account of the fish boat being so close on the shore and Rough Sea we could not do anything with our Power Surfboat. We went and got the Beebe McLellan Surfboat and run the anchor out for him and he could not haul himself off." Captain Bedford recorded that he then phoned to Frankfort for a tugboat; the Frankfort Coast Guard crew accompanied it to the site in their power boat, and the two crews worked together on the rescue. Bedford's men ran three lines from the fish tug to the tugboat before midnight, all of which parted during their efforts. They also broke one twelve-foot oar, Bedford reported in his log.

Like the military, the Coast Guard tended to operate "by the numbers." Thus, that fall, the district informed its keepers that official communications from the stations should no longer bear the name of the station. Only the station's number, "not its name which has been abolished," was to be entered on logs or other official papers. Thereafter, the Point Betsie Coast Guard Station was thus to be known as No. 262; the neighboring station at Frankfort harbor was No. 276; those names were to be featured on repainted station signs.

In 1916, the Coast Guard required station keepers and crews to be vaccinated for smallpox. A month before the station closed at year's end, several Point Betsie surfmen had to be vaccinated by Dr. C.P. Doyle two or three times to acquire the needed protection. Vaccinations for both smallpox and typhoid raised issues for Bedford and his crew. He reported that some of his men believed themselves too old for vaccination and the district superintendent, despite insisting that regulations did not provide exceptions on account of age, said he would seek clarification of the requirements from Washington. No relief seems to have been obtained.

Winter interrupted the new station's construction and the work was not resumed until mid-March, 1917. Meanwhile, Keeper Bedford put up posters soliciting local bids for window shades in the new station. His crew was busy in the spring, repairing the fence around the station boundaries and doing the grading around the building. The customary supplies were needed to sustain operations, and it was Bedford's job to procure many of them. He received posters advertising an opportunity for local businesses to provide Point Betsie Station with kerosene. He was to post the notices conspicuously, then to take them down at 2 o'clock on July 3rd, recording on the back side where the posters had been displayed and return them to the district office, along with any bids that had been received. The goal was to obtain three bids, the lowest of which was almost certain to be accepted.

In June, Bedford had to send Surfman Sandow to the town doctor to have his foot examined; having been run over by the boat wagon, Dr. Doyle said he would have to keep off his feet for several days. Another surfman was given five days of emergency leave time on account of his brother's drowning; a month and a half later the district superintendent ordered that same surfman to be placed under eighteen days' quarantine, including two days of liberty, for failing on two nights to properly record his lookout watch.

Captain Bedford and men at new station.
Courtesy of Claudia Lewis

Finally, Captain Bedford was officially notified on October 29, 1917, that "the building has been completed and accepted by Headquarters, and should therefore be occupied by the crew as early as possible." The old and new stations, each adorned with a distinctive cupola, briefly stood side-by-side. Bedford was instructed that when the old structure was torn down, its wood was to be sorted and piled neatly in anticipation of being re-used the following summer for a new boat building.[8]

View of new and old rescue stations from southwest.
Courtesy of Claudia Lewis

View of new and old stations from northwest.
Courtesy of Claudia Lewis

A month later, the crew demolished the old station and Bedford obtained permission to relocate the station's tall flagpole away from the new buildings. At year's end, Point Betsie Station was ordered closed until spring. The Keeper and a small crew, the No. 1 and one other surfman, were to remain at the station during the inactive period, caring for the building and equipment and monitoring coastal vessels operating on Lake Michigan when weather allowed.

New Coast Guard Station No. 276 and the Point Betsie crew the building and equipment and monitoring coastal vessels operating on Lake Michigan when weather allowed.
Courtesy of Claudia Lewis

Very soon thereafter, the Keeper was instructed to reopen the station on March 11, 1918, with his No. 1 and seven other surfmen, this complement being one man larger than normal because Bedford was to be retiring soon. Meanwhile, the district advised him that speaking tubes were to be installed in the new station to facilitate communication between the lookout atop the building and the first-floor messroom. The instructions were characteristically precise: "The tubing to be of tin 1" diameter, in 5-foot lengths; turns to be made with 1" diameter tin elbows; mouth pieces to be porcelain with whistle. The tube is made to be put together like conductor pipe and the joints to be soldered with rosin core flux solder wire." The lines were to be run "by the most practicable route," the work to be performed by the station's crew, with the assistance of the supervisor of telephone lines.[9] (This early "intercom" is still in place in the now privately owned historic home.)

Speaking tube in Coast Guard lookout, with Point Betsie Lighthouse in background.
Photo by author

∽

SOON THEREAFTER, THE NOTABLE BEDFORD ERA AT POINT BETSIE PASSED INTO HISTORY. On March 12, 1918, he advised the Coast Guard command, under the administration of the Navy Department during World War I, that his retirement address would be Frankfort, Michigan. He soon received a voucher for sixty dollars and twenty-one cents, reflecting his service during the month up to the date of his retirement, with just over nine dollars having been deducted from his gross pay to cover an insurance premium.

The curtain on his distinguished career came down on March 17. An initial entry in that day's account records his having granted five days' emergency leave to a surfman whose mother had died, then the log simply states, "Edwin E. Bedford Keeper Station No. 262 turned over all of the Public property temporarily to Ludwig Hendricksen Surfman No. 1 and retired at 12 midnight."

Like his distinguished great predecessor and mentor, Captain Miller, Captain Bedford enjoyed many years in Frankfort following his retirement. He had the financial advantage of the federal pension benefit which was denied Miller and others who had put in their years of service at an earlier time. As survivors of the lifesavers' glory years on the Great Lakes, both of them were highly respected in their community. People loved to visit with them about the "good old days" when the schooners and early steamships were so often in sight, and patrols nightly trudged along the beach north and south of Point Betsie as its piercing beam swept across the vast Lake Michigan darkness.

CHAPTER TEN

POINT BETSIE
BETWEEN WORLD WARS

The year 1918 found the United States deeply involved in the war in Europe and combating a catastrophic influenza epidemic at home. At the ten-acre federal reservation at Point Betsie Light and Coast Guard Station, however, customary activities were continuing, but with some significant changes in prospect.

Wartime economy measures became more meaningful when the commissioner of lighthouses accepted a recommendation from the district inspector to relocate two of the five Point Betsie fog signal air tanks, each forty-two inches in diameter and eight feet tall, to the station at Frankfort harbor for use in conjunction with a modern diaphone fog signal. Having five tanks had no practical benefit, the inspector contended, saying "the air whistle will operate fully as well using the three tanks which will remain. In fact, when the whistle is operated using but one tank, no difference can be distinguished in the sound." He also insisted that if Point Betsie's signal were also upgraded to an "air siren or Type G diaphone," three tanks would provide adequate capacity.

Both funds and steel would be conserved by making this change, as these tanks cost as much as three hundred dollars each, and were difficult to obtain during the "National Emergency." Using the agency's own personnel, the relocation expense would be just forty dollars, the commissioner added, and his superiors accepted his recommendation.

In early 1919, a field assistant for the Coast Guard visited its Point Betsie station to decide on a site for a new boat house. On March 26, 1919, command of the facility passed to Sigval B. Johnson, who had been serving in a New York facility; Ludwig Hendricksen, who had run the station on an interim basis after Ed Bedford's retirement, returned to the No. 1 position.

There were again troubles with the telephone line, the crew having to make repairs to three poles that went down in April and to the line that was broken in numerous places. Also laying a cement foundation for the new building that spring, the crew spent much of the summer constructing the boat storage facility. By fall, the men were busy laying track on which the launch wagon would be rolled between the new structure and the lake. At year's end, when the station was deactivated for the winter, Hendricksen was retired from active service.

On May 21, 1920, Sigval Johnson also began crossing out "Keeper" at the bottom of the old journal's printed forms, inserting in lieu "Boatswain (L)". The change was associated with the Coast Guard's adoption of the chief petty officer grade in May, 1920, the "chief" portion leaving no issue as to who was in charge of a facility. Former keepers of Life-Saving stations were given the rank of chief boatswain's mate, followed by a parenthetical "L" to denote lifesaving, thus clarifying that the individual was not affiliated with a sea-going or other Coast Guard unit. With the change, however, another tradition that had survived from the venerable days of the U.S. Life-Saving Service—the title of keeper—was swept away.

Johnson, who kept the station's log with a notably fine hand that an historian would one day appreciate, proved to be a relatively "short-termer" at Point Betsie. The following October, the crew helped him pack and crate his goods; he departed in the station's Beebe-McLellan power surfboat, heading for duty in the district office and leaving No. 262 under the temporary leadership of its No. 1, Fred J. Marsh.

On November 10, 1920, Boatswain (L) Abram Wessel arrived to take charge of the Coast Guard station, having been transferred north from his command at Grand Point Au Sable. Wessel and his wife Lillian, both of whom were Michigan-born, brought their family of five children to the point, the oldest of whom was eleven when they arrived. Abram's parents were from Holland; Lillian was the daughter of a Scandinavian couple. Initially, he would lead a Point Betsie complement of five surfmen; perhaps because of labor shortages in the area, he also had seven temporary surfmen who could fill in as required.

∽

SEVERIN DANIELSEN, A NEW KEEPER, HAD COME TO THE LIGHTHOUSE FROM CHICAGO IN SEPTEMBER, 1919, SUCCEEDING PHILIP SHERIDAN. Born at Stegen, Norway, in 1863, Danielsen, who never married, came

Lightkeeper Severin Danielsen.
Courtesy of Meridith Erickson

to the U.S. in 1888. He took up lighthouse work in 1898, serving ten years at isolated Poverty Island, off Lake Michigan's northern coast near Escanaba, where he started as 2nd assistant, earned promotion to 1st assistant and finally to the keeper's position. Thereafter, he spent five years as keeper at South Chicago Light and five more years at the Chicago Harbor Breakwater Light, after which he was transferred to Point Betsie. He would serve at the point for ten years, thus completing a distinguished thirty-year career in lightkeeping before retiring in May, 1928. After a post-retirement trip to Europe, he settled in Escanaba, his home until his death at age seventy-nine; he is buried in the city's Lakeview Cemetery.

John Peterson, a former summer resident at the point who remembered Danielsen as a "wonderful, saavy old man" and "excellent fisherman," recalled that the Keeper's understanding of Lake Michigan's currents were revealed in his warning against his superiors' decision to try to fortify the Point Betsie tower by substituting solid steel sheets for the existing staggered wooden pilings. The Keeper had warned his superiors that the proposed works' design, which they installed despite his concerns, would prevent the lake's powerful waves from flowing smoothly among the baffle-like barriers, and thereby cause erosion that would turn the point's then gradually curving shoreline into a peninsula. (The extent of land loss that has occurred over the years to the north of the lighthouse property lends some credence to his opinion.)

❦

OTHER THAN IN THE SUMMER, THERE WAS YET SOME SENSE OF ISOLATION AT POINT BETSIE, even though the surrounding area was becoming more substantially settled. The lands immediately surrounding the government tract were minimally occupied and generally remained in their wild state; the crews still enjoyed hunting right off the property. As late as 1923, a surfman was reported to have killed an owl with a four and one-half foot wingspan.

But people were living not far away, especially along nearby Crystal Lake during vacation months. Use of automobiles on the road (M-22) that ran northward out of Frankfort, between the western end of Crystal Lake and Point Betsie, was growing. As area residents were increasingly going to town by car, the lack of a good connection from the point to the state road was not only frustrating for the families residing there, but an inconvenience when supplying the two stations.

Taking on this cause, Danielsen wrote the Bureau of Public Roads in September, 1920, to see what help they might provide for improving the existing primitive route between Point Betsie and the highway, essentially a rough wagon path that he calculated at about 3,500 yards in length. Using a boat compass and a tape measure, he made a survey of the proposed road that year, demonstrating his commitment to the project. Despite the Light Station and Coast Guard Station having been at Point Betsie for many decades, Danielsen lamented that "...there has never been one cent of improvements made on the road" because "the Township of Lake is unable to make any improvements as they are without funds."

Danielsen continued, "There are 25 people living at this place and it is almost impossible for anyone to get in and out of here that is without walking; one half of the distance is through woods and the other half is over the sand." He suggested that both crews could help with the work, there being twelve men stationed at the point. The largest expense, he indicated, would be for tasks requiring a team of horses—grading and hauling gravel and clay. The Captain quickly won the support of his district superintendent.

Later that fall, the lighthouse personnel also took up the cause. A November 10 letter to the superintendent of lighthouses in Milwaukee detailed the cost at about $5000, taking into consideration the labor-cost savings that the two crews' work would yield. The letter reasoned, "This road will be used for hauling supplies to the Light and Coast Guard Stations, consisting of winter fuel, oil for fog signal engines, and kerosene lighting equipment, household supplies, etc., and travel incidental to transporting children to school at Frankfort, and for visiting town for mail and provisions."

Knowing that the authorities never wanted to slight the public relations factor, the appeal also sought to justify the project on grounds that the road would accommodate "...the great number of tourists at Frankfort each summer season from inland towns and cities of Michigan, Indiana, Illinois and Ohio, and in many instances more distant states, to visit Government stations of this kind who otherwise are in no position to become acquainted or learn of certain activities of Our Government for the welfare of the public generally."

Despite these justifications, the appeal prompted no quick response and the Coast Guard station was closed for the season at year's end. Wessel and two men were to remain at the isolated site, maintaining the facility and its equipment during the inactive period.

⤐

THE LACK OF A RESPONSE FROM THE COAST GUARD TO THE ROAD-BUILDING APPEAL MAY HAVE BEEN A HARBINGER OF THINGS TO COME, FOR MID-SUMMER, 1921, BROUGHT SOME JARRING NEWS. As Wessel wrote in his log, "Received orders at 4:00 P.M. to place this station in an inactive status as of July 1, 1921...." He recorded that he had implemented this instruction as of midnight and that several of his crewmen were immediately departing for other stations. Thus, irrespective of having so recently been awarded an outstanding new station building and having built a new boathouse to house the station's motor-powered rescue craft, the Point Betsie crew was being reduced to a total of just two or three men. The rationale behind this decision was visible—the advantages of powered rescue craft had ended reliance upon surfboats rowed by six or seven men, and with continued modernization of the Great Lakes commercial fleet, the frequency of rescue activity was much diminished and amounted mostly to aiding coastal fishing boats and pleasure craft. Another key factor, no doubt, was the redundancy posed by the Point Betsie and Frankfort harbor stations being just a few miles apart.

There were no men available at Point Betsie, and many other reduced stations, to continue the traditional beach patrols. Gone, too, was equipment such as the breeches buoy and life car whose use depended upon the availability of full crews. And the seemingly incessant drills through which surfmen had honed their rescue skills had become little more than a memory to be recounted by the old-timers, such as Captains Bedford and Miller and the men who had served in their crews and continued to reside in the area.

However, the Point Betsie Coast Guard Station still had its power surfboat to carefully maintain, its men being required to turn over its engine each morning to be sure all was in operational readiness. And they had a telephone line to check daily; with it, they could call the Frankfort Coast Guard to help assist a troubled mariner.

The men at the station continued to record the weather and surf conditions at four-hour intervals between 8 a.m. and 8 p.m. They tallied the passing vessels and inspected all station buildings and grounds every day, making repairs to the structures as required. They would record any unusual event in the log, of which there were few; each day's report was summarized merely as "Station in inactive status."

✍

IN CONTRAST TO THE COAST GUARD STATION'S DECLINING ROLE, THERE WAS A SPATE OF ACTIVITY AT POINT BETSIE LIGHT. Paving the way there, as at many other lighthouses, was the arrival of electricity which would make possible not only more powerful illumination but also the installation of more advanced fog signals and, ultimately, other new technological aids to assist mariners. Electrification, which started at the Statue of Liberty, generally reached lights as transmission lines and poles were being erected to carry power to outlying areas. Mariners would benefit from the improvements in navigational aids; the crews at light stations would experience reduced and less burdensome workloads. The latter many not have foreseen the manpower reductions that would gradually follow. And some of lightkeeping's lore would be lost as well; no longer would the keepers, in fair weather or foul, have to fuel their lamps every few hours.

The Lake Carriers' Association advised its members in 1920 that the superintendent of lighthouses had approved "...plans for increasing the efficiency of Point Betsie fog signal by the installation of electric power and oil driven machinery and diaphone signal of high grade."[1] The Bureau reported the purchase price of the new diaphone, powered by an electrically operated compressor (with a standby oil-operated backup system) as $3524, and permission was required from private owners to bring the power line from the state road to the fog signal building.[2]

The carriers' group anticipated that the work could be completed within a few weeks' time and the new equipment placed in operation for the 1921 navigation season. However, this job, like other previous work at the site, proved to be more substantial than predicted. According to an October 29, 1921, letter to the commissioner of lighthouses,[3] the job had required the dismantlement of the worn-out "Rumely" engines from the fog signal house so as to install the "new motors, oil engine, and air compressor." During the reconstruction a temporary six-inch steam whistle was put into use, the steam coming from a small boiler. The men pushed to get the new equipment into operation so the temporary device, which had to be set up outside, could be shut down before winter set in. The goal was to complete the electrification and modernization project so everything would be ready for the resumption of navigation in early 1922.

The temporary use of the steam whistle had drawn no complaints from mariners, it was later reported, and no problems in shifting to the new equipment were anticipated. The commissioner was advised, "The steamers more directly concerned in the light and fog signal at Point Betsie are the car ferries plying in and out of Frankfort, and inasmuch as the present characteristic of the Point Betsie fog signal is to be maintained with the diaphone, the only difference will be in the increased power of the signal and the difference in the sound." Consistent with that judgment, the Lake Carriers' Association was pleased that the large, type "G" diaphones had a sound radius "...several times that of the air whistle, and owing to operation of [the] station by electric power it will insure practically instantaneous service when weather is not entirely clear."[4]

Along with the more powerful fog signal, electrification would make possible a more powerful and dependable illuminant. A substantial increase in the light's rated candlepower was anticipated with the use of a two hundred-watt, one hundred ten-volt bulb within the station's fourth-order Fresnel lens.[5] The revolving flash mechanism continued to be driven by a descending weight that would need to be manually cranked back up to its starting point, a daily task taking close to fifteen minutes.

The official list[6] described the navigational aids in place at Point Betsie as a flashing white light with a ten-second period, the sweeping flash lasting for 1.3 seconds and the eclipse, or dark segment, lasting 8.7 seconds. This 1924 compilation showed Point Betsie's light to be the most powerful such beacon on this portion of Lake Michigan, with a rated candlepower of 70,000. Fifty-two feet above the lake's surface, the beam was said to be visible under normal conditions for fifteen miles.

The list also reported that the traditional pattern of the Point Betsie fog signal—its "characteristic" to use the proper term—had been changed to two blasts every thirty seconds, the first blast lasting one and one-half seconds followed by two seconds of silence, and a second blast for one and one-half seconds followed by a silent period of twenty-five seconds.[7] Mariners and many area residents quickly became accustomed to hearing blasts from two nearby shoreline sites—Point Betsie and Frankfort—and could readily identify each of them. Marking an important harbor entrance, Frankfort's sequence was more regular and frequent, two-second blasts followed by twenty seconds of silence.

The visibility of Point Betsie's electric-powered light soon became a subject of discussion. Correspondence in mid-July, 1925, indicates that the light was seen from across Lake Michigan by crew at Cana Island Light Station.[8] This seemed very doubtful to senior officials, but such reports continued to be filed. Almost ten years later, the keeper at Big Sable would report that on a June night he could see several lights, including Point Betsie's, about forty-five miles north, and the light at the Sturgeon Bay Canal, sixty-five miles across Lake Michigan. Under certain atmospheric conditions, it seems, such claims may have been valid despite the lights' more limited official ranges.

The benefits of electricity were realized somewhat later at Point Betsie's adjacent Coast Guard rescue station; it was not until the fall of 1926 that the Benzie County Power Company wired the station and supplied it with fixtures that headquarters had approved.

As at Coast Guard stations, telephone service was increasingly important to light stations, and keeping the service functioning was often a struggle. In the fall of 1922, an Ann Arbor car ferry is said to have carried the line away as it navigated through a relatively shallow passage at Frankfort harbor, and just days later a portion of the line to Point Betsie was buried in a landslide.

∽

AS 1922 DREW TO A CLOSE, THERE WAS ONE MORE SIGNIFICANT DEVELOPMENT AT THE COAST GUARD STATION. Captain Wessel reported that the station's power surfboat had been taken away to have a new engine installed, also noting that he had sprained his left wrist while launching the boat that day. There is no evidence that the boat was returned to the station; no further references are made in the logs to the daily ritual of turning over the boat's engines. Thus, to initiate a response to emergencies on the lake, the Point Betsie Station became totally dependent upon its communications link to the Frankfort crew, which stood ready to deploy its motorized rescue craft.

But that didn't mean that Point Betsie's "skeleton" crew would cease to follow tradition where it could. The men served as they were able, keeping the log, drilling with Morse Code and flags, reviewing the boating laws they were expected to help enforce, and practicing resuscitation, frostbite relief and other techniques as well as maintaining their facilities. The Point Betsie station crew was expected to help monitor Lake Michigan, especially northward over the popular route between the point and the Manitou Islands, past Platte Bay. A highlight each summer was the Chicago-Mackinac yacht race; the crew would spot and report by phone the arrival of the leaders off the point. To this day, people go to Point Betsie to try to spot the passing sailboats, sometimes close enough to the beach for the boaters and observers to greet one another.

∽

A MAJOR EVENT IN THE HISTORY OF FRANKFORT AND ITS CAR FERRY OPERATIONS OCCURRED IN THE WINTER OF 1923, when the *No. 4* wrecked against the south pier after having barely survived a wild night's storm on Lake Michigan. (The ship's struggle to reach Frankfort is depicted in a mural inside the Frankfort post office.) Captain Wessel recorded the weather on February 14 as featuring a "fresh to moderate Westerly gale" with snow and heavy haze on the lake, which at Point Betsie was ice-covered from the shore to about one hundred and fifty yards out. He recorded receiving a telephone call at about 8:30 a.m. with news that the ferry had hit the south pier. Leaving his recently arrived new No. 1 surfman, Edward F. Erickson, behind because he was suffering from the flu, Wessel left his station to be of assistance to the Frankfort crew as it faced this major crisis.

Arriving there about 10:30 a.m., he found the huge boat grounded just inside the outer end of the south pier, but fortunately in a position that eventually enabled her crew to descend to the ice-covered pier by ladders. The local Coast Guardsmen had faced a major challenge in this rescue; two men had nearly lost their lives in trying to get a line out to the ferry over the ice-choked waters. Wrote the local *Benzie County Patriot* several weeks later, "While it was not necessary to use the breeches buoy, it gave one a sense of security to know one could be rigged immediately if need be and that there were men trained for such an emergency, waiting to assist in every way possible." The crew having reached shore safely, Wessel returned to Point Betsie that afternoon after having tried to be available for service, but recording that no assistance had been rendered from his station.

∾

THE TWO POINT BETSIE CREWS FINALLY CAME TO THE REALIZATION THAT THE ONLY WAY THE ROAD TO THEIR STATIONS WOULD BE IMPROVED WAS BY TAKING MATTERS INTO THEIR OWN HANDS. In the fall of 1923, they obtained a team of horses for the task and got the project underway. With the justification that the road would be important to the people of Frankfort and the vicinity, businesses in the town were canvassed for funds with which to obtain gravel for the new surface.

Excited by the effort, the *Benzie County Patriot* described a passable road between the state highway and Point Betsie as "...an actual necessity as it will be a benefit to the families residing there and also for the great numbers of resorters and tourists that visit in this vicinity who think that a summer spent in this section of the country is not complete without a visit to these old established services of the Government." The story added, "It is also intended to make a tourist camp among the sand dunes where our vast number of summer visitors will be provided with unexcelled drinking water, modern rest room and one of the best bathing beaches on Lake Michigan." The paper voiced its own encouragement to the front-page news story, urging everyone "...cooperate to the best of our ability and give the boys at the Point every possible help in their undertaking."

Point Betsie Road at its junction with the state road (M-22), prior to paving.
Courtesy of Claudia Lewis

A serviceable road to Point Betsie was finally a reality in the summer of 1924, and the public promptly took advantage of it. More than three hundred people visited Point Betsie on an August Sunday; the *Patriot* reported that camp stoves, tables and benches were in great demand. Mention was made of the limited parking spaces that were available for the beach at the new road's end.

The increased visitations may have heightened both stations' determination to present a "spic-and-span" image. Now easily accessible to visitors, they had become the local showplace for the U.S. Government; buildings had to be in excellent condition and the grounds were to be tidy at all times. Despite their own station's vanishing capacity to serve mariners, the remaining Coast Guardsmen did their part. Yet another sign of the station's inactive status was that fall's transfer to Beaver Island of Point Betsie's no longer used launch carriage.

The station's telephone links, however, kept the station on its toes and enabled it to be of some benefit. On May 22, 1925, a call alerted Captain Wessel that a nearby farm was burning. With an adequate road now available, he and two assistant lighthouse keepers drove to the scene in his car and helped fight the fire by setting back-fires and digging trenches. And a few days later, the Captain reported that he had discovered a gas-powered boat adrift north of the station. "Called the Frankfort Station at once and requested that they come with the life boat to tow the disabled boat to Frankfort," he recounted, adding, "Stood watch until Frankfort crew got the boat to Frankfort. No assistance rendered from this station."

On the following June 18th there came another call, this one from Otter Creek some sixteen miles north of the station, reporting that five men had been out in a skiff the night before and had not returned. Wessel in turn called the Frankfort station and asked that they take their boat to search for the lost men. The Captain and his new No. 1, Kenneth Robinson, who had replaced the retired Edward Erickson, took the latter's car to Otter Creek.

Wessel wrote that upon arriving, they saw a group of people on the beach about a mile to the south. They hiked down and learned that the men had left the beach in a rotten skiff to lift some fishing nets; while attempting this, the boat had capsized. Two of the men, not being swimmers, had drowned immediately; another had headed for shore but also drowned. The fourth man had managed to hold onto the skiff, thereby saving his life. Two men's bodies had been found, but resuscitation efforts had failed. Surfman Robinson searched for the missing fifth man, even lifting the nets for his body, but it could not be located. Although the Coast Guardsmen had not gotten to the distant scene by car in time to save these victims, nor could they probably have done so by boat, the episode illustrated how the telephone and automobile had become key elements in the Point Betsie station's emergency response capability.

Point Betsie Lighthouse in the Danielsen era.
Courtesy of Meredith Erickson

❧

THE "RADIOBEACON" OR "RADIO FOG SIGNAL," AN IMPORTANT SHORELINE NAVIGATIONAL AID, WAS DEVELOPED IN THIS PERIOD, its first deployment on the Great Lakes coming in 1925 aboard the *Huron* lightship. The technology quickly proved highly successful; the *New York Times* soon reported that many vessels already had been equipped with radio compasses to make use of these transmissions.[9]

The radiobeacon transmitted its unique signal in Morse Code. A radio direction finder on board a ship could get a bearing off that signal from a substantial distance away—fifty to one hundred miles from the source—and the ship's position relative to the radiobeacon's direction could be determined. The equipment also served as a "homing" device, and operators of small craft found this capability, which was relatively inexpensive and simple to operate, useful in setting a course to a harbor.

Radiobeacons amounted to a substantial improvement in a light station's ability to serve vessels, especially in thick foggy weather when atmospheric conditions could mute the sound blasts or in storms when wave and vessel noise might prevent the crew from hearing the fog signal. This possibility was of such concern to the government that its official lists included warnings to ship captains that they ought not presume that they could hear an operating fog signal, at least not in sufficient time to avert a catastrophe to their vessel. A radiobeacon and direction finder yielded much more reliable information.

Within a year, the Lighthouse Bureau was pressing to deploy the radiobeacons widely. By the close of 1926, seven radiobeacons already were in operation on the often-foggy Great Lakes. That August, there came a recommendation for the device's installation at Point Betsie, given its critical location at the south end of the course into the Manitou Passage. The Lake Carriers' Association reported that year that materials had been assembled at Point Betsie and it was proposed to have a radiobeacon functioning there as quickly as possible. The task, projected to cost $6,500, was to install the new radio equipment in the west end of the fog signal building. The fog signal's air tanks that had been located inside the structure, where they were close to the electric compressor, were moved outside along the building's north wall. Two tall antenna towers were erected and two 200-watt transmitters, along with control panels and necessary generating capability, were put into operation.

On February 28, 1927, a telegram went to the lighthouse commissioner in Washington saying, "POINT BETSIE RADIOBEACON COMPLETED AND PLACED IN OPERATION MONDAY; CHARACTERISTIC DASH DOT DOT FOUR THIRTY TO FIVE, TEN THIRTY TO ELEVEN."

Men working atop one of Point Betsie's two radio towers.
Courtesy of U.S. Coast Guard

The 1927 *Light List* provided a description of Point Betsie Light Station's new service. During clear weather, the radio signals were sent between 4:00 and 4:30, both a.m. and p.m., and also between 10:00 and 10:30 a.m. and p.m.; in foggy conditions, the signal was broadcast continuously until the hazard dispersed. Broadcast on a frequency of three hundred kilocycles for sixty seconds, Point Betsie's own characteristic was a group consisting of a dot, two dashes and another dot, that being followed by one hundred and twenty seconds of silence and then the pattern repeated.

The new radio technology spread swiftly throughout the lakes; by the end of 1927 there were nineteen radiobeacons in operation, one of which was started by the Canadian Government and the rest by the U.S. Revealing the shipping industry's interest, two hundred sixty-two steamers were already equipped with radio direction finders by that time, and the system was expected to be installed in about one hundred more ships during winter lay-up.[10]

Sometimes a ship captain asked Danielsen and his successors to have Point Betsie's radiobeacon operated for a specific time to enable the on-board technician to calibrate the ship's equipment. In later years, when radiobeacons became so essential to navigation that they were operated continuously, there were beacons whose purpose was to accommodate such calibrations.

≼

KEEPER DANIELSEN'S DEPARTURE led to an unusual budget request for Point Betsie in 1928, when the superintendent in Milwaukee wrote to the commissioner to justify the purchase of an increased volume of anthracite coal for the station. "The former Keeper being a bachelor heated only one room and it was possible to get along with 24 tons but this Keeper has retired and a Keeper with family has been transferred to Point Betsie mainly for the reason that school facilities are available and with a family it will be necessary to heat the quarters…" Thirty tons would be an appropriate amount, he suggested, emphasizing, "The station is in the northern latitudes where severe winters are experienced and [it] operates throughout the year."

The new lightkeeper was German-born Charles E. Tesnow, who arrived with his wife Ida and young son Howard on May 24, 1928, to take charge of the station. A lighthouse veteran, Tesnow, like Peter Dues many years before, had served at Waukegan Harbor Light as 1st assistant. At about the same time Captain Wessel took on a new No. 1 surfman at the Coast Guard Station, Fred Wendel, Jr..

The need for yet more reliable telephone service to the lighthouse was becoming acute, and in August, 1928, the district superintendent urged the commissioner to approve a line that would run from Frankfort through the Coast Guard Station and on to the lighthouse, thus replacing the extension service that had linked the light and Coast

Guard stations. "This service will be at a cost of $30.00 per year exchange service…it will permit the receipt of radiograms at Frankfort and communication from the Radio Station [in Frankfort] to the Light Station in case a vessel desires the operation of the radio signal for any purpose. The telephone service will also permit transmission of radiograms received for the operation of the diaphone if required," the commissioner was advised.

By the following spring, the line had been installed, the commissioner being reminded in mid-May that the primary justification for this new direct service was so that "…radio messages can be received at the Radio Station, Frankfort, and transmitted by telephone to the isolated Light Station at Point Betsie for the operation of Radio Beacon."

∽

BOATSWAIN (L) WESSEL'S TENURE AT THE POINT BETSIE COAST GUARD STATION CAME TO AN END IN MID-1929; he signed the log for the last time on July 25 and was detached from the station after almost nine years of faithful service in what was likely a frustratingly austere time. The No. 1, Fred Wendel, was in charge until August 1, when Chief Boatswain's Mate (L) Fred D. Straubel, who was one of Wessel's surfmen at Grand Point Au Sable a decade earlier, arrived with his French-Canadian wife Darilla and their teen-aged son and daughter. Fred Wendel, who later in his career would lead the Grand Haven, Michigan station, continued as surfman, residing at the point with his wife Anna.

A compilation showing the Point Betsie Light Station's characteristics at the beginning of 1930 made mention that the station had been rebuilt in 1894 and that its 70,000 candlepower illuminant was of the "electric incandescent" type—meaning that its light was produced by a heated filament within a bulb. The year also brought a notable distinction to the lighthouse; it was awarded the Milwaukee district pennant as "…the station kept in the best condition and showing the most original and thorough attention," the local newspaper reported, adding that congratulations were in order for Keeper Tesnow and his two assistants, Henry LaFreniere and Robert McKillop.[11]

∽

THE YEAR 1930 ALSO FEATURED THE EFFORTS OF A PROMINENT PRIVATE CITIZEN TO SECURE THE RESTORATION OF A FULL CREW TO POINT BETSIE'S COAST GUARD STATION. Arthur P. Peterson, owner of Frankfort's *Benzie County Patriot* and a summer resident at the point, wrote an influential U.S. senator from Michigan, Arthur Vandenberg, urging him to press for returning the station to "active" status.[12] Peterson noted that the facility had been placed on the inactive list as a result of the "retrenchment" brought on by the financial burdens of the World War and been manned by only two men for about nine years. Being one of the oldest on this shore and having been rebuilt into one of the "better class stations," Peterson pled that the facility deserved higher recognition.

"During the schooner days it was also the scene of much activity and several thrilling rescues. Point Betsie is the most Western point in the northern part of the Lower Peninsula and is therefore a point where all north bound boats change their course and usually are very 'close in' and consequently one of the real danger points on Lake Michigan," he wrote. He also stressed that "Frankfort is the home of probably the largest and most important fishing fleet in Michigan working the year around… with most of the fleet going northward and past Point Betsie. The ice in winter time constitutes a real menace….There is also much pleasure boating in this vicinity and many tourists and resorters make land and water pilgrimages to the Point. The car ferry fleet at Frankfort in a measure are dependent upon this service." Hence, Peterson insisted, if the case were presented to the authorities in a "clear and forceful manner," he was sure "…that preparations would be made at once for speedily re-establishing a full crew at this very important point."

Senator Vandenberg replied that he would take the matter up with the Coast Guard commandant, Admiral Billard. Headquarters handled this "constituent service" request in the routine manner, seeking the views of its field officials in Grand Haven, Michigan. After reviewing the situation, they recommended against restoring the station to active status for the following five reasons: (1) there had been only twelve cases of assistance by the station, all of them minor, over a ten-year period, and not a single such instance in the prior year; (2) while all north- and south-bound boats using the Manitou Passage change course off Point Betsie, they are supposed to be about four and one-half miles offshore when doing so; (3) a point that would have surprised Captains Miller and Bedford, rescue equipment could not be placed there due to its "exposed location," and quite often conditions would prevent a motor lifeboat from being launched from that beach; (4) the Frankfort station is only a few miles away and South Manitou station is only twenty-three miles distant, and both would respond to a telephone alert from Point Betsie station with motor lifeboats that would be capable of assisting mariners in a rough sea, and (5) Point Betsie Light is only a few hundred yards away, and its light (the lens erroneously described here as "first-order"), fog signal and "master radio beacon" together serve to "…eliminate much of the danger of vessels stranding in this vicinity."

Given the above rationale, senior Coast Guard staff felt free to turn down the Senator: "I feel that you will agree that the conditions would not justify any action on the part of Headquarters contrary to the findings of the District Commander." Vandenberg, in turn, advised Peterson, "I doubt whether we could find it possible to change the Department's decision except as we could present convincing and specific testimony to combat the conclusions as here reported." In short, there was no realistic prospect of revitalizing the Point Betsie rescue station; it would simply have to hang on in its curtailed state, providing services to the extent its sharply diminished resources would permit.

⌀

MEANWHILE, THE LIGHTHOUSE'S ROLE AND OPERATIONS CONTINUED. 1931 saw a change made in the fog signal's characteristic. Two blasts would still be sounded, each of one and one-half seconds, every thirty seconds during the presence of fog off Point Betsie. Two seconds of silence would follow the first blast, and twenty-five silent seconds would follow the second one. But a new feature, presumably to give the Point Betsie signal clearer identity, would come every third minute: a five-second blast, with silence for one second, then a one-second blast followed by a silence of fifty-three seconds. For some unknown reason, this innovation didn't last long; by the time the 1936 *Light List* had been published, Point Betsie's traditional signal had been restored—just the pattern of two quick blasts every thirty seconds, with one short silent interval and a long one.

Another technological innovation at Point Betsie was also recommended—the synchronizing of Point Betsie's radiobeacon and fog signal. With this enhancement, made at Point Betsie, Chicago Harbor and Manitowoc (Wisconsin) Breakwater lights in 1931, by examining the difference in the time the two signals were received, a vessel could better determine its distance from the point.

This "distance-finding" procedure was explained in the 1939 *Light List* as follows: "Whenever the sound signal is operating a group of two radio dashes, a short and long, 1 second and from 3 to 5 seconds respectively, is transmitted every 3 minutes at the end of the radiobeacon minute of operation. A group of two sound signal blasts of corresponding length is sounded at the same time. When within audible range of the sound signal, navigators on vessels with radio receivers capable of receiving the radiobeacon signals may readily determine their distance from the station by observing the time in seconds which elapses between hearing any part of the distinctive group of radio dashes, say the end of the long dash, and the corresponding part of the group of sound blasts, say the end of the long blast, and dividing the result by 5 for statute miles." The text added, "The error of such calculations should not exceed 10 percent. For observations on aerial sound signals a watch with second hand is all that is needed, although a stop watch is more convenient."

As an example, the description cited the synchronized signals at Lansing Shoal Light Station: "…[I]f the interval between hearing the end of the long radio dash marking the end of the radiobeacon minute and the end of the long (5-second) blast of the diaphone is 30 seconds, the observer is 30 [divided by] 5 = 6 miles from the station."

On shipboard, attention to detail and frequent practice were both essential to a vessel relying on radiobeacons, the government advised: "Serious errors may result in bearings taken if other shipboard antennas are erected close to the direction finder after calibration or if the direction finder, ship's rigging or other equipment affecting direction finder performance is not maintained in the condition existing at the time of last calibration. Regular and frequent use of the direction finder under all conditions is one of the best means of insuring ability to obtain accurate bearings and that the direction finder is at all times in proper condition. Clear weather operating periods provide ample opportunity for such use."

The federal announcement contained one final bit of advice: "Full use should be taken of the opportunity for fixing positions by cross bearings on two or more radiobeacons which is provided through the convenient arrangement of stations as to frequency and sequence of operation and in most cases their favorable geographic location." Underlying all the jargon was a clear message: electronics were bringing important new responsibilities and benefits to both ship and lighthouse crews, and would ultimately produce major changes in lighthouse operations.

∽

SADNESS CAME TO FRANKFORT IN THE SPRING OF 1931 with news of the death, from a pneumonia attack at the age of 92, of Captain "Tip" Miller. Among area residents with personal knowledge of the lifesavers, Miller, the four-decade veteran leader of the crews at Point Betsie and Beaver Island, and former island lightkeeper as well, was a legendary figure.

Upon leaving the lifesaving station in 1908, the Captain and his Bridget had retired to a simple home on five acres at the north end of Frankfort, from which he frequently walked about a mile into town to buy groceries and mow lawns or perform other odd jobs to supplement the couple's slim financial resources.

Efforts to pass private legislation to procure pension benefits for this distinguished man were unsuccessful, prompting the *Grand Rapids Herald* in its 1929 feature on this beloved couple to observe, "All Frankfort wants to know why." (Despite having exceeded the thirty years' service on which pension eligibility was based in the Coast Guard after 1915, Miller was denied coverage.) And, as if they hadn't already faced enough challenges in their eventful lives, their house burned down many years after their retirement, taking most of their possessions with it. So at almost ninety years of age, the Captain himself had erected a small pre-fabricated replacement.

The Millers observing their 60th wedding anniversary.
Courtesy of Claudia Lewis

Miller's front-page obituary in the *Benzie County Patriot* recounted his passing in LaCrosse, Wisconsin, where he had been visiting a granddaughter almost a year after the death of his beloved Bridget. He had known grief too well; over their many years together, the couple had buried eight of their ten children. The paper reported that "…a goodly company stood with bared heads…as a group of stalwart young men, wearing the uniform of the Coast Guard service of the United States, brought ashore, from the Ann Arbor Carferry *No. 7,* the casketed remains of Captain Harrison Miller, the first captain of the first Coast Guard station on Lake Michigan."

A Mason for more than a half century, Miller's body laid in state in Frankfort's Masonic temple, the *Patriot* reported, "under the colors of our country, which he honored by his long years of service." The writer added, "It was his joy to have with him during these last days one of his old comrades in the service, Captain Bedford of Frankfort, who remained with him to the last and then accompanied the body of his friend on its return to this place which for so many years had been his home and where everybody was his friend, so that his loss is the common sorrow of all of us."

Following the funeral service in Frankfort, Miller's body was taken to Charlevoix and received by his home lodge which, with his association extending back to 1877, had granted him life membership. There he was buried alongside most of his family.

Miller family cemetery plot, Charlevoix, Michigan.
Photo by author

In a front-page story, the *Charlevoix Sentinel* lauded Miller's lifesaving service: "At its best the work…was fraught with danger, such as only a member of the old time life guard can fully appreciate. Especially hazardous when during a storm ships were driven upon rocky shores and wrecked and loss of human life imminent. In this duty many acts of extreme bravery; practically facing death in his activities, he is authentically credited with having saved more than 100 lives and so credited in government records, wherein heroic deeds, brave acts and intelligent effort bear witness to his faithful performance of duty assigned to him." [13]

The paper's tribute also took a personal tone: "His record as a citizen is above reproach and he is remembered by the earlier generations as a jovial, kindly hardworking man, interested in his local community as one ready to extend a helping hand to unfortunate neighbors and friends, while the few old residents of his time now living and residing here always looked forward to his visits to Charlevoix.… He was of sturdy type, carried his years well and on his last visit…in late summer of 1930 appeared more like a well preserved man of sixty-five, although his age was ninety-two."

Irrespective of the Coast Guard station's "inactive" status, Miller's old stamping ground at Point Betsie continued to attract lots of visitors. In preparation for the 1931 summer season, the buildings were painted. Early that summer the *Benzie County Patriot* reported, "At times there are twenty-five cars parked at the turn-around and the beach lined with parties enjoying roasts. The dunes and their picturesqueness have provided subjects for the artists' brush and each year sees its classes of naturalists studying its flora." Poignantly and presciently, the writer added, "In truth the Point has come to mean as much to the land farer as it has to the sailer for the past eighty years."

❧

COAST GUARD STATION NO. 262 CARRIED ON in its limited operating status. Shortly before Christmas of 1931, Chief Boatswain's Mate (L) Straubel was reassigned to the district commander. His position as officer-in-charge at the Point Betsie station was assumed by CBM (L) William Dipert, with Clifford Plowman, who had arrived in mid-1930, as No.1, his only surfman.

In the early spring of 1932 a fish tug operating out of Frankfort, the *Seabird*, had engine trouble off the point. The lighthouse crew spotted the boat and telephoned the Frankfort station whose crew immediately responded, thus demonstrating again the existing arrangements' emergency response capability.

A crisis of another sort, one much closer to home, came on the first of August when the Diperts awakened at 1 a.m. to discover a raging fire in a nearby privately-owned garage that was situated immediately adjacent to a structure used by the Coast Guard as a garage and carpenter shop. The building could not be saved, but the crew managed to get two automobiles out. Using their hoses and pumping from the lake, the crew kept the fire from spreading to the nearby Coast Guard boathouse and a privately owned cottage. The Frankfort fire department responded as well, and the fire was out within a couple of hours.

❧

AN IMPORTANT PERSONNEL CHANGE OCCURRED AT THE LIGHTHOUSE IN 1933 with the arrival on April 1, from the light at Racine Reef, Wisconsin, of Edward M. Wheaton to succeed Charles Tesnow as keeper. This appointment opened a new and important thirteen-year era at Point Betsie. Wheaton's first assistant was Henry LaFreniere, who had joined Tesnow from the Beaver Islands in 1928; the second assistant was Nels Nelson, who had arrived in November, 1931, from South Manitou Island, where he had worked at the Coast Guard's lifesaving station. First assistant Nelson and his wife Augusta were to have six children, one of whom

(Melvin) would eventually follow in his father's footsteps at both Point Betsie and the Frankfort station. The LaFrenieres had one son, Chuck.

The residential quarters at Point Betsie were hardly spacious or luxurious; in this era, the officer-in-charge, Ed Wheaton and his wife, lived in the two-bedroom apartment on the west end; the LaFrenieres were upstairs on the east end and the later- arriving Nelson brood somehow managed initially in a one-bedroom apartment, later acquiring somewhat more space after some remodeling.[14] The residents then were dependent on two outhouses just east of the lighthouse, near the coal storage structure from which they carried fuel to the house. Feeding a family of eight on an assistant lightkeeper's salary surely presented Nels and Gusty Nelson with quite a challenge; the children would help out by spreading nets in the lake right in front of the house, catching great quantities of delicious fish.

Comprising a truly memorable team, these three men would serve together at the point for many years. One usually finds their activities recounted in the log not by their individual names, but by their rank: "Keeper did so-and-so" or "1st asst. or 2nd asst. did such-and-such"—apparently Wheaton, a very conscientious keeper who was devoted to the point, believed in preserving this formality.

Cheboygan native Ed Wheaton began his lightkeeping career at about nineteen years of age. He spent about four months in the winter and spring of 1904 as the second assistant at North Manitou Light, then joined Keeper Ingvald Olsen at the isolated light on Waugoshance Shoal, a crib light erected off the coast of northern Lake Michigan. He served there for seven years. In August, 1909, he married Elvira Doyle, who was also from Cheboygan. They soon had a daughter, Thelma, but Ed's wife died when she was yet an infant. The motherless baby girl may have been cared for by her grandmother, Edward's mother Martha, for a number of years.

In 1911, Ed Wheaton became 1st assistant at the Sturgeon Bay Canal Light, where he remained for about seven years until his promotion in 1918 as keeper of the pier light in Milwaukee. At the time of the 1920 U.S. Census, 35-year old Ed, widowed, was living in that city's Third Ward. Subsequently, he was 1st assistant at the Chicago Breakwater Light; from there he moved back north as keeper at Racine Reef in 1930, and proceeded to Point Betsie, where many years later he would close out his career.

Along the way, Wheaton had re-married; he and his second wife, Elizabeth, had his daughter Thelma, with them. But Ed apparently was so visibly devoted to the child that his wife apparently became jealous of their relationship; perhaps to show that she wanted a greater measure of his affections, she took the unusual tactic of changing her own first name to the child's, Thelma. So, forever after, there was "Big Thelma" and "Little Thelma" within the family.[15] By the time the Wheatons were at Point Betsie, the daughter had essentially left home.

Ed's father, a Civil War veteran, had died when Ed, one of six children in the family, was but a pre-teen; during his years at Point Betsie, Ed used his leave time each summer to care for his aging widowed mother in Cheboygan, visiting her and performing household chores. Sometimes he would bring a young niece, "Gertie," back with him to play with a young Nelson girl for several weeks.

Point Betsie Light tower and antenna, circa 1930, with wooden shore protection.
Courtesy of Benzie Area Historical Museum

ON SEPTEMBER 11, 1933, WHEATON RECORDED IN THE LOG THAT AFTER ATTENDING TO HIS CUSTOMARY MORNING DUTIES, HE HAD BEGUN CONSTRUCTION OF A STONE PORCH AT THE SOUTHWEST CORNER OF THE KEEPER'S QUARTERS. The credit for this project goes to Ed Wheaton and his assistant, Nels Nelson; to this day, their craftsmanship and dedication are revealed in the porch and stone planters on the station's grounds. Building the porch was no small undertaking, as it involved constructing a base and foundation for the walls, and hauling to the site loads of beach sand and a huge quantity of Lake Michigan stones—attractive, appropriately-sized and shaped ones selected with care by the Nelson children. The individual stones were placed by hand to form the porch's decorative walls. Recently

Edward Wheaton
Courtesy of Paul and Joanne Wheaton

restored, the artistically designed and well-constructed porch continues to serve as the front entrance to the historic keeper's quarters.

Wheaton's work with beach stones brings to mind another intriguing story. Some years ago a gravestone, bearing only the word "Mother" and dates, was found in the sand and brush behind the Point Betsie lighthouse. The discovery led to much speculation about who was buried there, and the mystery was recounted in a local paper which happened to be seen by Ed Wheaton's nephew. The story piqued his curiosity, motivating him to get in touch with an older cousin who was more familiar with family matters. She immediately solved the case, recalling that after his mother's death, Ed had made a marker for her grave out of stones and concrete. Upon completing this masterpiece, he found it to be too heavy to load into his car; he was sadly forced to leave the fruit of his labors right where he built it. Even though the mystery has been solved, the story remains a favorite among visitors.[16]

&

WITH THE NATION IN THE GRIP OF THE DEPRESSION, Wheaton had closed the light's record of 1933 on December 31, with the message, "Retiring the old year with Mr. E. Wheaton, Keeper, Mr. H. Lafrenier 1 asst and N. Nelson 2 asst. All well and hope it will find us the same at the end of 1934."

Unfortunately, however, for the Point Betsie community as a whole, that was not to be; the two crews found themselves sharing the sorrowful word, on the first of December, 1934, of the death of Jack Dipert, son of Captain and Mrs. Dipert, who had followed his father's footsteps into the Coast Guard and was stationed at Muskegon. Carrying a crew of twenty-five across Lake Michigan from Milwaukee, the *Henry W. Cort*, a three hundred fifteen-foot ore carrier, was driven against the Muskegon breakwater by gale-force winds. When the stricken vessel's lights were spotted through the storm, the station's captain and three members of his crew boarded their power surfboat and went out to investigate. Having difficulty finding the *Cort*, the rescue craft was itself swamped among the surging waves and Dipert was drowned; the other rescuers managed to lash themselves to the boat and eventually made it to shore. Jack Dipert's loss brought home to the Point Betsie community the grim reality underlying the old lifesavers' motto, of which every crew member at a coastal rescue station was—and even today is—surely mindful: "You have to go out, but you don't have to come back."

❧

LIGHTNING STRUCK the Coast Guard boathouse the following summer while the Diperts were away, the strike running from there to the pump house and then to the station itself, where it fortunately did little damage. The winter of 1936 must have revived memories of past fierce days at the point. In mid-February, Captain Dipert recorded that he had left the station to get the mail; with snow blocking the highway, he had to walk the ice-covered beach to Frankfort and back, the trip taking much of the day. The rugged winter, however, little altered life at the station; a few steamers continued to pass, and the crew kept up their regular duties, including the periodic cleaning and overhauling of the station's rifles and pistols (a reminder of the agency's military affiliations), and the daily ritual of checking the telephone line. On one day, Captain Dipert and Surfman John Quinlan, Plowman's successor, had to repair seven telephone breaks to restore the station's vital contact with Frankfort.

❧

MORE NOTEWORTHY DAYS LAY AHEAD; 1937 would bring several developments of interest to Point Betsie. The first of these was the death, at age 83, of Captain Bedford on April 11. One of the most notable of Point Betsie's lifesavers, both as its No.1 and as its officer-in-charge, he was also much respected in the Frankfort community. Wrote the *Benzie County Patriot* upon his passing, "Probably no one had more friends than did Capt. Bedford. Always genial and friendly, he had a greeting for all he met and it was a pleasure to meet him." The paper recalled the Captain had served "...during the days of the schooner and he could tell many a tale of his experiences." Fittingly, the pallbearers came from both the Point Betsie and Frankfort Coast Guard stations and lighthouses. He and his family are buried in Crystal Lake Township Cemetery (North), on the road between Frankfort and Point Betsie.

In September of 1937, a Canadian vessel, the *J.H. Redfern*, was caught in a gale for two days and ultimately sank about four miles off Point Betsie, imperiling the lives of its fifteen-man crew. Fortunately, they were all rescued by Coast Guardsmen from the Frankfort and South Manitou Island stations, with the service's cutter *Escanaba* standing by. The ability of these two facilities to serve the Point Betsie area—and the point station's redundancy—had again been demonstrated.

∽

EVERY GREAT RIDE MUST COME TO AN END. Doubtless, Captain Bedford and others in the Coast Guard community could foresee, with much regret, the demise of the storied Point Betsie rescue station. The end came only months after Bedford's death; on December 14, 1937, Captain Dipert logged his completion of the customary duties and at 3 p.m., penned the epitaph, "Point Betsie station was decommissioned." As the *Benzie County Patriot* put it more eloquently, Dipert and his assistant "...locked the door, nailed up the shutters and for the first time in 60 years the Point was without a coast guard and finis was written to another chapter, rich in the romance of lake lore."[17]

Captain Fisher of Frankfort's Coast Guard station publicly criticized the closing, saying he and his men had depended on Point Betsie's vantage point for reporting fish tugs or other vessels delayed or in distress. A potentially grave situation three years earlier offered an example of such collaboration; a fish tug, described as "helpless because of a disabled motor," was adrift off Point Betsie and poor visibility prevented the Frankfort station's lookout from monitoring the boat's position and condition. Station Frankfort asked the Point Betsie post to observe the craft; the latter reported that distress signals were being raised on the boat, which fortunately was subsequently recovered by the Frankfort crew.[18] Nonetheless, Fisher's protestations were of no avail.

Dipert spent the next year as No. 1 at the Ludington station, where he had served prior to his Point Betsie stint, then retired from the Coast Guard. John Quinlan served out his career, retiring in 1947. Interestingly, just four months after the Point Betsie station's demise, the end also came for the North Manitou Island station.

∽

THERE SOON AROSE THE QUESTION OF THE DISPOSITION OF THE POINT BETSIE COAST GUARD BUILDING. A notice was issued advising the public that the station house would be formally abandoned and declared surplus property. The decision to dispose of the property came after the Lighthouse Service's district office had examined blueprints and photographs to see if it might be a useful addition to the lighthouse's own holdings. The agency reasoned:

The building stands some seven hundred feet distant from the Lighthouse Reservation. Although this distance would be inconvenient in inclement weather and for other considerations for Keepers residing in the building in its present location, this distance is not considered of sufficient inconvenience to warrant the expense of moving the building along the beach....

In other words, the expense of moving the station building close to the lighthouse, where it would provide better housing for the lightkeepers and their families, was not justified. Nor did the government foresee any economic gain in a sale of the property on which the station stood; the district superintendent wrote to the commissioner of lighthouses, "No particular advantage would accrue...in disposing of the Coast Guard property separate from the structure as the property is remote from any town, is, in general, non-productive soil and would be worth no more than any other parcel similar in size in the vicinity as the site for a cottage or summer home." Today's seekers of shoreline property might find this dismissive assessment surprising.

The district superintendent did acknowledge that the station was in excellent condition, and he recognized that with rearrangement of a number of interior walls and the installation of another kitchen and bathroom, the building could provide quarters for two lightkeepers, one on each floor. The problem was, there were three keepers at Point Betsie Light. He noted that the original keeper's quarters in the lighthouse had been enlarged years before, but that the space was inadequate for housing three families of average size. Plans had been developed to reconfigure the interior to more equitably distribute the space; the existing arrangement gave the keeper six rooms, the first assistant only three rooms, while the second assistant had four. The installation of inside plumbing fixtures was also within the budget, he reported. So, rather than having to fund the maintenance of two buildings—the lighthouse and the relocated Coast Guard residence—the district favored using its available funds to improve the lighthouse living spaces. Thus, the Lighthouse Service passed up the opportunity to request transfer of the former Guard Station, and the station and shoreline site soon became eligible for purchase as surplus property.

∽

ON JULY 1, 1939 – JUST ONE MONTH SHORT OF THE SESQUICENTENNIAL OF THE LIGHTHOUSE SERVICE'S FORMATION IN AUGUST, 1789—THE BUREAU OF LIGHTHOUSES AND ITS RESPONSIBILITIES, ALONG WITH

THE LEADERSHIP OF THE COMMISSIONER OF LIGHTHOUSES, WERE ABRUPTLY TRANSFERRED out of the Commerce Department, its bureaucratic home for almost forty years, and into the U.S. Coast Guard, a Treasury Department agency. With a stroke of President Roosevelt's pen—a reorganization which many veteran lightkeepers deeply resented—America's lighthouses were placed under the Coast Guard's multi-purpose management.

The lighthouse community greeted the announcement with sadness, certain that the distinguished agency's identity and traditions would be swallowed up in a larger bureaucracy. As had many keepers of the old lifesaving stations almost twenty-five years earlier when the Coast Guard had absorbed their own historic agency, many lightkeepers now became chief boatswain's mates. And, with the passage of time, the retirements of Lighthouse Service veterans led to light station assignments of relatively young, less experienced men whose services were not always highly regarded by the "old pros". There was even some subsequent suspicion that assignments to lights were handed out to men less skilled in other Coast Guard functions. But while such skepticism can be understood in the face of the Lighthouse Service's rich past and the depth of pride typically placed in its heritage by the agency's "long-timers," Coast Guardsmen gradually proved themselves capable heirs of a great service tradition.

At Point Betsie, however, the personnel situation was stable, but life was not entirely uneventful. The night of April 30, 1940, surely was an exciting one for the Wheatons and other point residents, for shortly after midnight his niece, Ruth Meggitt Steele, gave birth to twin boys in the keeper's quarters.

SHORTLY BEFORE CHRISTMAS, 1940, there occurred an intriguing event which shows how swiftly time's passage erodes memories. Mid-November brought a fierce gale to the area on Armistice Day, a storm often described as the most powerful to hit communities and mariners up and down Lake Michigan's eastern shore. Several weeks later, someone walking the Platte Bay beach found an unusual wooden structure, an oak frame with long spikes, like comb teeth, running fully around it. No one apparently had a clue as to what this was, but there were lots of guesses. Placed in a prominent town window, it took a passing Coast Guardsman to identify the item correctly as a "faking box" used to wind a Lyle gun's shot-line so that the projectile would fly smoothly off the beach when fired to a vessel in difficulty. In one of the last uses of a Lyle gun in this region, one had been fired when the *City of Flint*, a Pere Marquette railroad ferry, had been driven aground at Ludington by the great storm. The box had somehow gotten away and come ashore after drifting nearly seventy miles north.

In about 1940, when the boathouse collapsed, the Coast Guard sought to enhance the protection of Point Betsie Light from the lake's erosive forces through the installation of new sheet pilings—a portent of greater efforts soon to come. But as sometimes happens with such installations, while apparently serving the immediate purpose, the works may have contributed to additional cutting away of the shoreline.

∼

HISTORY TELLS US THAT THE COAST GUARD SOON HAD MUCH MORE SERIOUS ISSUES TO BE CONCERNED ABOUT. A plot plan shows that in early 1942, consideration was given but apparently not pursued, to siting an "aerial identification platform" on the former rescue station tract. The customary operational routines at Point Betsie and other light stations had been suddenly shattered on December 7, 1941, by the shocking development that Wheaton dutifully logged: "Japan made an early morning air raid on Pearl Harbor…" and the next day he followed that notation with the entry, "United States declared war on Japan 12:30 P.M. The vote for war in Congress was unanimous, with one exception, Mrs. Rankin voted against war."

During the following winter of 1942, the Point Betsie and Frankfort communities lost another much respected couple who were part of the Light's great tradition of service, Phil and Grace Sheridan. Like many other veterans of Point Betsie service, the Sheridans had returned to Frankfort in their retirement after he had finished his career at the Michigan City, Indiana, pier light. The later years were not kind to this distinguished keeper and his spouse; seriously ill and confined to bed for his last four years, Phil Sheridan passed away at the Marine hospital in Chicago, where he was

Phil Sheridan and wife Grace at Pt. Betsie

Courtesy of Stephen Sheridan

taken after his wife, herself fatally ill, could no longer care for him. The Sheridans were buried in Crystal Lake Township Cemetery (North).

In that same year, well-known former Point Betsie surfman, Charles Gaul, passed away; three years later, Frank Jeffs, another much recognized veteran of the station's active days, was gone. The spring of 1943 brought word of still another loss, that of veteran lightkeeper Severin Danielsen, living in retirement at Escanaba in the Upper Peninsula. The passing years were taking their toll among Point Betsie's storied figures.

◦෨

BY THE SUMMER OF 1943, FOLLOWING A SEVERE SPRING STORM THAT YEAR, THE EROSION SITUATION AT POINT BETSIE HAD BECOME A MAJOR CONCERN. Keeper Wheaton reported that if the old sea wall in front of the lighthouse had not been replaced by a steel wall, the spring gale—one of the worst storms this veteran coast-watcher had ever seen—would have undermined the structure and destroyed its foundation. As it was, the shoreline, sidewalk and concrete driveway between the lighthouse and old Coast Guard station had been broken up by the encroaching surf.

Cyclically high water levels on Lake Michigan were combining with changes in the immediate area's currents stemming, in the judgment of the experts at Frankfort's Luedtke Engineering Company, from the steel wall that had been installed to protect the lighthouse. The shore on both sides of the lighthouse, including the property to the south adjacent to the former Coast Guard station, was seriously scouring. Its owner sought the marine engineering firm's assistance in protecting his property, but was advised that unless the Coast Guard—operating then under wartime naval administration—undertook further protective work that was also needed at the lighthouse, his property and summer home would fall victim to the ravages of the lake.

The Luedtke firm bid on the project and was advised of its bid's acceptance in 1943, but frustrating bureaucratic delays in the government's contracting formalities prevented the job from being started that fall despite the company's warning that it would be impossible to proceed with the work during harsh winter weather. That proved to be the case. The poor condition of the Point Betsie access road (preventing delivery of a crane to the site), the lack of availability of stone for filling between the new protective bulkhead extension and the existing works after heavy snow had covered the ground, and the especially severe icing that year combined to block the job until the spring of 1944.

Ice at the tower base, January, 1944.
Courtesy of Alan K. Luedtke

1944 protective bulkhead, with man working on tower.
Courtesy of Alan K. Luedtke

View from north of bulkhead, fog signal building, air tanks and antenna tower.
Courtesy of Alan K. Luedtke

AS WORLD WAR II DREW TO A CLOSE, THE COAST GUARD WAS ACTIVELY SEARCHING FOR ABOUT FIVE HUNDRED ACRES OF PROPERTY IN BENZIE COUNTY, hoping to establish a search-and-rescue base for both land-based planes and amphibian craft that would enhance the efficiency and performance of its marine response capabilities. It was anticipated that about seventy-five men would be assigned to such a facility. Two sites, several miles south of the Frankfort-Elberta area near Upper and Lower Herring Lakes, and the other between Little Platte Lake and Lake Michigan to the northeast of Point Betsie, were under consideration. Meanwhile, some thought was given to basing an amphibian rescue plane in Frankfort. However, on November 15, 1945, the Naval Air Station in Traverse City was decommissioned; the facility was then re-commissioned as a Coast Guard Air Station, from which it still continues to provide vital helicopter rescue services that cover much of Lakes Michigan and Superior.[19] Among the station's early leaders was Frankfort native Robert Johnson, son of former Point Betsie Coast Guard station boss Sigval Johnson.

Many aspects of American life had been changed by the impact of World War II. There would be no return to the isolationism which had characterized the nation's policies between the world conflicts. As for Point Betsie, the sense of isolation that had lingered from the light station's formative period was virtually gone, except when vicious winter storms interrupted motor vehicle travel. Important services to mariners from that key vantage point, however, would be maintained for many years.

CHAPTER ELEVEN

FROM WORLD WAR II
TO THE PRESENT

The last half of the twentieth century brought many changes to Point Betsie Light, culminating with the station's being relegated largely to history. Through the years, the availability of vastly improved navigational aids gradually reduced mariners' reliance upon lighthouses and fog horns. And fast, sea worthy boats as well as helicopters allowed the Coast Guard to consolidate rescue services while generally maintaining the effectiveness of their emergency response capabilities. At the conclusion of this transitional half-century, the only Coast Guard responsibility at the Point, aside from its continued ownership of an adjacent vacation cottage, was the minimal task of servicing, as needed, the tower's rotating automatic light.

Yet, one ought not understate the significance of the past six decades within Point Betsie's long story. Most of the Coast Guardsmen who served at Point Betsie subsequent to World War II, as well as current visitors and the volunteers and local officials who are now charting the landmark's future role, have known the station only during this gradual reduction of its navigational significance. But this reality hasn't dampened anyone's enthusiasm about the place. The crewmen and families who lived at the point from the war years until the station's residential closing had a chance to share in a bit of America's maritime history. And it is clear that even though light-tending didn't hold much career potential for those men, they evidently much appreciated their Point Betsie assignment.

❧

ALTHOUGH THE HISTORIC ADJACENT RESCUE STATION SAT EMPTY, THE LIGHTHOUSE REMAINED AN ACTIVE PLACE DURING THE WAR AND FOR SEVERAL DECADES AFTERWARD. For example, at times during the summer of 1942 the numerous tasks at the lighthouse and fog signal building were handled by four men: Captain Wheaton himself; his long-time first assistant, Henry "Hank" LaFreniere; Nels Nelson's replacement, Jerry Conley, who transferred from the North Manitou Shoal light station after Nels Nelson's re-assignment to South Chicago, and Claude Harrison of the Frankfort Coast Guard Reserve, who helped out as needed at Point Betsie.

The Wheaton era was the last in which Point Betsie light's crewmen served together for much of their respective careers. They performed their duties throughout a significant period, when they and other lighthouse men made the transition into the Coast Guard. "Cap" Wheaton was in charge between 1933 and his retirement in 1946. LaFreniere retired in the mid-1940s after spending twenty-seven years at the station, and Nelson served there for a decade, until his 1941 transfer. These three veteran lighthouse men and their families were a close community; each was thoroughly experienced in Lake Michigan navigational needs, well versed in all lighthouse operations and committed to Point Betsie's specific mission. The team's professionalism was much respected.

Hank and Hattie LaFreniere had met on Beaver Island and married there, her birthplace. A native "downstater" whose family had moved to the island, he entered the Lighthouse Service on Squaw Island, northwest within the Beaver archipelago. Their son, Chuck, was born and spent his infancy on that island and his youth by Lake Michigan at Point Betsie, which may explain his own career path. After high school in Frankfort, he worked on the Ann Arbor boats until serving on Army ships during the war, earning his captain's stripes. He returned home to the ferries after the war, soon becoming a captain and sailing for the line until his sudden death, in 1968, from heart failure suffered aboard the *Viking* as it prepared to depart Frankfort harbor.

Nels and Gusty Nelson with granddaughter, Virginia.
Courtesy of Paul Marcussen

Henry and Hattie LaFreniere with infant son, Chuck.
Courtesy of Sally Pryce

The LaFrenieres' grand niece treasures her vivid memories of frequent childhood visits to Point Betsie. She recalls that she was only about a year old when she began visiting the lighthouse with her parents during her spring and summer vacations. "When I was very young, Aunt Hattie would wake me early and dress me in front of the big shiny coal stove", she recounts. "Then Uncle Hank would take me on his morning chores – raising the flag, feeding the hummingbirds, helping me up the tower steps and holding me up while I turned off the switch. He would polish the lens and wrap the cloth around them. Then, we would head back to the kitchen for breakfast."[1]

Only after she was a little older did she think positively toward the station's horn. "I thought it was a monster," she recalled, adding, "Aunt Hattie discovered if she did not dust under the furniture, I would do it for her with my clothes, as they would find me hiding from that fog horn." While some people wish they could yet hear those old fog horn blasts, her reaction was hardly unique. Author Steven Karges, writing of lighthouses across Lake Michigan in Door County, Wisconsin,[2] notes that some people found those deep tones melancholic, likening them to a cow's pathetic call to a lost calf. He also recounted the experience of a foreign visitor to Sturgeon Bay who recuperated from an illness at the home of friends near a light station. She became so distressed by the piercing tones that she immediately left for her distant home.

The local newspaper published an early 1940s story involving LaFreniere and a friend; it seems that farmers living near Point Betsie were being warned, albeit tongue-in-cheek, to be cautious "…about letting the animals roam the dunes this fall if [these men] are anywhere in the country." The story reported that LaFreniere had told his friend about a deer track he had just discovered—the biggest, he said, he had ever seen. The story continued, "While discussing it they looked up across the dunes and… sighted a group of three doe. They started toward the animals and it was not until they got within a few feet of them they discovered they had tracked down three of the nicest heifers you could imagine." That the paper carried such an anecdote is testimony to the good feelings townspeople held for these faithful Point Betsie crewmen.

Having received fond farewells from the community in December, 1945, "Cap" Wheaton and his wife left the Point to serve as a navigation aids instructor in Detroit, where the Coast Guard had begun holding training classes for new recruits. The assignment proved to be briefer than expected, however, for within less than a month, they were back at Point Betsie where he concluded his career the following June. Having served a total of forty-two years in the Lighthouse Service and the Coast Guard, the Wheatons retired to Florida, where he died in 1954.

The LaFrenieres retired to South Haven, Michigan. Sadly, Hank died in 1962 at a lighthouse medical facility that was situated at a Kentucky prison, separated from Hattie by the substantial distance and her inability to travel there. Nels Nelson devoted thirty-seven years to lighthouse work in both agencies, including, in addition to his long service at Point Betsie, work on both Manitous and the Fox Islands, at South Chicago, and finally at Frankfort's pier light. He retired in 1947, operating a marina in the local harbor and offering rides in a speedboat made by Higgins, a company whose boats became famous during World War II. He was widowed in 1959 and died in Frankfort in 1962 at age seventy-eight.

Winter of 1944, on post card Mrs. Wheaton made.
Courtesy of Paul Marcussen

IN ADDITION TO THE BULKHEAD INSTALLATION IN 1944, A SUBSTANTIAL REMODELING PROJECT WAS UNDERTAKEN AT THAT TIME. It was then that the building's exterior acquired its existing character; in conjunction with a reconfiguration of the second floor, two south-facing dormer windows were added at the western and eastern ends of the building. Both first- and second-floor apartments were modified to arrange for new kitchens, bathrooms and bedrooms, thereby significantly improving the two assistant keepers' living quarters. Subsequently, two no longer used chimneys over the assistants' section of the original lighthouse were removed. (During a 2006 renovation of the lighthouse's exterior, the building was restored to its mid-1940s configuration and colors, the task requiring the removal of dozens of layers of paint. For historical accuracy, replicas of the two missing brick chimneys were erected.)

A building just behind the lighthouse that had been used to house coal, was relegated to various storage needs in the station's later years. A privy that had been located immediately next to its north end was removed, and a garage that had been built originally as a boathouse was relocated to the lighthouse driveway entrance.

A major change in the light's mechanism was also made in 1944, when an electric motor was installed to rotate the light, replacing the old weight-driven mechanism. The change relieved the crew from the burden of climbing the stairs every few hours for the necessary re-winding. Point Betsie Light continued to rotate every 10 seconds, flashing across the sky for 1.3 seconds, then eclipsing for 8.7 seconds. As is generally true of new technology, this modernization, while reliable, was one of several changes that would pave the way for eventual personnel reductions.

The diaphone fog signal and radiobeacon remained important navigational aids. Twice every thirty seconds, the horn would sound its distinctive pattern through the megaphone-like trumpet extending from the building's west wall toward the lake: a one and one-half second blast followed by two seconds of silence, then another one and one-half second blast followed by a silent twenty-five seconds. The radiobeacon sent out its dot, dash, dash, dot pattern on 290 kilocycles; the fog horn and radiobeacon were synchronized every three minutes for distance-finding aboard vessels that were so equipped.

✑

WITH THE END OF THE WAR, IN 1945, CAME WIDESPREAD DISPOSALS OF COAST GUARD PROPERTIES THAT IN POST-WAR AMERICA WERE REGARDED AS SURPLUS TO FUTURE NEEDS. In fact, as of the end of June, 1946, only sixty-one lifeboat stations were still in "active" status throughout the United States, a far greater number of these old rescue stations having already been shut down.

A final reminder of Point Betsie's long record of lifesaving service came in November, 1947, with the retirement of John Quinlan after thirty-three years' service in the Coast Guard and two years with the old Lighthouse Service. He had enlisted in the Coast Guard at Beaver Island, serving eighteen years there before being transferred to the Point Betsie Coast Guard Station, which he later helped William Dipert shut down. Quinlan finished out his long career by working at both the Frankfort Coast Guard Station and Point Betsie Light.

✑

THE SHUTTERED POINT BETSIE RESCUE STATION WAS BACK IN THE LOCAL NEWS AT THE WAR'S END. Having been vacant for about nine years and officially "inactive" for more than a decade before that, the station was advertised for disposal in late 1945. Bids were invited, with the presumption that the structure would be promptly dismantled. But fortunately for history, the handsome building survived. It was acquired by neighboring families residing in New Castle, Indiana, the Arvid Zetterbergs and Dixon Oberdorfers. The Zetterberg family were long-time summer vacationers in the area and owned adjacent Point Betsie property; in part, they intended the additional parcel to memorialize their son, Lieutenant Pierre Zetterberg, who had loved Point Betsie as a young man, and had been killed in action in Germany just prior to the end of the war in Europe.[3]

Another Zetterberg son, Steven, recalled that when his family had first come to Point Betsie, some two decades prior to the purchase, the Coast Guard was still supplying its station from boats that tied up at a dock out in front. Then under the command of Abram Wessel, the property was always in "great shape," he says, just as the formal records would imply. Wessel and his assistant had diligently maintained the property, even though their capacity to assist mariners was by that time seriously diminished. The road was still gravel-surfaced and mostly single-lane, with several sandy turn-outs where vehicles could pass. Zetterberg also recalled keeping a shovel handy with which to dig out stranded cars. He remembered that the Coast Guard had a fine workshop in a shed by the boathouse, where he and other Point Betsie children would make model boats, and that lightkeeper Wheaton had helped his mother fortify and expand their chicken house.[4] The residents at Point Betsie were truly a community.

In 1962, the old Coast Guard station and surrounding property was sold to another Indiana neighbor of the Zetterbergs, Thomas B. Millikan, as a summer cottage. A small cottage immediately next to the old station recently has been known as the "Captain's Quarters," but it housed the No.1 surfman (the only crew by that time) and his family as the Wessels and their "passel of kids" resided in the main building. Throughout the ensuing years, the Millikans have been dedicated to retaining the station's historic structural features, making only minor interior changes to meet their needs. Through the generosity of the Zetterberg family, close to one hundred acres of Point Betsie's natural landscape also have been protected under the ownership and management of The Nature Conservancy.

ᦕ

TO RETURN TO HISTORICAL NARRATIVE, a manpower shortage in the Coast Guard in the latter days of World War II and subsequent years forced the agency to curtail operations at a number of its locations. Shortly after the war's end, the

Coast Guard placed its South Manitou Island station on "inactive" status, despite its important location within the Manitou Passage, insisting its air rescue services based at Traverse City could cover the region in conjunction with boats based at other area stations. The authorities also said that in the event a large vessel experienced serious trouble, an eighty-three-foot cutter would be dispatched from Charlevoix, along with—if need be—another cutter from Grand Haven and the icebreaker *Mackinaw* based in Cheboygan, on the Lake Huron shore. Such assurances, however, were not very comforting to commercial fishermen then running their tugs in these waters, as many of them had not yet been equipped with radio transmission equipment and had valued the island-based station's presence.

At the lighthouse, Coast Guardsman Louis Bauchan arrived for duty in 1947, soon after Ed Wheaton's retirement. The station was fortunate to be served by him, if only for about five years until his transfer to Hawaii. Bauchan had joined the Lighthouse Service in 1935, during the Depression, serving first as a cook on the tender *Sumac;* he also spent ten years as keeper at Lake Michigan's St. Martin Island station, during which time Roosevelt incorporated the lighthouses in the Coast Guard and Bauchan became a "Coastie" to continue lightkeeping. His career took him to several other Great Lakes lights besides Point Betsie, and also aboard the Coast Guard's original Great Lakes icebreaker *Mackinaw*, now decommissioned after being replaced by a new vessel of the same name. Spending his retirement years in Cheboygan, Bauchan passed away in the spring of 2003 at the age of ninety-one; he was believed to be the longest surviving veteran of the old Lighthouse Service. That he had valued his stint at Point Betsie was attested to by the family's request that contributions in his memory be made to support the lighthouse's preservation and restoration. The respected *Lighthouse Digest* published a fitting tribute to him, saying that his legacy "…will go down in history, there will never be another like him; he will be dearly missed. Not only was he part of the 'Greatest Generation,' he was a hero of it."[5]

✎

IN 1948, THE COAST GUARD MADE A NOTABLE CHANGE IN POINT BETSIE'S FOG SIGNAL, ADDING A SECOND "TRUMPET" TO PRODUCE BLASTS OF TWO TONES, ONE HIGH AND ONE LOW.[6] The "characteristic" of Point Betsie's signal—its sequence—was not changed; it would still produce a group of two blasts, lasting one and one-half seconds, every thirty seconds, one followed by five seconds of silence and the next by twenty-five seconds of silence. The radiobeacon and fog signal remained synchronized, allowing vessels to use them for distance-finding.

The value of converting to two tones was that lower tones carried a greater distance than higher tones did and the lower tone in a two-tone system would be heard longer than a diaphone's traditional "grunt." This was an improvement, to be sure, but it didn't entirely overcome what the Coast Guard repeatedly acknowledged to be "inherent defects" in fog signals. The 1972 *Light List* contained typical advice to mariners, saying that fog signals "...can never be implicitly relied upon, and that the practice of taking soundings of depth of water should never be neglected" when their vessel is sailing near land. The photo below, taken in 1953, shows the dual system's two trumpets on the west side of Point Betsie's fog signal building:

Second trumpet as installed at the peak of the main roof.
Courtesy of Pat and Bill Forney

ANOTHER WELCOMED CHANGE AT POINT BETSIE IN THE "FIFTIES" was the black-topping of Point Betsie Road by the Benzie County Road Commission. In preparation, the road had been rebuilt and partly re-routed. This would prove to be a major convenience to visitors as well as the crews continuing to reside there.

Among the men early in that decade were George Parrot, who was officer-in-charge of the station, and assistants Bert McKinney and Charlie Payment, who had been transferred there from Frankfort. The latter's son, Louis Payment, has written of his family's arrival and rich experiences at their father's new duty station.[7] Like many other "Coasties," the Payments were a Coast Guard family; not only was Charlie a career man, but so was his father-in-law. Charlie met his wife on Mackinac Island when the two men were stationed there.

> *The night we arrived at our new home, we were not prepared for the sound that welcomed us. Our first night...would be spent with very little sleep. It was a foggy night and the fog horn was blasting. We had all heard*

the sound of a fog horn before but hadn't heard it at such close proximity. I'm sure we all wondered how we could be expected to live with that kind of noise. I'm sure if someone had told us we would get used to it, we would have told them they were crazy. As odd as it seems, however, that is exactly what happened. We found that after we had made that adjustment, we would hear the first blast and then become oblivious to the following reports. I know that's hard to believe, but it's true. And we found when Dad retired and we moved to Empire, we all missed the sound of Point Betsie's fog horn. On nights when the weather conditions were right and the Point's foghorn was sounding we could hear its familiar signature call in Empire. When we would hear it, we always felt a sentimental twinge of longing for those days living at Point Betsie.

Life for the children of the three families then living at the station, Louis Payment recalled, was truly special—in his words, "...perfect for a pre-adolescent boy. Every day held the promise of a new adventure. I've always been happy we didn't know what television was. If we had owned a television, I doubt if we would have enjoyed the life we knew. We knew, without being told, that if we wanted to have any fun we'd have to generate it ourselves. We also knew that if we got into a fight with our 'buddy' it had better be a short one because we didn't have an alternate pal to turn to."

Among his favorite memories was walking Point Betsie Road to M-22, the highway, to get the school bus:

It was a one mile walk, but we always enjoyed it. There was often wildlife or some new discovery to look forward to on the fifteen-to-twenty minute walk....On days when the weather was bad enough to warrant it, one of the men would give us a ride. On days when the lake was really kicking up, the waves would hit the breakwall in front of the buildings and the water would just explode, sending a spray high enough to cover the roof of our two story living quarters. If we didn't time it right we would get a second shower when we stepped outside. Mom, when describing to friends what these heavy waves were like, would explain how the dishes in the cupboards would rattle. In the winter the spray would create a coating of ice on everything. The ice reflecting the sunlight would sparkle on the buildings and shrubs giving the scene a look of something from a children's fairy tale.

There were chores for the older children. Louis wrote he would not likely ever forget taking turns with the oldest boy in the "Chief's" family in the important task of removing the dust cover from the "huge fresnel lenses" and turning on the light at the proper time. On Saturdays, it was his job to swab the floor of the kitchen, hallway and bathroom with hot water and "G.I. soap", working with a scrub brush on his hands and knees. After the washing, the floors were rinsed and left to dry, then waxed. This was the level of cleanliness demanded by the Coast Guard's lighthouse inspectors.

The lighthouse basement, which was where lines were strung for drying the families' laundry, was a popular play area for the station's children. They played in their stocking feet, he recalled, because the men "...scrubbed and waxed those floors and they weren't about to clean up the marks from a bunch of kids' shoes."

Louis Payment's memories of the fog signal building, which also housed the station's radiobeacon equipment, are instructive. The building contained large diesel engines that would provide power in the event of a failure on the line to the point, as well as the compressor that powered the horn. He remembered a long workbench and an impressive array of tools and equipment:

> One long wall was taken up with an ominous bank of radio equipment. It's front was a metal wall of lighted dials, large black knobs, toggle switches and an untold number of other gizmos and gadgets that were far beyond my understanding. On one end there was a large clock with a long pendulum. The loud ticking sound was usually the first thing you heard when you entered the building. There were other electronic bell sounds and occasionally there was a message that would come in on short wave or ship-to-shore radio. I can also remember the identifying Morse code signal that was broadcast around the clock. It was one short, two longs and another short. Its audible sound was 'di-dah-dah-dit." This impressive radio equipment stood about eight feet high and was probably thirty feet long. It was three feet deep and there was a narrow passageway that went between the radio and the main wall, allowing room for a man to go behind for maintenance purposes. There was a chain stretched across the entrance to this passageway with a metal sign hanging from it warning DANGER—HIGH VOLTAGE!"

The neatness of the "radio shack" impressed Louis, who recalled that its cement floors were mopped each day and frequently given a fresh coat of "regulation battleship gray" paint. He added:

> The walkways were delineated by black, corrugated, rubber mats. Periodically, on sunny days the mats were taken outside and painted with a thinned-out solution of black enamel paint and fuel oil. When the paint dried, those mats looked like they were brand new. The diesel engines were kept just as clean as the floors. I can remember being fascinated by the fuel lines, exhaust piping and all kinds of other pipes that were painted in bright red, yellow, black and blue. This form of color coding indicated what each pipe was for. To a young boy's eyes, this building was more than impressive, especially when its appearance was coupled with the smells of fresh paint, G.I. soap, floor wax and diesel fuel.

Louis Payment's recollections are vivid testimony of life at Point Betsie in the light station's halcyon, mid-twentieth-century years. He acknowledged, "I've always felt sorry for kids who didn't grow up with access to the outdoor offerings we enjoyed…. We had it all. Lake Michigan at our doorstep, where we fished and swam, miles and miles of sugar sand beaches, rolling dunes with low spots where small lakes and ponds would form, islands of heavy forest surrounded by sand dunes and large wooded stands that we never did fully explore. Buddies at school were always asking if they could come out for a weekend of camping and exploring."

᪥

IN 1958, THE STATION'S BARN, WHICH HAD STOOD JUST EAST OF THE LIGHTHOUSE, WAS SOLD to a nearby property owner who incorporated the structure, topped with a small cupola, within his summer cottage.

By 1960, the U.S. *Light List* specifically noted that there were resident personnel at the Point Betsie station—an unusual entry that could be interpreted as a commentary on the extent to which the automation movement was sweeping through the Great Lakes stations. The crew maintained a long, popular tradition—weekend "open houses" and occasional other visitor sessions.

This was also a time when both federal and state governments were wrestling with the issues associated with ensuring that additional shoreline areas of particular significance might remain open to public use. Point Betsie was identified in the spring of 1960 as an attractive site for a possible state park, but Michigan's shortage of funds quickly curtailed that discussion. However, efforts to protect miles of Lake Michigan shore to the north of the point, including beaches covered by Point Betsie's legendary patrols, proved successful in 1970 with the enactment—after a decade-long battle in Congress—of federal legislation creating the Sleeping Bear Dunes National Lakeshore. Overlooking the Manitou Passage and surrounding waters, the park contains about thirty-five miles of mainland shore and the two Manitou Islands. It includes the exemplarily restored lifesaving station at Glen Haven, which features seasonal demonstrations of rescue techniques and opportunities for visitors to participate in reenacted beach patrols.

In 1961, the National Music Camp at Interlochen, located between the Point Betsie area and Traverse City, purchased approximately ninety acres at the point, including almost one-quarter mile of Lake Michigan shoreline, from the widow of A.P. Peterson. The camp subsequently used the land for a number of years for recreational activities prior to selling the property. An interesting aspect of the Peterson sale is that it included close to twenty acres adjacent to the lighthouse that had constituted the last tract in Michigan—and one of the last shoreline tracts, if not the very last one in the country—to qualify for treatment under the famous Homestead Act of 1862.

Noticing in the early 1920s that the value of Michigan land suited to vacation purposes was starting to increase in value, Peterson, had studied the area townships and found that this parcel had somehow been passed by during decades of homestead activity. He had staked his claim, just as an early settler would have done, and in early April, 1924—for three cents, then the price of a stamp—had forwarded his application to the secretary of the interior in Washington. The department had initially denied his bid on grounds President Calvin Coolidge, on April 24 of that year, had withdrawn all government-owned land on the coasts from the homestead process. But the persistent Peterson had sought the assistance of a U.S. senator from Michigan, who had ascertained that the application had reached the secretary one hour prior to the effective time of the Coolidge order. After living on the property as settlers for seven months a year for five years, in 1929 the victorious Petersons, having "proved" their claim, had received an official certificate confirming their ownership.[8]

≈

1962 SAW THE LAST TECHNOLOGICAL IMPROVEMENTS at Point Betsie Light. As detailed in the 1962 and subsequent issues of the *Light List,* the light's candle-power was boosted from a rating of 70,000 to 350,000, and the station's fog signal was changed from a two-toned diaphone to a two-toned diaphragm, still sounding its pattern twice every thirty seconds. The newer equipment passed compressed air over metal diaphragms, creating a vibration that would yield a sound sometimes described as rather wail-like. By a number of years thereafter, the horn had ceased to be two-toned, and its characteristic had been very slightly modified to produce two, two-second blasts every thirty seconds, with silent intervals of two seconds and twenty-four seconds.

1963 brought the deaths of two well-known Point Betsie figures. Keeper John P. Campbell, a full-blooded Cherokee who served at the point from 1958 to 1963, passed away that August, and Sigurd M. Frey, a former Ann Arbor captain who had spend his early working years in the Coast Guard at Frankfort and Point Betsie, died near year's end.

≈

ABOUT THIS TIME, THE COAST GUARD DISCONTINUED MANY REMAINING LOOKOUT TOWERS. The increasing use of radio equipment on the Great Lakes meant that men no longer needed to spend hours scanning the waters, waiting for signs of trouble. Visual signaling, by which early lakes mariners had called for help, was no longer a common practice, and vessels with modern navigation equipment had no need to navigate by hugging the shore, where they were at risk of striking submerged rocks and shoals. In fact, according to an account in the *Benzie*

County Patriot,[9] assistance reports for 1962 in the Ninth Coast Guard District showed that only ten percent of the "...distress situations were actually reported by the lookouts at the lifeboat stations. The remainder were reported to the Coast Guard either by the distressed boat itself, by other crafts in the area, or by people observing from the shore....(A)ll of the emergencies which were first observed by the lookout were soon reported by telephone calls from people observing along the shore."

Commander Vance K. Randle, who headed the district's search-and-rescue branch, summed up the situation this way: "The homes along the shore, with their large picture windows overlooking the lakes, often afford these people a better vantage point to observe lake activity than most of our lookout towers." The message was clear: many of the forty lifeboat stations that then remained on the Great Lakes would cease tower activities, and some would be closed altogether. At only a few stations, especially those overlooking congested waterways and port entrances where collisions were a greater risk, would the lookout tradition survive.

Yet another movement away from historic practices came with the Coast Guard's announcement in mid-1964 that its stations would no longer be known as "lifeboat" stations. The terminology had outlived reality. As for Point Betsie Light, the day was long past when its crew would have a boat at the site; nor had the station received its supplies of fuel, food, construction and maintenance equipment, and even its box of books, from lighthouse tenders such as the *Dahlia* and *Hyacinth* for many years. The crew and the station's goods were easily moved to and from the site over roads. There being no rescue boats at the lighthouse, any emergencies involving small boats on Lake Michigan continued to be handled by the Frankfort station and the Coast Guard's airborne crews operating from Traverse City.

This diminished status proved frustrating—and possibly even costly to human life—on a Saturday in late September, 1967, when thousands of fishermen from all over Michigan and nearby states descended upon nearby Platte Bay in what came to be known as "coho salmon mania." This was the first year of fishing following the state's successful program of planting alewife-eating salmon in Lake Michigan. Many anglers not accustomed to Great Lakes conditions, reacting as might be expected to widespread news reports of the initial catches, brought to these waters small boats unsuited for rough conditions. Others likely knew better, but brushed those concerns aside in their eagerness to go for the big fish. All of them were to find themselves challenged as never before, especially those boaters who had launched their craft in Frankfort harbor and headed north around Point Betsie to Platte Bay in the morning's beautiful conditions.

That afternoon, generally without benefit of warning, the fishing enthusiasts were suddenly hit by a vicious storm that swamped many of their boats. Opting to escape the chaos in the bay and at the mouth of the Platte River, some boaters tried to run their crafts to safety on the beach near Point Betsie or, if able to proceed farther, within the safety of Frankfort's piers. The shore at Point Betsie became littered with wrecked and abandoned small craft. For the lighthouse crew and members of their families, this was a nightmare coming tragically true; with no boat at hand and no other means of aiding the trapped boaters, they watched helplessly as some of the fishermen were tossed into the angry surf. Seven men died in that tragedy, which doubtless long remained in the minds not only of the light station's personnel but of the persons who, upon having heard news reports, rushed to Platte Bay in hopes they could assist the boaters in any way they could. While Coast Guardsmen from Frankfort and Traverse City did their best to bring these fishermen home safely, this sad episode is a poignant reminder of the historic role of Point Betsie's rescue crews in assisting area mariners. It also invites speculation as to how these lifesavers might have helped boaters that day had their station still existed.

❧

THE U.S. COAST GUARD UNDERWENT ANOTHER MAJOR ADMINISTRATIVE CHANGE IN 1967 WHEN IT BECAME PART OF THE DEPARTMENT OF TRANSPORTATION under President Lyndon B. Johnson. Despite considerable concern that the agency lacked adequate status and resources in the new department, the Coast Guard remained there until it became a core element of the Department of Homeland Security, created by President George W. Bush and Congress in the aftermath of the attacks of September 11, 2001.

❧

IN 1969, POINT BETSIE LIGHTHOUSE WAS PLACED ON THE NATIONAL REGISTER OF HISTORIC PLACES, a step which ultimately would support local efforts to preserve this most historic of Benzie County's structures. In the mid-1970s, a three-car garage, originally a boathouse that had been situated at the entrance to the lighthouse property, was torn down. It was replaced several years later with a new, more convenient garage sited just east of the lighthouse residences. Having a garage was a major relief to the residents who, during winters after the original structure had been removed, had often found their vehicles heavily coated with ice from moisture blowing off the lake.

From the mid-twentieth century to the conclusion of Point Betsie's manned operation, a "Coastie's" typical duty at the light would be for a few years, at most.[10] All of them, together with their families, are significant in the light's recent history; their experiences, told proudly by their descendants, contribute to Point Betsie's story. To illustrate, it must have been far from dull in the early '50s during William O. Mathews' charge; in addition to this Boatswain's Mate 1ˢᵗ Class and his wife and four children, two of his assistants lived in the lighthouse with their families. The building's residents then totaled sixteen children and six adults; a third assistant lived—quite understandably—in Frankfort.

A former Coast Guardsman who served at the point in 1947 probably spoke for many others, both before and after his service, when he wrote, "I have often thought of how great it would have been to raise our daughter and son at Point Betsie." Looking back in retirement, he added that he thanks Point Betsie "…for being instrumental in getting a good job after leaving the Coast Guard. I…became an operating engineer in an industrial power plant. I was told my experience in the lighthouse was a big factor in getting the job." It is clear that he thoroughly enjoyed his stint; among his memories were meals served him by the wife of the officer-in-charge. Single at the time, he recalled that she was a fine cook, and that without her kindness he thought he might have starved.[11]

◈

SURELY, THERE IS SOMETHING APPEALING IN THE SPIRIT EXUDED BY BM3rd EDWARD R. ZANE III as he welcomed the year of 1971 during his midnight duty in the tower:

"Beginning my watch, the Coders are perfect and so are the Clocks. Point Betsie's light, bright and clear, is ready to guide ships through another safe year."

But not always was everything in such fine order; about three weeks later, Zane's entry in the log noted that the crew had been unable to operate the main light due to a lack of voltage from the transformer. But, as they say, what goes around comes around. "An oil lamp was used as the emergency lighting while other necessary steps were taken to correct the failure to the light," he reported.[12]

The 1972 *Light List* included Point Betsie's radiobeacon whose tone could be heard within a fifty-mile range, and diaphragm horn with its traditional sequence. Another possibly useful nighttime landmark was also noted on that marine guide—Frankfort Aero Light, a beacon on the bluff above nearby Crystal Lake that was primarily intended to guide planes to the town's general aviation field.

From Point Betsie's tower, Coast Guardsman Zane opened the year of 1972 with poetic thoughts:

It is the first few minutes of the new year and I've arrived at the beacon full of laughter and cheer.

The beacons are perfect and the light is clear on this first watch of the New Year. Now that you know we are working right, you must wonder who has the watch on this cold windy night? Well, I must say he is full of good cheer, 'cause it's BM3 Zane for the fourth straight year![13]

The entry in the 1974 *Light List* differs notably from the 1973 version in that no reference is made to the diaphragms. Records indicate that the Coast Guard discontinued the station's fog signals sometime in late 1973 or early 1974; about two years later, the crew was told to get rid of the then-obsolete equipment—the horns and tanks, compressor and generator—and clean up the facility.[14] Never again would those mournful, yet still fondly recalled deep tones be heard by mariners or residents scattered among the dunes or even miles away, along Crystal Lake's shores. Newer technologies—radio, loran, radar, and, most recently, global positioning satellites—had driven traditional, but fondly recalled air-powered horns, to extinction.

≈

LAKE MICHIGAN AGAIN ROSE TO HIGH LEVELS IN THE MID-1970s AND '80s, smashing at both the lighthouse's protective apron and neighboring shoreline structures. In April, 1973, the privately-owned former Coast Guard rescue station was seriously imperiled from surf rolling under its porch. The owner added pilings to try to save his precious structure, but fears for its survival remained. Wrote the *Benzie County Patriot* at the time, "Man and his inventions are waging a gallant fight, but whether they will be victorious in this fight with the rising angry waters of Lake Michigan is an unanswered question." The pounding resulted in the need for major repairs to the Light Station's concrete breakwall; as for the rescue station, while it survived this particular threat, eleven years later the owners had to resort to more drastic action which had first been discussed forty years earlier—jacking up the handsome sixty-five-year old building and rolling it back from the lake, across the sand, to a new, secure foundation.

As the following photos illustrate, 1977 again brought severe winter conditions to Point Betsie:

Ice-coated antenna tower, and deactivated fog signal building.
Courtesy of Marc A. Phillips, USCG Ret.

North antenna tower undermined by winter's erosive force.
Courtesy of Marc A. Phillips, USCG Ret.

❧

BY THE EARLY 1980s, THE AUTOMATION OF LAKE MICHIGAN LIGHTS WAS NEARLY COMPLETE. Driven by economics, the Coast Guard insisted that automation, having been achieved at ninety percent of the nation's four hundred and fifty lighthouses, had saved eighteen million dollars. Two nearby island lights, South Manitou Light and South Fox Light, had been automated in 1959, and it was inevitable that one day Point Betsie's manned operation would give way to a sensor. That innovation, in place of a residential crew, would assume the task of turning on and off the beam, then produced by the 1,000-watt quartz-iodine bulb rated at 184,600 candlepower, illuminating the tower's three-foot tall, six-sided lens.

Even in this latter era, a Point Betsie assignment was attractive, especially to married men. Boatswain's Mate 1st Class Steve Sherman said in a 1980 interview, "When this assignment opened up, I jumped at it…It's considered good duty—much better than shipboard duty or working at a SAR (search-and-rescue) station—because you get to live with your family."[15] Added Sherman, who shared life at the point with his wife Carla, eight-year-old son and their golden retriever, "And we really like it out here…the peace and quiet, especially in winter. There are almost no cars at all coming out here during the winter." He knew that the light would one day be fully automated, as nearly all others on the lake had been by that time, but expected that it would still be "…necessary to have someone living at the station even when the equipment is more or less running itself."

When the Shermans had moved to the light in early 1979, three families, with five dogs among them, shared the house. Sherman described their thick-brick quarters as comfortable and cozy despite the lighthouse's exposure to the elements. As he described Point Betsie life, "The waves sound like a heartbeat, but sometimes the waves sound as if they are going to come right through the walls. You hear the pounding, but you get used to it." It took some time to get used to the beacon, he acknowledged, which reflected off nearby trees, its light momentarily and repeatedly illuminating their bedroom.

Sherman reported that he was kept "pretty busy" maintaining the station buildings and equipment, keeping up the grounds, filling out weather reports and "pushing paper." On weekends and holidays in summer, Sherman would conduct public tours, telling visitors of the light's operation. To serve at Point Betsie was a bit like living in a fishbowl; Sherman said that nearly every time they looked out the window after they first arrived at the station, they would see artists and photographers at work—"…people pointing cameras at the place. It was a little weird at first…probably bothered my wife more than it did me. But I don't think it bothers her any more."

Soon thereafter, Sherman moved on, replaced that spring by CBM 2nd Class Scott Sandy, an Oklahoman who, assisted by California native Machinist Mate 2nd Class Neil Martinek, would be the light's last official residential keeper. The latter was headed for duty on a Coast Guard cutter after completing his Point Betsie duty. In an interview with a *Detroit Free Press* writer in late February, 1983, with the light's automation at hand, Martinek somewhat lamented his impending reassignment, saying "Working and living in a lighthouse has been 'very good duty'…but you have to have initiative because you have to define your own job. I'd like to stay. I never get bored here. I've got all kinds of projects in the works. I kind of like being off boats. I'm not crazy about boats. As far as duty goes, you're not going to get better than this.'"

These final Point Betsie crewmen, along with their spouses and children, were notable descendants in the line of service compiled by men such as Alonzo Slyfield, Peter Dues, Phil Sheridan, Severin Danielsen, Ed Wheaton and the light's other dedicated lightkeepers and their families. All of them were conscious of the light's rich legacy, and left Point Betsie with their own memories. Said Martinek shortly before automation, "It's more of a tradition than a job, in many ways."

In the spring of 1983, local electricians came to Point Betsie to install the sensor that would replace the light's keepers. Even the electricians were caught up in the nostalgia of the event; as one of them told a reporter, "Automating the light was on the sad side for me. Looking at the worn steel treads on the spiral staircase where so many Coast Guardsmen had made their way to the top every day to polish the brass rail and shine the lens and clean the glass"…he wondered if the "'grand lady' would miss the human touch."

Automation was not initially intended, however, to abruptly terminate the Coast Guard's use of the lighthouse's residential quarters. Personnel working at the nearby Frankfort station were expected to continue to reside in the three apartments with their families. One of the first of these families to do so was Chief Boatswain's Mate Joe La Rue, Frankfort's "heavy weather coxswain." He and his family had been living in the upstairs rear apartment, but when Sandy and Martinek departed for other assignments, the La Rues, who had two children, were assigned to the larger keeper's apartment. This "luxury" living was not without some responsibility; if the automatic mechanism failed, he had to turn the light on each evening and off each morning. True to the traditions of lightkeeping, when his Frankfort duties conflicted with this task his wife substituted for him.

The Point Betsie entries in the 1983 and 1984 *Light Lists* referred only to the station's light characteristic, its flash every ten seconds, and to the radiobeacon and on-site antenna. And by the mid-90s, more reductions in service had occurred; the 1996 list no longer included the radiobeacon and antenna and simply described Point Betsie as a "standby light of reduced intensity."

In the winter of 1996, time finally caught up with the old mechanism which had turned the station's lens, powered by an electric motor for a half-century after the original weight drive had been replaced. The beautiful Fresnel lens was taken from the tower and placed in storage, to be preserved for history. As in most other light towers, the Coast Guard replaced it with a modern acrylic system, a 250-millimeter Vega VRB-25 beacon whose twelve-volt, tungsten filament lamp yields a light that can be seen some fourteen-to-fifteen miles out on the lake. Around and around the mechanism goes, night and day, illuminated from dusk to dawn. An internal changer automatically replaces a burned-out bulb from an inventory that will last for more than a year.

THE COAST GUARD WAS SOON EMBARKING ON ANOTHER ROUND OF COST-CUTTING, ULTIMATELY INTENDING TO SURRENDER CONTROL OF POINT BETSIE AND MOST MICHIGAN LIGHTS. In Point Betsie's case, the circumstances leading to this action stemmed primarily from problems with the heating system as well as the necessity of maintaining chlorinating equipment for the station's well water. Since an on-site presence was no longer required to maintain the light, the agency concluded in 1997 that the costs of continuing to occupy the residential quarters were no longer justified. Also, residents who weren't needed to maintain the light may not have felt the same emotional attachment as had their predecessors. As an officer-in-charge of the Frankfort station is known to have complained—quite accurately—on behalf of the point's residents, "The winter is a real killer. The drive must be plowed at least twice a day, and it's not just snow. Once the wind starts blowing off the lake, the ice forms, not in inches but in feet, on everything, the buildings, the driveways, the roads.... One guy left his car out of the garage one night and the next morning it was literally encased in ice and it stayed that way until spring."[16]

A CENTURY AND A HALF HAVE PASSED SINCE THE LIGHT-HOUSE BOARD ALERTED MARINERS IN THE FALL OF 1858 TO A NEW COASTAL LIGHT ON LAKE MICHIGAN'S POINT BETSIE. DESPITE THE INEVITABLE CHANGES BROUGHT BY TECHNOLOGICAL ADVANCES AND BUDGETARY PRESSURES, THAT GUIDING LIGHT STILL SHINES. Not many lighthouses reach a sesquicentennial, especially while continuing in service to mariners. But when the sun nightly sinks below the vast western horizon at this special spot, visitors routinely look to see if, as Mr. Zane affirmed, "Point Betsie's light, bright and clear, is ready to guide ships through another safe year."

There is a continuity that people find at Point Betsie, whether they are just admiring the handsome lighthouse or walking the adjacent beach with families, lovers, friends, or alone. It's not that the beauty of this place doesn't change, or that the station's purpose hasn't markedly diminished over time, nor even that its visitors don't themselves change in ways for which they might or might not wish. It is that irrespective of whatever those changes may be, many people find joy, peace and a vital sense of renewal in this pilgrimage. Wrote one devoted frequent visitor, "Nature's lesson is written large and dramatically here, All must yield to Nature's incessant forces...." But he also appreciated Point Betsie's enduring gift:

Another generation will come to this place with the same needs to face
the inland sea and to hunker down here in the sun.

They will not be disappointed, and
They will come to love and understand
the meanings of this place,
as we have. [17]

And may we always be grateful, too, for the dedicated and courageous men who served, night and day, at the lighthouse and rescue station, and for the families who shared their commitment to safety on our sea. All of them have an important place in Point Betsie's rich story, and their exemplary legacy deserves our lasting respect.

Every night at sunset....
Greg Hultman, photographer

ACKNOWLEDGMENTS

I want to express my deep gratitude to persons who share my commitment to the preservation and interpretation of Point Betsie Light and its historic lifesaving and lightkeeping missions. Many descendants of the men and women of Point Betsie have shared their memories and family accounts either with me personally or with The Friends of Point Betsie Lighthouse, Inc., and in so doing have helped to enrich our understanding of the importance of this site in the maritime and social history of the Great Lakes region generally, and particularly of the waters associated with the Manitou Passage.

To persons who have expressed their interest in Point Betsie through service in its Friends group, led by President Amy Ferris with the steadfast support and cooperation of Benzie County Administrator Chuck Clarke, I express my thanks. Your interest in my research over the years has been an important source of encouragement for me. I have also benefited from my association with the Ann Arbor-based architectural firm of QUINN EVANS, whose experts in restoration faithfully guided most of the preservation and restoration project at the historic light station.

My research has taken me to many libraries and archives whose holdings and staff services have made this book possible. With respect to federal facilities, I wish to acknowledge Susan Abbott of the National Archives and Records Administration in Washington, D.C., together with Charles Johnson and their colleagues there and in College Park, and Scott Forsythe and his associates at NARA's Midwest regional facility in Chicago. The Historian's Office at U.S. Coast Guard headquarters in Washington was another valuable source, as well as the Library of Congress. At the state level, the Library of Michigan, and the Clarke Historical Library at Central Michigan University were helpful, as well as the Historical Collections of the Great Lakes at Bowling Green State University headed by Archivist Robert Graham. Other valuable repositories were the Michigan Maritime Museum in South Haven, the Great Lakes Historical Society in

Vermilion, Ohio, and the Lake Carriers Association. Colin MacKenzie and his Nautical Research Centre in Petaluma, California, provided access to scarce or otherwise unavailable materials.

Never to be overlooked, numerous local library resources within and beyond our county were essential to my research. These include the Benzie Area Historical Museum and the Benzie Shores District Library in Frankfort, where Cathy Carter, Cindy Collier and Julie Morris, making skillful use of inter-library loans as well as the facility's own holdings, helped me in my quest to leave no promising stone unturned.

Descendants of Point Betsie's lightkeepers and lifesavers as well as former personnel of the U.S. Coast Guard who themselves served there, have contributed much to my understanding of life at the site through fifteen decades. Sometimes these gifts have taken the form of memories recounted or genealogical clarifications provided; other times they have been as seemingly insignificant as a question posed to me that has led to new discoveries. I apologize that I am unable to include all such names, but I now greatly thank everyone for his or her contribution, large or small, to my work, either directly or to the endeavors of the Friends of Point Betsie Lighthouse, Inc., whose expanding archives are represented here.

For my account of Alonzo and Alice Slyfield and their lightkeeping son Edwin, many thanks are extended to Marcia Case and her family, to Myra Elias, Jan and Katie Condon, and Sue Whitcomb—not to overlook Charles, another son of that great lightkeeper and his steadfast spouse, whose own memoir offers an irreplaceable window on those early formative years at the light station. For historical materials and precious memorabilia relating to the legendary lifesaving Capt. Harrison "Tip" Miller and his wife Bridget, the Friends group and I are deeply grateful to Ted Hansen and his immediate family, and to Verna Vigland. I am indebted to Claudia and Pete Lewis for use of her family's materials on Miller and his successor, Capt. Edwin Bedford, and for her careful reading of my entire manuscript.

I thank Stephen Sheridan for materials relating to longtime Keeper Philip Sheridan and other members of his distinguished extended family of Great Lakes lightkeepers. Special thanks are also due Meredith Erickson for essential material on lightkeeper Severin Danielsen. And for my insights into the life and service of distinguished lightkeeper Edward Wheaton, I gratefully acknowledge the contributions of Paul and Joanne Wheaton. I want to express particular gratitude to Sally Pryce, whose own love of Point Betsie and her memories and memorabilia have enriched my appreciation of point life during the long service of Assistant Lightkeeper Hank LaFreniere and his wife Hattie. I also thank Christina Spencer for sharing insights into another wonderful Point Betsie assistant, Medad Spencer.

Finally, sincere thanks to Steven Zetterberg, to the late John Peterson and his family, and to Dee Miller and the Millikans for insights into their respective families' experiences at the point. Among several accounts of former Coast Guardsmen, thanks are also due the Payment family and Marc Phillips for sharing rich memories and valuable photos from their service at the light, and to Alan Luedtke for pictures and materials relating to his family's important construction work there.

If, upon reading the book or these acknowledgements you feel that you or your relatives were left out, please accept my apologies. The gap was inadvert; your interest in Point Betsie's stories, and each individual's part in its history, is most heartening to me. Errors of omission or commission are my responsibility alone, but as they come to my attention I will learn from them, and through the work of the Friends, the interpretation of Point Betsie's historic missions will be enhanced.

Finally, and perhaps most importantly, there are some especially personal thanks to extend. First, for the many friends who have heard me recount my Point Betsie discoveries and encouraged me to keep going—you all know who you are, and you have my deep appreciation. Special recognition is owed to the talented Betsy Youngblood, who volunteered to serve as my editor—and did so most conscientiously until moving from the area—and to Hilary Turner and Frankfort's Bayside Printing for their aid and counsel. I also extend appreciation to Grant Brown who, while researching and writing his own fascinating history of Lake Michigan's Ann Arbor Railroad car ferries, read the manuscript and exchanged thoughts with me along the way. I also thank Brian Lewis for his interest in Point Betsie, his enthusiastic response to the manuscript and his key role in its publication.

I have been greatly blessed by family support. Brother-in-law Norman Kenney assisted my review of the lifesaving station's daily logs; son-in-law Mathew Thomson patiently answered computer-related questions. My daughters Susan and Anne, together with their own families, have grown in their appreciation of Point Betsie even as they have encouraged me in this labor of love. Their careful thoughts and support has been invaluable. And to my dear wife Peggy, I owe more than I can say. A woman of great talent and artistry, she's been a tireless reader and listener; without her support I might not have started out on this trek, and very likely would never have finished it. To all of you, I truly hope you've enjoyed Point Betsie's story, and will join me in sharing your appreciation for this beautiful place and its significance in Great Lakes history.

Jonathan P. Hawley

Acknowledgments

Jonathan P. Hawley in lantern room.

NOTES

Preface

1. A characteristic, if nonetheless fictional comment illustrating Point Betsie's significance to mariners, in "One Degree West," a story by noted Great Lakes writer George P. Wakefield in his volume, *Lure of the Lakes: A Taste of the Great Lakes (2001)*.
2. *The New York Times,* August 16, 1855, p. 1.
3. *The New York Times,* August 16, 1856, p. 1.
4. Information provided by the Lake Carriers' Association of Cleveland, Ohio, which represents operators of U.S.-Flag vessels on the Great Lakes.
5. Currently, the largest vessels are frequently unable to carry capacity loads, owing to low water levels in certain Great Lakes channels and ports.

Chapter One

1. *Notices to Mariners of or changes to aids to navigation,* 1857-59, p. 10; Records of the U.S. Coast Guard, Record Group 26, National Archives Building, Washington, D.C.
2. From the party's field notes of April 22, General Land Office, Bureau of Land Management, U.S. Department of the Interior.
3. *In Waiting for the Morning Train: An American Boyhood,* historian Bruce Catton linked "Betsey" to the original name of the small interior lake (now known as Green Lake) from which this stream flows some fifty miles, the name having been chosen by the lake's first white settler in honor of his wife. He wrote, "So it was Betsey's River at one end, and Aux Bec Scies at the other, and before many years Betsey won out...."
4. In order to minimize confusion, the author uses "Betsie" except where faithfulness to quoted sources requires an alternative.
5. Robert H. Ruchhoft, *Exploring North Manitou, South Manitou, High and Garden Islands Of The Lake Michigan Archipelago,* p. 51.
6. Myron H. Vent, *South Manitou Island: From Pioneer Community to National Park,* p. 8.
7. Henry R. Schoolcraft, *Narrative Journal of Travels Through the Northwestern Regions of the United States Extending from Detroit through the Great Chain of American Lakes to the Sources of the Mississippi River in the Year 1820.* Mentor L. Williams, ed., p. 262.
8. Justin L. Kestenbaum, *Modernizing Michigan: Political and Social Trends, 1836-1866,* p. 115.
9. *A Trip Through the Lakes of North America; Embracing a Full Description of the St. Lawrence River,*

Notes

Together With All The Principal Places On Its Banks, From Its Source to Its Mouth: Commerce of the Lakes, Etc., p. 108.

10. Steve Harold, *Shipwrecks of the Sleeping Bear,* p. 40.

11. Theodore J. Karamanski, *Schooner Passage: Sailing Ships and the Lake Michigan Frontier,* p. 35.

12. Ibid., p.36.

13. Ibid.

14. Ibid.

15. Kenneth J. Vrana, ed., *Inventory of Maritime and Recreation Resources of the Manitou Passage Underwater Preserve,* p. 2—3.

16. Ibid., p. 2—17.

17. Ibid.

18. Harold, op. cit., p. 1.

19. Frank Barcus, *Freshwater Fury,* pp. 66-67.

20. David Swayze, *Shipwreck: A Comprehensive Directory of Over 3,700 Shipwrecks on the Great Lakes.*

21. Mark L. Thompson, *Graveyard of the Lakes,* p. 21.

22. Ibid., jacket

23. Harlan Hatcher and Erich A. Walter, *A Pictorial History of the Great Lakes,* p. 95.

24. Thompson, op. cit., p. 17.

25. Ibid., p. 21.

26. Ruchhoft, op. cit., p. 73.

27. Ibid.

28. David T. Dana (ed.), *A Fashionable Tour Through the Great Lakes and Upper Mississippi: The 1852 Journal of Juliette Starr Dana,* p. 67.

29. Ruchhoft, op. cit., p. 74.

30. Ibid., p. 172.

31. Weed's account appears in J.B. Mansfield Vol. I, *History of the Great Lakes,* 1972 reprint, pp. 211-213.

32. William H. Ohle, "Manitou, the vanished county," *Chronicle* (Historical Society of Michigan), Spring, 1978.

33. Other lights would be established over time, first at South Fox Island to the north of the Manitous, in 1868, and at North Manitou Island in 1898. The latter tower was replaced in 1910 with a lightship moored in the passage, then with a concrete-based "crib" and light atop in 1935.

34. T. Michael O'Brien, *Guardians of the Eighth Sea: A History of the U.S. Coast Guard on the Great Lakes,* p. 15.

35. In 1910, Congress and President William Howard Taft abolished the Board and created a civilian-led Bureau of Lighthouses in the Department of Commerce and Labor (the Labor component later won independent Cabinet-rank status). In 1939, President Franklin D. Roosevelt ordered the lighthouses transferred into the U.S. Coast Guard, which had been formed in 1915 as part of the Treasury Department. During the presidency of Lyndon B. Johnson, the Coast Guard was shifted into the newly established Department of Transportation; it is now a key component of the Department of Homeland Security.

36. O'Brien, op. cit., p. 16.

37. Francis Ross Holland, Jr., *America's Lighthouses: Their Illustrated History Since 1716,* p. iv.

38. Michigan Site File No. 5, Records of Point Betsie Lighthouse, National Archives.

39. Ibid.

40. *U.S. Statutes at Large and Treaties,* 32nd Congress, Second Session, pp. 240-241.

41. Michigan Site File No. 5, National Archives, contains relevant materials and the reservations are identified on a survey by the U.S. Bureau of Land Management.

42. Identified as Parcel #1 in a 1930 Federal Real Estate Board questionnaire; Site File No. 5.

43. Record Group 26, Lighthouse Board List of General Correspondence, 1791-1900, National Archives.

44. James D. Richardson, *Messages and Papers of the Presidents, 1789-1879*, Vol. V, p. 214.

45. Ibid., p. 265.

46. *Contracts*, Vol. 2, 1853-57, Lighthouse Board, Bureau of Lighthouses, National Archives.

47. Perry Francis Powers, *A History of Northern Michigan and Its People*, p. 360.

48. *Annual Report*, Lighthouse Board, February 1, 1858, pp. 122-123, National Archives.

49. U.S. House of Representatives, 35th Congress, 1st Session, Ex. Doc. No. 101, *Expenses of Light-House Service Northwestern Lakes*, as reprinted by Nautical Research Centre, Petaluma, CA.

50. *Report of the Secretary of the Treasury on the State of the Finances for the Year Ending June 30, 1859*, a facsimile produced from the original by the Nautical Research Centre, Petaluma, CA

51. Dr. M.L. Leach, *A History of the Grand Traverse Region*, pp. 133-134.

Chapter Two

1. Hans Christian Adamson, *Keepers of the Lights*, p. xvi.

2. *Annual Report of the Lighthouse Board, 1858*, p. 7.

3. J. B. Mansfield, *History of the Great Lakes,* vol. 1, p. 364.

4. Francis Ross Holland, *America's Lighthouses: An Illustrated History*, p. 14.

5. *Instructions For Light-Keepers of The United States, 1852*, facsimile produced from the original edition by the Nautical Research Centre, Pentaluma, CA.

6. Department of Commerce, Lighthouse Service, *Instructions to Employees of the United States Lighthouse Service, 1927.*

7.. Dennis L. Noble, *Lighthouses & Keepers: The U.S. Lighthouse Service and Its Legacy*, p. 92.

8. Ibid., p. 117.

Chapter Three

1. Charles B. Slyfield, "A Brief Account of the Life of Charles B. Slyfield," May 9, 1912 (unpublished), p. 6.

2. H.R. Page & Co., *The Traverse Region: Historical and Descriptive, With Illustrations of Scenery....* p. 308.

3. Ibid.

4. Ibid.

5. Allen B. Blacklock, *History of Elberta*, p. 3.

6. Slyfield, op. cit., p. 7.

7. Ibid., p. 8.

8. Ibid., p. 13.

9. Ibid.

10. Lighthouse Board, "Report on State of Finances," p. 60

11. Lighthouse Board, Annual Report, November 6, 1868, p. 378. A reference to Point Betsie within the Board's discussion of Michigan's Big Sable Light, in its subsequent 1869 annual report, offers further insight into these structural problems. The Board therein warned of the need to pay close attention to the sand about Big Sable's foundation so as to avoid a repeat of the serious deterioration which had occurred at Point Betsie where sand was blown away from the foundation, permitting it to erode and thus jeopardizing the building's integrity.

12. Slyfield, op. cit., p. 14.

13. Ibid., p. 16.

14. Ibid., pp. 17-18.

15. Ibid., p. 18.

16. October 19, 1872, entry in "Journal of Lighthouse Station at Point Betsey, Michigan," Arthur C. Frederickson

Collection, Historical Collection of the Great Lakes, Bowling Green State University.

17. Slyfield, op. cit., p. 18.

18. November 4, 1873, entry in "Journal," as above.

19. November 14, 1873, entry in "Journal," as above.

20. October 13, 1868, letter from Light House Inspector T.H. Stevens to Rear Admiral Shubrick, chairman of the Lighthouse Board, in Lighthouse Board General Correspondence Files, National Archives.

21. March 15, 1878, entry in "Journal," as above. Myron H. Vent, in his publication, *South Manitou Island: From Pioneer Community to National Park*, describes the accident slightly differently, saying that the family had accepted a ride from a friend. The boom's swing knocked Keeper Sheridan into the water, according to this account, probably rendering him unconscious; his body was never found. Mrs. Sheridan clung to the boat with one hand, her other holding the baby. By the time the friend had found a rope in the capsized boat with which to tie them to it, they had drifted away. The friend held on as the boat drifted; he landed on North Manitou Island the following day. This version adds that the Sheridan's two older children, probably able to comprehend the tragedy which they had observed from a lighthouse window, persistently searched the beach, weeping and scanning the water for the bodies of their parents, which were never recovered.

Chapter Four

1. *Annual Report of the Operations of the U.S. Life-Saving Service for the Fiscal Year Ending June 30, 1876*, p. 28.

2. Letter Book, Record Group 26, National Archives, as cited in Frederick Stonehouse, *Wreck Ashore: The United States Life-Saving Service on the Great Lakes*, p. 12.

3. J.B. Mansfield, *History of the Great Lakes*, reprinted 1972, p. 379.

4. J.H. Merryman, *The United States Life-Saving Service – 1880*, pp. 8-9.

5. Built as a gift to Point Betsie Lighthouse by Daniel Sanders, a close friend of Robert and Marilyn Conrad, original members of the board of The Friends of Point Betsie Lighthouse, Inc.

6. The U.S. Life-Saving Service Station at Sleeping Bear Point, now a key part of Sleeping Bear Dunes National Lakeshore, is a nationally recognized, outstanding restoration by the National Park Service, which also maintains the remains of other lifesaving stations on the Manitou Islands, which lie within the park's boundaries. Tours and other activities are regularly conducted at the site, giving visitors an opportunity to see a station's equipment and to observe simulated rescue operations.

7. Journals kept by Alonzo J. Slyfield as keeper of Point Betsie Lighthouse are in the Arthur C. Frederickson Collection at the Historical Collections of the Great Lakes, Bowling Green State University (OH).

8. The journals of Point Betsie Life-Saving Station, as well as others from stations on the northwestern lakes, are maintained at the National Archives and Records Administration's Great Lakes Region Office in Chicago, Illinois.

9. Some punctuation and capitalization have been added by the author to assist the reader.

10. From demonstration of the Lyle gun and its operation, conducted by the staff of the Sleeping Bear Dunes National Lakeshore.

11. Ibid.

12. Lifecar displayed at Sleeping Bear Dunes National Lakeshore's Glen Haven Life-Saving Station.

13. *Annual Report of the U.S. Life-Saving Service, 1881*, pp. 19-36. The rescue is depicted in a video, "The Wreck and Rescue of the Schooner J.H. Hartzell," produced in 1988 by Bauer Productions of Traverse City, MI. It is also featured in Dennis L. Noble's excellent study, *That Others Might Life: The U.S. Life-Saving Service, 1878-1915*, and in Frederick Stonehouse's comprehensive history of Great Lakes lifesaving as cited above.

Chapter Five

1. Daily logs of the U.S. Life-Saving Service and U.S. Coast Guard's rescue stations at Point Betsie are located within Record Group 26 at the National Archives' Great Lakes regional facility in

Chicago, Illinois.
2. General Correspondence file, NARA, Washington, D.C.
3. NARA, Washington, D.C., Letter Book 547, p. 492.
4. Records of the case, "The People of the State of Michigan vs. Thomas E. Matthews," are in the files of the Benzie County Clerk.

Chapter Six

1. Alta Lawson Littell, "Saw 43 Years in Coast Guard Service: Capt. Miller Figured in Scores of Great Lakes Tragedies," *The Grand Rapids Herald*, November 24, 1929.
2. Ibid.
3. *The Benzie Banner*, July 3, 1891.
4. Larry and Patricia Wright, *Great Lakes Lighthouses Encyclopedia*, p. 316.

Chapter Seven

1. Second annual report of the Board of Managers of the Lake Carriers' Association (1893).
2. From an interview with Dr. John Spencer, in the Traverse City *Record-Eagle*, August 7,1981.
3. Letter to Mr. F. O'Donnell, in unpublished journal, December 18, 1889.
4. Letter to Lieut. James Rogers, U.S. Revenue Marine, in unpublished journal, December 2, 1889.
5. Letter to Capt. Robbins in unpublished journal, December 5, 1892.
6. Letter to S.I. Kimball in unpublished journal, August 21, 1893.
7. Letter to Dr. R. Mead, Manistee, Michigan, in unpublished journal, *circa*. 1890
8. Ibid., March 29, 1892.
9. These two letters to Keeper Miller are among in-coming correspondence to Point Betsie Life-Saving Station in records at Historical Collections of the Great Lakes, Bowling Green State University, Ohio.
10. September 9,1894 letter to Miller, in-coming correspondence, Historical Collections as above.
11. March 21, 1894 letter to Miller from District Superintendent Robbins, Historical Collections as above.
12. Entry in unpublished Miller journal
13. Dog oil is a product that continues to be produced in England under that name. Now a blend of vegetable and mineral oils that is recommended for animals and people, its name stems from its initial use in conjunction with the massaging of racing greyhounds. A predecessor product is said to have been made by rendering waste animal fats, including those of deceased dogs.
14. October 14, 1899, letter, in-coming correspondence, Point Betsie, Historical Collections, as above.
15. Annual report of the Board of Managers of the Lake Carriers' Association (1898).
16. *Annual Report of the U.S. Life-Saving Service, 1899*, Historian's Office, U.S. Coast Guard, Washington, D.C.
17. Also published in the *Grand Rapids Herald,* Nov. 24, 1929.

Chapter Eight

1. From the research library of the Michigan Maritime Museum, South Haven.
2. Correspondence of the Lighthouse Board, March 9, 1907, National Archives and Records Administration. Washington, D.C. At this time, the official name of the lighthouse agency was the Light-House Establishment, which was then part of the Department of Commerce and Labor.
3. From in-coming Point Betsie correspondence, Historical Collections of the Great Lakes, Bowling Green State University, Bowling Green, Ohio.
4. From the collection at The Library of Michigan, Lansing, Michigan.
5. Historical Collections of the Great Lakes, op. cit.
6. Ibid.
7. Ibid.

8. Lake Carriers' Association annual report, 1910, p. 64.

9. Ibid., 1913, p. 87.

10. The author is indebted to Terry Pepper, president of The Great Lakes Lighthouse Keepers Association, for his helpful comments on Point Betsie's chime whistles.

11. Point Betsie correspondence, NARA, Washington, D.C.

12. Ibid.

Chapter Nine

1. In-coming correspondence to Point Betsie Life-Saving Station, Historical Collections of the Great Lakes, Bowling Green State University, Bowling Green, Ohio

2. Ibid.

3. Ibid.

4. Ibid.

5. Ibid.

6. Ibid.

7. Ibid.

8. This boathouse, pictured in the previous chapter, replaced a smaller one that had been built about 1905, featuring a similar, two hundred-foot rail launch-way extending into the lake.

9. Historical Collections of the Great Lakes, op. cit.

Chapter Ten

1. Lake Carriers' Association annual report, 1920, pp. 107-8.

2. Correspondence in the files of the National Archives and Records Administration, Washington, D.C.

3. Ibid.

4. Lake Carriers' Association annual report, 1921, p. 93.

5. The enhancement of the light's power may not have taken effect immediately upon electrification, as the Lake Carriers' Association's annual report in 1924 indicates that the light's intensity as a result of the new power source occurred "during the season of 1924."

6. *U.S. Light List*, 1924.

7. The change, which took effect on April 1, 1922, took place in conjunction with the operation of the new Point Betsie diaphone at the beginning of that year's navigation season.

8. Ibid.

9. *The New York Times,* December 19, 1926.

10. Lake Carriers' Association annual report, 1927, p. 199.

11. *The Benzie County Patriot,* February 13, 1930.

12. Letter of August 9, 1930, from Arthur Peterson to U.S. Senator Arthur Vandenberg. The Senator's substantive reply on October 14, 1930, enclosed a letter he had received from Captain B.M. Chiswell, acting commandant of the Coast Guard, dated October 6, 1930. Letters were made available to the author by the family of Arthur Peterson.

13. *The Charlevoix Sentinel,* March 31, 1931.

14. According to an interview by Gloria C. Sproul, published in the *Benzie County Weekly Express/Press Box* on March 17, 1983, for their final years in residence at the Point the Nelson family had moved into the large Coast Guard station sometime after its 1937 closing and the transfer two years later of the lighthouses into the Coast Guard.

15. Interviews with Gertrude Kline, a niece of Edward Wheaton, on September 25, 2003, and her nephew, Paul Wheaton, and his wife, Joanne, on that date and on September 13, 2007.

16. When the mystery was reported in the *Traverse City Record-Eagle,* Paul Wheaton's telephone call to his

cousin, Gertrude Wheaton, served to put these cousins in touch with each other, so Ed Wheaton's handiwork had an unintended, heart-warming benefit.

17. *The Benzie County Patriot,* late December, 1937.
18. *The Benzie County Patriot,* February 1, 1934. The boat involved was the Rubier-Cooper fish tug.
19. Lake Carriers' Association annual report, 1946, p. 126.

Chapter Eleven

1. Correspondence from Sally Pryce, Ann Arbor, MI.
2. Steven Karges, *Keepers of the Lights: Lighthouse Keepers & Their Families, Door County, Wisconsin – 1837-1939,* pp. 295-6.
3. *The Benzie County Patriot,* November 29, 1945.
4. Telephone interview Steven Zetterberg, March 11, 2006.
5. *Lighthouse Digest,* June, 2003.
6. Lake Carriers' Association annual report, 1948, p. 144.
7. The source of material on Charles J. Payment's years at Point Betsie, and his colleagues, is a September 14, 2004, letter to The Friends of Point Betsie Lighthouse, Inc. from F. Louis Payment.
8. The *Detroit News* pictorial section, September 16, 1945.
9. The *Benzie County* Patriot, June 13, 1963.
10. Records are scant for some years, but other known "officers-in-charge" from the latter 1950s until the cessation of the light's residential management in the early 1980s included William O. Mathews; John P. Campbell; Hubert C. Jackson; Robert Hansard; Wilbur G. McVay; Glynn Butler; David H. Marphree; Keith Norden; Kenneth P. Rachford; Edward R. Zane III; George D. Milligan; Marc Phillips; Tom Wilson,Steve Sherman and Scott Sandy. Inspection records throughout these years repeatedly indicate that the station's buildings, equipment and grounds were maintained in exemplary fashion by its crews. The tone of the report expressed by Captain R. M. Moss following his 1953 visit was not unusual: "This station is in excellent condition in all respects. It is a credit to the Coast Guard and the personnel assigned deserve credit for its condition.
11. Letter to The Friends of Point Betsie Lighthouse, Inc. from Russell Pagel, June 7, 2004.
12. Point Betsie Light Station log, January 19, 1971, at NARA, Washington, D.C.
13. Ibid., January 1, 1972.
14. Correspondence with Marc Phillips, officer-in charge of Point Betsie Light Station, December 1975-June 1978. He said he tried the horn just one time, while his baby, now grown, slept; the son still can't stand loud noises! Phillips added, "Am I glad I wasn't stationed there when that thing was working."
15. The *Record-Eagle,* Traverse City, Michigan, August 11, 1980.
16. Huffstutler, Steven, USCG, *International Lighthouse Magazine* "Will Point Betsie Light Be Lost?" on file at Great Lakes Historical Society.
17. From "Ode to the Point Betsie Beach" by Douglas A. Noverr in the summer of 1986, published in the *Ad-Visor Community Weekly,* July 21, 1986.

BIBLIOGRAPHY

Books

Adamson, Hans Christian. *Keepers of the Lights*. New York: Greenberg Publisher, 1955.

A Trip Through the Lakes of North America, Embracing a Full Description of the St. Lawrence River, Together With All the Principal Places on Its Banks, From Its Source to Its Mouth. New York: J. Disturnell, 1857.

Bald, F. Clever. *Michigan in Four Centuries*. Revised edition. New York: Harper & Brothers, 1961.

Barry, James P. *Wrecks and Rescues of the Great Lakes: A Photographic History*. San Diego: Nowell-North, 1981.

Baucus, Frank. *Freshwater Fury*. Detroit: Wayne State University Press, 1986.

Benzie Area Historical Society. *Shared Moments: A Journey Through Time*. Gaithersburg, MD: Signature Book Printing, 2007.

Bixby, Florence and Pete Sandman. *Port City Perspectives: Frankfort, Michigan at 150 (1850-2000)*.

Blacklock, Allen B. *Blacklock's History of Elberta*.

Case, Leonard L. *The Crystal Gazer*. The Benzie Area Historical Society, 1985.

Catton, Bruce. *Waiting for the Morning Train: An American Boyhood*. Garden City, NY: Doubleday & Company, 1972.

Craker, Kathy Nickerson. *They Came to South Manitou Island*. Chelsea, MI: Bookcrafters, 1983.

Crowner, Gerald E. *The South Manitou Story*. 1982.

Dana, David T. III (ed.) *A Fashionable Tour Through the Great Lakes and Upper Mississippi: The 1852 Journal of Juliette Starr Dana*. Detroit: Wayne State University Press, 2004.

Harold, Steve. *Shipwrecks of the Sleeping Bear*. Traverse City, MI: Pioneer Study Center, 1984.

Hatcher, Harlan. *The Great Lakes*. New York: Oxford University Press, 1944.

Hilton, George W. *Lake Michigan Passenger Steamers*. Stanford, CA: Stanford University Press, 2002.

History of the Great Lakes. Two volumes. Reprinted. Cleveland, OH: Freshwater Press, 1972. Original author, J.B. Mansfield. Chicago, IL: J.H. Beers & Company, 1899.

Holland, Francis Ross, Jr. *America's Lighthouses: Their Illustrated History Since 1716*. Brattleboro, VT: The Stephen Greene Press, 1972.

Howard, John. *The Story of Frankfort*. Frankfort, MI: The City Council, 1930.

Hoyt, Susan Roark. *Lighthouses of Northwest Michigan*. Chicago: Arcadia Publishing, 2004.

Hyde, Charles K. *The Northern Lights: Lighthouses of the Upper Great Lakes*. Lansing, MI: TwoPeninsula Press, 1986.

Johnson, Robert Erwin. *Guardians of the Sea: History of the United States Coast Guard, 1915 to the Present*. Annapolis, MD: Naval Institute Press, 1987.

Karamanski, Theodore J. *Schooner Passage: Sailing Ships and the Lake Michigan Frontier*. Detroit: Wayne State University Press, 2000.

Karges, Steven. *Keepers of the Lights: Lighthouse Keepers & Their Families, Door County, Wisconsin—1837-1939*. Ellison Bay, WI: Wm Caxton Ltd, 2000.

King, Irving. *The Coast Guard Expands, 1865-1915: New Roles, New Frontiers*. Annapolis, MD: Naval Institute Press, 1996.

Kozma, LuAnne (ed.) *Living at a Lighthouse: Oral Histories from the Great Lakes*. Great Lakes Lighthouse Keepers Association, 1987.

Leach, M.L. *A History of the Grand Traverse Region*. Traverse City, MI: The Grand Traverse Herald, 1883.

Methley, Noel T. *The Life-Boat and Its Story*. London: Sidgwick & Jackson Ltd., 1912.

Noble, Dennis L. *Lifeboat Sailors: The U.S. Coast Guard's Small Boat Stations*. Washington: Brassy's, Inc., 2000.

———. *Lighthouses & Keepers: The U.S. Lighthouse Service and Its Legacy*. Annapolis MD: Naval Institute Press, 1997.

———. *That Others Might Live: The U.S. Life-Saving Service, 1878-1915*. Annapolis, MD: Naval Institute Press, 1994.

O'Brien, T. Michael. *Guardians of the Eighth Sea: A History of the U.S. Coast Guard on the Great Lakes*. Honolulu: University Press of the Pacific, 2001.

Peterson, Douglas. *U.S. Lighthouse Service Tenders, 1840-1939*.

Annapolis and Trappe, MD: Eastwind Publishing, 2000.

Peterson, William D. *United States Life-Saving Service in Michigan*. Chicago: Arcadia Publishing, 2000.

Powers, Perry F. assisted by H.G. Cutler. *A History of Northern Michigan and Its People*. 3 volumes. Chicago: Lewis Publishing Co., 1912.

Putnam, George R. *Lighthouses and Lightships of the United States*. Revised edition. New York: Houghton Mifflin Co., 1933.

——. *Radiobeacons and Radiobeacon Navigation*. Washington: U.S. Department of Commerce, Lighthouse Service, 1931.

Quinn Evans / Architects. *Historic Structures Report: Point Betsie Light Station*. Ann Arbor, MI, 2005.

Quaife, Milo M. *Lake Michigan*. Indianapolis: Bobbs-Merrill Co., 1944.

Ratigan, William. *Great Lakes Shipwrecks and Survivals*. Revised edition. New York: Galahad Books, 1960.

Rogers, Joseph H. *South Manitou Island: A Field Trip Sourcebook and Guide*, 1933.

Ruchhoft, Robert H. *Exploring North Manitou, South Manitou, High and Garden Islands of the Lake Michigan Archipelago*. Cincinnati: The Pucelle Press, 1991.

Rusco, Rita Hadra. *North Manitou Island: Between Sunrise and Sunset*, 1991.

Sapulski, Wayne S. *Lighthouses of Lake Michigan: Past and Present*. Manchester, MI: Wilderness Adventure Books, 2001.

Shanks, Ralph; Wick York and Lisa Woo Shanks (ed.). *The U.S. Life-Saving Service: Heroes, Rescues and Architecture of the Early Coast Guard*. Petaluma, CA: Costano Books, 1996.

Schoolcraft, Henry. *Narrative Journal of Travels Through the Northwestern Regions of the United States Extending from Detroit through the Great Chain of American Lakes to the Sources of the Mississippi River in the Year 1820*. Mentor L. Williams (ed.) East Lansing, MI: The Michigan State College Press, 1953.

Shelak, Benjamin J. *Shipwrecks of Lake Michigan*. Black Earth, WI: Trails Books, 2003.

Sheridan, James E. *Saugatuck: Through the Years, 1830-1980*. Detroit: Harlo Press, 1982.

Sladek, Benjamin J. *Shipwrecks of Lake Michigan*. Black Earth, WI: Trails Books, 2003.

Sproul, Gloria C. "Point Betsie more than lighthouse for those who grew up there," *Benzie County Weekly Express/Press Box*, March 17, 1983.

Stonehouse, Frederick. *Great Lakes Lighthouse Tales*, 1998.

——. *Haunted Lake Michigan: Ghosts, Shipwrecks and Scary Mysteries of a Great Lake*. Duluth: Lake Superior Port Cities Inc., 2006.

——. *Wreck Ashore: The United States Life-Saving Service on the Great Lakes*. Duluth: Lake Superior Port Cities Inc., 1994.

Swayze, David D. *Shipwreck: A Comprehensive Directory of Over 3,700 Shipwrecks on the Great Lakes*. Boyne City, MI: Harbor House Publishers, 1992.

Tag, Thomas A. *Big Sable Point Lighthouse*. The Big Sable Point Lighthouse Keeper's Association, 1997.

Thompson, Mark L. *Graveyard of the Lakes*. Detroit: Wayne State University Press, 2000.

The Traverse Region, Historical and Descriptive, With Illustrations of Scenery and Portraits and Biographical Sketches of Some of Its Prominent Men and Pioneers. Chicago: H.R. Page & Co., 1884.

The United States Lighthouse Service, 1923: Washington, Department of Commerce, Lighthouse Service, 1923.

Vrana, Kenneth J. (ed.) *Inventory of Maritime and Recreation Resources of the Manitou Passage Underwater Preserve*. East Lansing, MI: Department of Park, Recreation and Tourism Resources, Michigan State University, 1995.

Vent, Kenneth J. (ed.) *South Manitou Island: From Pioneer Community to National Park*. 1973.

Wakefield, George P. *Lure of the Lakes: A Taste of the Great Lakes*. 2001. Available from the Great Lakes Historical Society, Vermilion, OH.

Weiss, George. *The Lighthouse Service: Its History, Activities and Organizations*. Baltimore: The Johns Hopkins Press, 1926.

Wright, Larry and Patricia. *Great Lakes Lighthouses Encyclopedia*. Erin, Ontario: The Boston Mills Press, 2006.

Unpublished Source
Slyfield, Charles B. "A Brief Sketch of the Life of Charles B. Slyfield" (1912).

Newspapers
Ad-Visor Community Weekly, Beulah, MI.
Benzie County Weekly Express
The Benzie County Patriot and *The Benzie County Record-Patriot*
The Benzie Banner
The Charlevoix Sentinel
The Grand Rapids Press
The Ludington Daily News
The New York Times
The Traverse City Record-Eagle

Libraries And Other Historical Research Facilities
Beaver Island Public Library, Beaver Island, MI.
Beaver Island Historical Museum, Beaver Island, MI.
Benzie Area Historical Museum, Benzonia, MI.
Benzie Shores District Library, Frankfort, MI.
Benzonia Public Library, Benzonia, MI.
Clarke Historical Library, Central Michigan University, Mount Pleasant, MI.
General Land Office, Bureau of Land Management, U.S. Department of the Interior, Washington, D.C.
Great Lakes Historical Society, Vermilion, OH.
Historical Collections of the Great Lakes, Bowling Green State University, Bowling Green, OH.
Historian's Office, U.S. Coast Guard Headquarters, Washington, D.C.
Lake Carriers' Association, Cleveland, OH.
The Library of Congress, Washington, D.C.

Library of Michigan, Lansing, MI.

Ludington Public Library, Ludington, MI.

Michigan Maritime Museum, South Haven, MI.

National Archives and Records Administration; Washington, D.C., College Park, MD and Chicago, IL.

Nautical Research Centre, Petaluma, CA.

Osterlin Library, Northwestern Michigan College, Traverse City, MI.

Traverse Area District Library, Traverse City, MI.

INDEX

Index

fog signal, 82

Sheridan, Aaron, lightkeeper, 58

Sheridan, Lyman, lightkeeper, 145

Sheridan, Philip, assistant lightkeeper, 145

Slyfield, Alonzo J., lightkeeper, 45-48

Spencer, Medad, Point Betsie assistant lightkeeper, 120, **120,** 147

   Beaver Island Head Light lightkeeper, 119

Spider lamp, 30

Stibitz, Charles, Point Betsie assistant lightkeeper, 147

Straubel, Fred, USCG, Point Betsie, 188, 194

Strang, James J., 14-15

Surfboats, **137**

   Beebe-McLellan, 153, 155, 167, 168, 169

   Buffalo, 91

   Francis, 60-61

   Long Branch, 91

   Monomoy, **63**, 63n5, 125, **125**, 133, 155,

Sweet, Alanson, lighthouse construction firm, 21-23, 25

T

Taft, William H., U.S. president, 19n35

Tesnow, Charles E., Point Betsie lightkeeper, 187-88

Three Bells, schooner, 132-33

Two Brothers, sloop, 133

   U.S. Coast Guard

   assignment to U.S. Department of Transportation, 220

   assignment to U.S. Department of Homeland Security, iv, 220

   establishment (1915) 69, 150, 161

   log-keeping instructions, 163-64

   neglect of duty terms, 165

   physical fitness requirements, 165

proposed search-and-rescue air base, 205

transfer of U.S. lighthouses to (1939), 69, 201

Traverse City, Michigan, air station, 205, 220

V

Vandenberg, Arthur, U.S. senator, 188n12, 189-90

W

Wallis, Point Betsie surfman, 166

Washington, George, U.S. president, 16, 30

Weed, Thurlow, 13-14

Wendel, Fred Jr., USCG, Point Betsie, 187-88

Wessel, Abram, USCG, Point Betsie, 175, 178, 181-82, 184, 187-88, 212

Wheaton, Edward M., USCG, Point Betsie lightkeeper, 194-97n16, **197**, 202-03, 207, 209

Wilson, Woodrow, U.S. president, 154

Women's National Relief Association, 134-35

Z

Zane, Edward R. III, USCG, Point Betsie, 221-22, 226

Zetterberg, Arvid family, 212